The Duke of Lennox, 1574–1624

The Duke of Lennox, 1574–1624

A Jacobean Courtier's Life

David M. Bergeron

EDINBURGH
University Press

Edinburgh University Press is one of the leading university presses in the UK. We publish academic books and journals in our selected subject areas across the humanities and social sciences, combining cutting-edge scholarship with high editorial and production values to produce academic works of lasting importance. For more information visit our website: edinburghuniversitypress.com

Edinburgh University Press Ltd
The Tun – Holyrood Road
12 (2f) Jackson's Entry
Edinburgh EH8 8PJ

Typeset in 10.5/13pt Sabon by
Manila Typesetting Company

A CIP record for this book is available from the British Library

ISBN 978 1 3995 0044 9 (hardback)
ISBN 978 1 3995 0046 3 (webready PDF)
ISBN 978 1 3995 0047 0 (epub)

Contents

Figures

Acknowledgements

I have the happy task of thanking a number of individuals, some of whom I have never met, and institutions. One of the joys of undertaking such a research project as this biography is that knowledge expands through contact with people, archives and books. I begin with people.

Julian Goodare of the University of Edinburgh has been exceptionally supportive and helpful, providing contacts and information about the subject of Scotland in the late sixteenth century. Maureen Meikle graciously agreed to read the chapter on Scotland and thus saved me from errors. I corresponded with Adrienne McLaughlin about her interest in Lennox and benefited from her helpful published article about him. Robert Maxtone-Graham alerted me to a document in the National Records of Scotland and provided me with his transcription of it. Jamie Reid-Baxter sent me helpful references. Amy Thompson and Nicole Winard graciously helped me decipher a particularly difficult document from the National Records of Scotland. I owe much to the support of Alan Stewart of Columbia University for his belief in me and this project, his constructive observations about it and for his excellent biography of James, *The Cradle King*, which illuminated my path and provided practical information.

Several libraries and archives made this project possible. I am especially grateful to the British Library, the National Archives (Kew), the Bodleian Library, the National Records of Scotland, Spencer Research Library of the University of Kansas and the Government Documents section of the university's library system. I would be remiss without calling attention to the wonderful HathiTrust database; this resource provided exceptional and sometimes hard to get materials. For help with illustrations I thank the National Portrait Gallery of London, the Folger

Shakespeare Library, Westminster Abbey, the Spencer Research Library and the Society of Antiquaries of London.

I have benefited also from speaking about parts of this biography at several meetings of the Mediterranean Studies Association, the Southeastern Renaissance Conference and the London Shakespeare Seminar, the last one at the kind invitation of my friend Gordon McMullan of King's College. At all of these sessions I seemed to be talking about new material for most people; this assured me that I was perhaps pursuing a worthwhile and largely ignored topic.

The indomitable Pam LeRow of the Media Digital Services, University of Kansas, worked her usual wonders with the computer and thereby made my life much easier. She has both tolerated me and helped me for several decades now. She sensibly decided to retire before this project came to an end. But Eric Bader has plunged in and helped in the last phase, and for that I am grateful.

Friends have contributed in ways not always obvious. I single out a few: Lucia Orth, John Head, Ardith and John Pierce, Gene and Judy Bauer and Gaywyn Moore. These dear friends have tolerated discourses about Lennox and managed to be interested. Several of my ideas have been tried out on them. I remember vividly sitting in the back of a van en route from Trieste, Italy to Pula, Croatia and speaking at considerable, perhaps inordinate, length to Lucia and John, who raised probing questions and made suggestions. All of these friends have enriched my life beyond measure. I end by naming with unstinted gratitude my husband Geraldo de Sousa, whose unending and unerring love and support have sustained me in this and all things.

TUDORS (England)

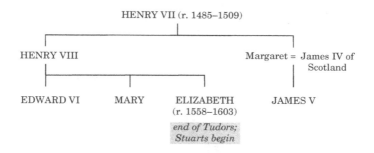

HENRY VII (r. 1485–1509)

HENRY VIII   Margaret = James IV of
                                           Scotland

EDWARD VI   MARY   ELIZABETH   JAMES V
                           (r. 1558–1603)
                           end of Tudors;
                           Stuarts begin

STUARTS / STEWARTS (Scotland)

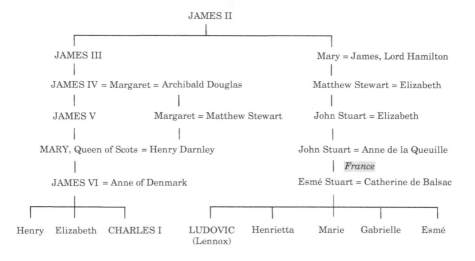

JAMES II

JAMES III   Mary = James, Lord Hamilton

JAMES IV = Margaret = Archibald Douglas   Matthew Stewart = Elizabeth

JAMES V   Margaret = Matthew Stewart   John Stuart = Elizabeth

MARY, Queen of Scots = Henry Darnley   John Stuart = Anne de la Queuille
                                   France

JAMES VI = Anne of Denmark   Esmé Stuart = Catherine de Balsac

Henry   Elizabeth   CHARLES I   LUDOVIC   Henrietta   Marie   Gabrielle   Esmé
                              (Lennox)

Introduction: 'nearest to the king'

In 1609 an obscure Italian, Antimo Galli, published a book in London, *Rime di Antimo Galli*, a multi-stanza poem dedicated to Elizabeth Talbot-Grey, daughter of Gilbert Talbot, Earl of Shrewsbury. Galli responds to a performance of Ben Jonson's *Masque of Beauty*, held at Whitehall in January 1608.[1] The poet, in addition to offering comments about the masque, also surveys the audience, enumerates the persons present and writes about them in the poetic stanzas. Of course, the attendees constitute a 'who's who' of the Jacobean court. His eye lights on Ludovic Stuart, Duke of Lennox, whom he describes thus in stanza 81: 'And that one you see there is the Duke of Lennox: grave in countenance and of courteous appearance. He is a greatly esteemed knight, and, believe me, is gifted with great prudence and intelligence.'[2] Such a view echoes throughout many documents and publications. The perspective of the Stuart royal family can be captured in Princess Elizabeth's comment when she learns of Lennox's death in early 1624. She writes from The Hague to her friend Thomas Roe: 'you know how well I loved him', a view shared by other members of this family.[3]

Who was this Ludovic Stuart, Duke of Lennox (1574–1624), so celebrated by many observers and writers? I argue that he was the most important courtier in King James VI of Scotland's court in both Scotland and England in the forty years, from 1583 to 1624, that he faithfully served the king, never returning to his native France to live. James trusted no one more than Lennox. This biography offers substantial evidence of this claim as it explores his political, diplomatic and personal life, which included an interest in the arts.

I have been captivated by Lennox's story for some time. King James requested that his French cousin, the nine-year-old Ludovic, come to Scotland to serve him. Thus, in November 1583, Ludovic arrived there, leaving behind his mother and four siblings. In a sense, Ludovic came to Scotland to replace his father, Esmé Stuart, who had served James from 1579 to 1582, when forced by the Scottish nobles and the church into exile and a return to France. James immortalised his love for Esmé in his poem *Phoenix*, published in 1584, a thinly veiled allegory of their relationship. I am haunted by the image of the young Ludovic coming to a foreign land, having never before travelled outside of France, knowing little of Scotland's culture, politics and language. But James immediately granted him the title of Duke of Lennox, which his father had had. The king also began to reward him with several important court positions. This process culminated in 1589 when James put the fifteen-year-old Lennox in charge of the three-person commission appointed to govern Scotland while the king travelled to Denmark to marry Princess Anne. Lennox presided over a time of quietness in the kingdom, a remarkable achievement given the fractious and contentious natures of the Scottish noblemen. In the space of a mere six years Lennox headed the government, a stunning political feat and indicative of James's trust in him, a trust well placed, as subsequent years show.

My interest in King James and the Stuart court through research and publication has occupied me for more than thirty years, beginning with *Shakespeare's Romances and the Royal Family* (1985) through *Royal Family, Royal Lovers* (1991) and *King James and Letters of Homoerotic Desire* (1999). In my most recent *Shakespeare's London 1613* (2017), Lennox began to emerge for his importance and participation in the major court events of that year. Clearly I needed to come to terms with him in ways that I had not before – hence this biography, which fills a surprising gap. No sustained study of Lennox's life exists, despite his prominence and importance. Over the course of forty years Lennox became for James a confidant, trusted advisor and friend. We cannot fully understand the reign of King James without knowing about Lennox and his unparalleled importance. We cannot ignore his omnipresence in most of the significant events of the Jacobean era.

ORGANISATION OF THE BIOGRAPHY

This biography unfolds from Lennox's arrival in 1583 to his unexpected death in February 1624. The first chapter explores his time in Scotland (1583–1603), the formative moments in his young life. The king showered him with desirable positions and political responsibilities, as mentioned above. Lennox during this time also went on diplomatic missions to France and England. In 1601 he had a personal audience with

Queen Elizabeth I, whom, of course, James never met. The queen wrote to James in glowing terms about Lennox. He had his share of conflicts: political, personal and sometimes physical. This chapter also explores Lennox's two marriages, the first cut short by the wife's death and the second an unhappy one that seemed to last too long. Documentary evidence, not previously reported, reveals that Lennox fathered an illegitimate son while in Scotland. Lennox's siblings also arrived and settled in Scotland. When James learned in March 1603 that he had been named King of England, he immediately wrote to Lennox asking him to accompany him to the new kingdom.

Chapter Two focuses exclusively on major events in the royal family's early years in England (1603–12) and Lennox's involvement. His hand can be found in almost all that shaped their lives, participating actively with them. Lennox was, for example, central in the festivities of 1606 for the visit of King Christian IV of Denmark, Anne's brother. The years 1610 through 1612 concentrate on Prince Henry, beginning with festivities that surrounded his investiture as Prince of Wales (1610) and leading to his tragic death in November 1612. In Henry's funeral, Lennox served as 'chief supporter' to Prince Charles, the chief mourner.

The next chapter begins with the preparations for and the celebration of Princess Elizabeth's wedding to Prince Frederick of Germany on 14 February 1613, as the court turned away from Henry's death. Lennox participated fully in all the activities associated with the wedding, including escorting Frederick into the chapel and the princess out. At the king's request, Lennox then accompanied the princess to her new home in Germany. Elizabeth reported to the king that Lennox's company had given her 'unutterable pleasure'.[4] In 1616 he was central in the events associated with Charles's investiture as Prince of Wales. Through these years, Lennox had to confront the presence of two successive 'favourites' of the king: Robert Carr and George Villiers. He skillfully navigated this potential minefield. No other courtier had a better, long-lasting relationship with the royal family than Lennox.

In Chapter Four, 'Diplomacy, Politics and the Arts', I write about Lennox's involvement in politics in England and his commitment to and participation in the arts. Immediately on arriving in England, King James named Lennox to the Privy Council and to the Bedchamber, which Lennox headed; thus, from these positions Lennox could exercise considerable power. James dispatched him back to Scotland several times to wrangle with the Scottish Parliament. The king also sent him to France to strengthen the ties between the two countries and, in 1613, to negotiate possible marriage arrangements for Charles. Lennox regularly entertained foreign ambassadors and occasionally intervened on their behalf. They understood his importance. In 1616 James made Lennox Lord High Steward, in charge of managing the royal household. After receiving the title Earl of Richmond in 1613, Lennox joined Parliament, whose members often sought his advice. James rewarded him with the title Duke of Richmond in 1623, making him the only courtier to hold two ducal titles, underscoring his unsurpassed importance for the king. Shrewd politician, ambitious and sometimes ruthless, but also beloved by the royal family, Lennox carefully negotiated political and diplomatic challenges.

Lennox demonstrated considerable interest in the arts, especially dramatic arts as patron and performer. He became, for example, patron of his own theatre group, the Duke of Lennox's Men, which apparently performed mainly outside of London. Lennox developed a keen interest in court masques, arranging for the first one in the Jacobean court in 1604. He performed as a dancer in several of Ben Jonson's masques. In 1619, documentary evidence reveals his attendance at a performance of Shakespeare's *Pericles* at Whitehall. James appointed Lennox to a three-person commission to rebuild the Whitehall Banqueting House, which had burned down in early 1619. Few courtiers in the Jacobean era could surpass Lennox in his commitment to the arts.

Chapter Five, 'Last Years: Good and Ill Together', contains three parts: marriage, letters and death. In 1621, Lennox married Frances Howard, widow of Edward Seymour, just a few weeks after Seymour's death, indicating a likely ongoing affair. This was the third marriage for both, a more pleasant experience than the previous ones. Lennox, of course, had been a highly desirable target for marriage: handsome, witty, wealthy and with ducal titles. During this time, Lennox wrote numerous letters to friends, revealing additional qualities about himself. In these circumspect letters, Lennox nevertheless expresses his love and respect for these friends and he did not hesitate to ask for favours.

Lennox's unexpected death on 16 February 1624 and his extravagant funeral created quite a stir. He died in his sleep, but this did not prevent the publication of various narratives that offered details of his death. Elegies and accounts of funeral preparations followed. The king postponed the opening of Parliament, and the country got ready for the equivalent of a state funeral, which took place on 19 April in Westminster Abbey after a long procession through London. Thousands lined the streets. The Archbishop of Canterbury presided and John Williams, Bishop of Lincoln, preached. No one could disagree with John Chamberlain's contemporary assessment that Lennox was 'magnificently enterred'.

John Hacket, in another account, describes Lennox as 'affable, humble, inoffensive, whose wit and honesty kept him great and much belov'd of all'.[5] The funeral and elegies confirm this judgment. The Italian Galli had correctly assessed Lennox as 'a greatly esteemed knight'.

BIOGRAPHY AND HISTORY

Constructing a biography, a form of history, places the writer at the mercy of the surviving evidence. The further back in history, the more difficult this becomes. Lennox's contemporary Sir Philip Sidney had a dim view of the enterprise. He suggests that a historian is one 'loden with Mouse-eaten records, authorising himselfe (for the most part) upon other histories, whose greatest authorities are built upon the notable foundation of Hearsay'.[6] Fortunately, I have not come upon 'Mouse-eaten records', nor am I dependent on hearsay. Copious primary, contemporary records exist for a life of Lennox, although I am fully aware of gaps. I have resorted on occasion to surmises, based on the context and the probability of his participation in some event. I embrace Hayden White's view in his *Tropics of Discourse*: 'Histories are not only about events but also about the possible sets of relationships that those events can be demonstrated to figure'.[7]

My biography of Lennox depends on manuscript, archival, published contemporary accounts and records, and modern compilations of documents from the time. Because no extended study of Lennox or biography exists, I have had to create this account from the ground up. Therefore, I have relied heavily on primary materials. I have consulted original materials found in the British Library, the National Archives (London), the National Records of Scotland and the Bodleian Library. A document from the National Records of Scotland, for example, provides a kind of 'pre-nuptial' agreement between Lennox and his second wife, Jean Campbell. Personal letters from Lennox to friends offer insight into friendly relationships; these letters come primarily from the National Archives and form the basis of an exploration of letters in the final chapter. Other letters crop up throughout the chapters. No gathering of all of Lennox's letters exists. I also make generous use of published primary materials, such as various reports from the Historical Manuscripts Commission, the Salisbury MSS, the state papers of Scotland and Venice, the Laing MSS in the University of Edinburgh Library, John Chamberlain's letters, etc. From *The Register of the Privy Council of Scotland*, for example, I discovered documentation that confirms the existence of Lennox's illegitimate son. These rich materials provide the building blocks for this book.

The Second Lord in Shakespeare's *All's Well That Ends Well* observes that 'the web of our life is of a mingled yarn, good and ill together' (Act IV, scene iii, lines 70–1).[8] Certainly the web of evidence about Lennox reveals the truth of that statement. Lennox, like all people, certainly experienced joyous occasions and ill events: for example, the wonderful celebrations for Prince Henry's investiture as Prince of Wales in 1610 and then, two years later, his tragic death and mournful funeral. A biography of necessity confronts the 'mingled yarn' of a life. I take my cue, in part, from Hilary Mantel's brilliant *Wolf Hall* and the words near its conclusion: 'It's the living that turn and chase the dead. The long bones and skulls are tumbled from their shrouds, and words like stones thrust into their rattling mouths: we edit their writings, we rewrite their lives'.[9] I am trying to rescue Lennox's life from neglect. I am indeed chasing his bones; I rewrite his life.

Notes

1. For a discussion of this account, see John Orrell's 'Antimo Galli's Description of *The Masque of Beauty*', *Huntington Library Quarterly*.
2. Translation of the Italian by Maria Dougu from the *Masque Archive: Masque of Beauty* # 26 in the online version of the *Cambridge Edition of the Works of Ben Jonson*.
3. Nadine Ackkerman (ed.), *The Correspondence of Elizabeth Stuart, Queen of Bohemia*, 1:445.
4. Ibid., 1:123.
5. John Hacket, *Scrinia Reserata*, p. 173.
6. Quoted in Bergeron, *Royal Family, Royal Lovers*, p. 13.
7. Hayden White, *Tropics of Discourse: Essays in Cultural Criticism*, p. 185.
8. All quotations from Shakespeare in this book come from *The Complete Pelican Shakespeare*, Stephen Orgel and A. R. Braunmuller (eds).
9. Hilary Mantel, *Wolf Hall*, p. 602.

1

Scotland: Phoenix, Maturation, Transitions

'THEY CALL ME LENNOX'.

Summoned by his cousin King James VI of Scotland to join the Scottish court, the nine-year-old Ludovic Stuart left his familial home in France and arrived in Scotland in November 1583, where almost immediately he received the title of Duke of Lennox. Little did he know that for the rest of his life he would remain in Scotland and then England, never returning to France to live. In fact, he had few ideas about what lay ahead. He was, after all, only nine years old and had never travelled before. He had, however, in the early months of 1583 in France, sat at the knee of his suave, savvy but dying father and learned a smattering of things about Scotland and its king. Now, unknown to Ludovic, he would spend his life fulfilling his father's unrealised potential, indeed exceeding what his father had imagined for himself and for Ludovic. But bereft of the comfort of home and the support and love of his mother and siblings, Ludovic's mood vacillated between excitement and fear – not to mention bewilderment.

This is the story of his forty years on an island, known as Great Britain, living in an exile that became his life. Three images help capture Lennox's importance over the course of forty years. First, his arrival. He landed at Leith on 13 November, accompanied by a few Scottish nobles, such as the Master of Gray and Thomas Livingstone. From there the party moved the following day to Kinneil, where the seventeen-year-old King James was in residence. James welcomed the young boy warmly, embracing and kissing him. Soon followed the granting of the title of Duke of Lennox, one that his father, Esmé Stuart, had held during his earlier service to the king. Together the group moved to Edinburgh and Holyrood Palace, where Lennox took up residence. An auspicious beginning.

In the cool of the early morning on 24 March 1603 the lives of James and Lennox changed forever: Queen Elizabeth I drew her last breath and the path to the English crown opened for James finally and irrevocably. On the night of 26 March, thanks to Robert Carey's epic ride from London to Edinburgh, James received word at Holyrood Palace that the queen had died and that he had been proclaimed King of England. Within three days the king wrote to Lennox, asking him to accompany him to this new country and new opportunity. In April, they began the journey down the Great North Road towards London, pausing many times to receive the adulation of the English people.

Twenty years later, in 1623, King James welcomed the Spanish ambassador to court on 20 July. A report of the meeting at court notes James's relatively modest dress, accented with a 'most rich and transparent diamond' in his hat, befitting a great monarch. When he entered the Chapel Royal, the report notes, Lennox accompanied the king; and the king leaned upon him. A perfect image of James's love and need of Lennox, who, after all these years, still occupied a central place in the court and in kingly favour: confidant and loving friend. King and kinsman had travelled a long journey together, something that the young nine-year-old could not have imagined.

ARRIVAL

Why did a nine-year-old boy from France, son of Esmé Stuart and Catherine de Balsac d'Entragues, born on 29 September 1574, leave his native land and come to Scotland in 1583? Lennox's journey began with his father, Esmé Stuart, Seigneur d'Aubigny, who died in May 1583. Esmé had himself left France in 1579, as a thirty-seven-year-old French courtier, presumably at the request of the Scottish Privy Council who sought someone to guide their teenaged king (now thirteen years old); Esmé left behind a wife and five children. Arriving at Stirling Castle in September 1579, he received an immediate and enthusiastic welcome from the young King James VI. A contemporary account reports: 'No sooner did the young King see him, but in that hee was so neare allyed in bloud, of so renouned a Family, eminent ornaments of body and minde, tooke him up and embraced him in a most amorous manner'.[1] From that moment on their relationship deepened as James showered him with titles and gifts, including the title Duke of Lennox, the only duke in all of Scotland. The king made Esmé a member of the Privy Council, Gentleman of the Bedchamber and governor of Dumbarton Castle. A relationship of mutual love also developed, to the chagrin and worry of the Scottish nobles and Kirk and to the alarm of English authorities. Esmé was the son of John Stuart, brother of James's grandfather and one-time regent, the Earl of Lennox, and first cousin to James's father, Henry Stuart, Earl of Darnley. James had no brothers or sisters, and his mother, Mary, Queen of Scots, had been driven into exile when James was scarcely a year old. He would consciously know his mother only through letters and reports. The familial connection to Esmé was clearly part of the attraction; his 'eminent ornaments of body and minde' only enhanced James's attraction to him. Their intimacy, whatever its precise nature, alarmed some. From the late seventeenth century through to the twentieth-first century historians have wrestled with this issue. One, writing in the mid-twentieth century, refers to James's 'perverted love for Lennox' and says that Esmé's influence 'was malignant'.[2] James would not agree with that assessment. The young king had felt very much alone. Into this familial vacuum Esmé moved and eventually filled it with love, respect and loyalty. Interestingly, Esmé apparently made no effort to bring his wife to Scotland; perhaps he had intended initially to stay only a short time. In any event, her absence suited James.

Esmé's motives remained suspect, as he established contact with Mary and sought to find help for her cause; such an overture to her became well known to both the Scottish lords and the English. Some imagined that he had come to Scotland to pave the way for more Catholics to enter the kingdom and for them to gain new liberties and power. Something slightly disingenuous, if not deceitful, lingered in his actions. But James did not care. He allowed Esmé to manage the royal household, put him in charge of many political operations and listened attentively to his advice. Only one thing stood in the way of Esmé's complete sway over the young king: his religion. But Esmé soon took care of that, converting to Protestantism and thus outflanking the Scottish church's opposition to him. James's love for him increased, for he understood this religious conversion as a sign of Esmé's love for him.[3]

Eventually the Scottish nobles and churchmen grew weary of Esmé's influence and political power, which had gone largely unchecked. Indeed, he had become the king's chief political advisor. Queen Elizabeth had also begun to worry about Esmé's influence. When the Scottish Kirk could no longer batter him about his Catholicism they devised other schemes to discredit him. In late summer 1582, the 'Lords Enterprisers', as the opposing group called itself, succeeded in literally separating James from Esmé as James hunted near Ruthven Castle at which the Earl of Gowrie persuaded him to rest. This 'Ruthven Raid' of conspirators in late August captured James and held him as prisoner for many months, despite his protestations. The Enterprisers believed that whoever gained possession of and maintained proximity to the king's body would secure the desired power. Robert Bowes, English ambassador to Scotland, reported back to Burghley on 26 August: 'Those noblemen obtained the possession of the King's person without the privity of the Duke [Esmé] and Arran'.[4] Removing Esmé from James's person suited their purposes perfectly. The Enterprisers claimed that they took James against his will in order to 'protect' him from Esmé's devious wiles. They regularly moved James, thereby pretending that he was not in fact a prisoner. They achieved by violence what they could not by persuasion and policy.

For the first time in nearly three years James and Esmé experienced a serious breach in their relationship. James remained anxious for Esmé to rescue him but Esmé was frustratingly powerless to save the king. The noblemen made clear that Esmé had only one option: to leave Scotland. Reluctant and guilt-ridden, James bent to their pressure and agreed to Esmé's exile. The experience did not dampen his love of Esmé. On 21 December Esmé began his journey to France, going by way of England. Although many people, including James, assumed that he would return in a few months that did not happen.

Esmé arrived in France a broken man, reviled by the French court and largely ignored by his wife, from whom he had been separated for three years. The surviving letters that he wrote to James just before his departure in December capture the poignancy of their situation, even as they document Esmé's devotion to and love for James. He writes: 'For whatever might happen to me, I shall always be your very faithful servant'. He insists that if his breast should be split open, James would find engraved on his heart the words 'fidelity and obedience', not 'words of inconstancy and disloyalty'.[5] He had served the king with his whole heart. In fact, he had given and hazarded all that he had. In this state of brokenness, Esmé's health failed.

Letters moved back and forth from Scotland to France but they could not conquer the separating space; indeed, nothing could assuage the loss that both men felt. Esmé's health worsened and death loomed. On the day of his death, 26 May 1583, Esmé 'at seven of the clocke . . . caused to write a writting to the King's Grace, shewing his Grace the estate he was at, desiring him to be good to his barnes [children], and to tak upon his Grace the defense of them'.[6] This letter James eventually received. But he also got something else: Esmé's embalmed heart. David Calderwood reports, 'he was bowelled, the same night, his heart takin out, the bodie putt in a leadin kist, . . . and on the morne conveyed away secreetlie'.[7] Esmé determined that his heart should be sent to James, rather than being left in France. This act powerfully testifies to and underscores his love for James, making literal what had been a metaphor.

The news of Esmé's death took a while to reach Scotland; it took the king even longer to accept it. For weeks no one at court dared broach the subject. Bowes writes to Sir Francis Walsingham on 9 June 1583: 'The report of the death of Lennox cannot get any credit in this realm, chiefly with his friends'.[8] But evidence mounted, and his death gained credence. Bowes reports on 31 July that James issued a proclamation that confirmed Lennox's 'good behaviour, and that he died a good Christian protestant' (p. 537), a point that James intended for the Scottish Kirk in particular. James did not wallow in grief for long; he decided instead to take action. First, he successfully escaped his captors in June 1583, just a month after Esmé's death. Second, he responded aesthetically by writing a poem, *Ane Metaphoricall Invention of a Tragedie called Phoenix*, typically referred to as *Phoenix*, which he published in his first volume of poetry, *The Essayes of a Prentise in the Divine Arte of Poesie* (1584). He thereby made public to a reading audience his recreated, imaginative version of desire. *Phoenix* offers a thinly veiled allegory of his love for Esmé Stuart. Through the covert allegory of this poem, James voices deep desire for his cousin, including homoerotic desire.

The poet's role in *Phoenix* bifurcates into narrator and participant; at moments they are, of course, the same. Another person lurks around this poem: namely, James the adolescent king, who poses as the narrator of a simple fiction about a phoenix. Within the poem the narrator becomes more than a conduit through whom the story flows: he expresses judgement, displays emotion and responds with action, but all restricted by the confines of the allegory. By this beautiful Arabian bird of the poem James clearly intends Esmé, who like the bird endured attack and eventual death. Everything in the poem speaks of the narrator's desire for the bird: its beauty, its soaring power, its brightness that rivals the sun, its attractiveness perceived by others and finally its helplessness as it comes to seek refuge from attack. The *Phoenix* thus forever links the two cousins in a fiction that adumbrates their personal lives; it recollects with lamentation and consolation the loving relationship of James and Esmé Stuart, including its sharp edge of desire.[9]

James closes the 280-line poem with a 'L'envoy' section of three stanzas, which serves as an address to Apollo and offers a way out of the tragedy that he has presented. The poet hopes that something may happen to assuage his grief; he urges Apollo: 'so heir / Let them be now, to make ane *Phoenix* new / Euen of this worme of *Phoenix* ashe which grew'.[10] If indeed a new phoenix can emerge from the ashes of the former

one, 'My tragedie a comike end will haue'. Ludovic Stuart will be the
new phoenix in James's life. James completed his grief not only by escap-
ing and writing a poem about his love for Esmé but also by inviting the
young Ludovic to the Scottish court and into his life. By recalling the lost
and dead love, he recuperates beauty, wonder and desire in the poem. By
summoning Ludovic, James enlarged his life, making it open to renewing
and hopeful possibilities that point toward reassuring comedy. Phoenix
can replace phoenix. Only new life can supplant and fulfil the *Phoenix*.
From early on the young Ludovic understood this poem, its relevance
and resonance for his life, and his role as the new phoenix. Ludovic, the
new heir, substitutes for his father. The phoenix funeral pyre has yielded
another phoenix.

But early life in this new country would not be simple or easy. Bowes,
who had been well acquainted with Esmé, reported back to Sir Francis
Walsingham on 23 November 1583 on Ludovic's new lodging, which
reflects a kind of Scottish roughness. James Stewart, Earl of Arran, 'had
lodged Lennox in the chamber of Holyrood House wherein Bothwell
[Francis Stewart] used to lie, and hastily broke open the door and cast
forth Bothwell's furniture, which is taken offensively by Bothwell'.[11]
Welcome to Scotland! Young Ludovic had never experienced such behaviour. Furniture being cast into the street must have frightened him. He
had no background in such violence, having lived a nurturing, sheltered
life in France. He would have to grow up fast.

Fortunately, King James's response to Ludovic and his obvious care of
him contrasted with the royal Scottish noblemen. Bowes reports that the
king 'is in suche excedynge good lykynge of this child, as he spareth not
to kisse hym openly and very often' (CSPS, 6:660). Bowes also reports on
29 December that the last Convention at Edinburgh acted 'to authorise
the young Duke of Lennox to sit at the King's table and how himself and
his possessions should be governed' (6:685).

On 1 December 1583 King James had issued instructions for the education and maintenance of Lennox. This document confirms the king's
desire to have Lennox served at his own table, being served of his 'own
kitchen and from his cupboard'.[12] This instruction grows from the king's
determination 'to have him remaining in his highness's own house and
company'. In this document King James outlines the function of numerous servants, including Gilbert Moncreiff, appointed to be Lennox's
tutor, in charge of the boy's education, 'to have the charge of his instructions in letters and good manners'. Moncreiff also oversees Lennox's
diet and should 'lie in his chamber when the said Mr Gilbert shall think
meet'. John Cavallione, 'his gentleman servant', should 'attend upon and

serve him at his table, and to instruct him in his bodily exercises and pastimes, when the said Mr Gilbert shall find the time convenient therefor, to lie nightly in the Duke's chamber' (454). James's instructions include the names of several other servants who will assist Lennox in various ways. James also lists the payments to be made to them. He promises:

> his Majesty is content and promises that, from this forth, his highness will remit the said Duke's affairs to the order of his tutor and persons foresaid ordained to assist him, and will hold back his hand from granting or subscribing any thing contrarious to the said order. (455)

On 9 December 1583, the Privy Council learned of the transfer of the dukedom of Lennox and earldom of Darnley from the sheriff of Dumbarton, John Earl of Montrois, to Lennox and his tutor, the Earl of March. The report records that the sheriff 'has now "voluntarlie and benevolentlie" demitted [relinquished] these honours, "seeing the noble and michtie [mighty] Lord Lewes [Ludovic], now Duke of Lennox, is now becum in this realme"'.[13] All the property and rights now belong to Lennox, who may 'enjoy the saides offices and manrent [homage]'. Therefore, 'proclamation of the premises is ordered at the market cross of Glasgow, charging the inhabitants of the said dukery, earldom, barony, and city to obey the said Duke of Lennox and his tutor in the said offices and manrent [support]' (Reg. 3:614–15).

Not all was sweetness and light. Janet Scott, Lady Ferniehirst, writes to Mary, Queen of Scots, on 25 November that 'The Kirk of Scotland are as evil affected to this young Duke as ever they were to his father, and cry out as fast against him as ever they did against the other'.[14] Lennox soon became aware of this opposition and he rather unexpectedly and quickly struck out at his father's adversaries, blaming them for Esmé's death. Lennox seems readily to be adapting to life in this new country by remembering his father's travails and mistreatment in Scotland. He is growing up fast. Evidence of this maturing appears in a letter that Lennox wrote to George Douglas in France in September 1584, not quite a year after his arrival. Lennox informs Douglas that Queen Mary has been instructed to

> request the King of France to acknowledge her son as King of Scotland in such form as has been advised, and with him ratify and confirm the ancient league. To this effect letters are directed to the Queen of Scots that will satisfy her desire. (CSPS, 7:340)

Now, only ten years old, Lennox has begun to function politically or at least as a transmitter of desired political action.

Like his father before him, Ludovic had a presumed and sometimes obvious connection to Mary. Monsieur Fontenay wrote to the queen on 15 August 1584, after a visit with the young Lennox. He reports:

> I have visited on your part the little Duke of Lennox, who is a very nice child, and promises much from his good nature. I gave him a sermon as small as himself to keep him in the continuance of our religion, and in the respect and fidelity that he owes to the service of your majesty.[15]

The French courtier puts his finger on what will be for Ludovic, as for his father before him, an ongoing struggle over religion. Fontenay adds: 'I find him very affectionate and desirous to serve you one day' (271), which turns out to have been more wishful thinking than a reality. Also, 'According to your majesty's commandment, I have recommended him to the King, who holds him as dear as his own child'. Yet, Fontenay fears, justly, that some of the Scottish nobles may try to work against the young Lennox, who has, after all, entered a fraught personal and political world. The Frenchman urges Mary to write to her son James to recommend Lennox to all 'the faithful friends and servants who are affectionate to him as they were to the Duke of Lennox, his father' (272). A month later, Mary responded to Monsieur Fontenay on 28 September: 'First, recommend on my part to my son, with all the favourable intercession that you can, the young Duke of Lennox, that he may be preserved in all the goods of his late father and others with which since he could have been gratified' (CSPS, 7:341). In a little over two years, the question of Lennox's service to Mary will be resolved by her death, although the matter of his religious allegiance will linger, at least in the minds of the Kirk.

In 1596, the Scottish poet John Burel dedicated his collection of poems to Ludovic, Duke of Lennox, great Chamberlain of Scotland, wishing for him long life and happy success. Burel writes further: 'And sen ze are, the onely sonne and hair, / Sprung from the synders, of that Phoenix rair', so must Ludovic serve God and their sovereign king.[16] Others revere his renown and acknowledge his descent from and perpetuation of the phoenix.

Apparently, this young phoenix, arriving into the presence of King James in November 1583, did not feel intimidated or daunted by his figurative and real responsibility as heir to his father and potential heir to the Scottish throne. From the beginning, James showered him with most of his father's titles, including the crucial one, Duke of Lennox. 'They call me Lennox'. He became a member of the King's Bedchamber, Privy Council and Lord Chamberlain of Scotland for life. Heady recognition for this child. The scant evidence suggests that Ludovic handled these privileges and duties with equanimity, despite his youth and inexperience. Wrenched from his comfortable familial life in France he suddenly stood at the centre of Scottish politics but embraced by the king's love. A few months after his arrival, Lennox carried the royal crown to the opening of Parliament in 1584, a sure sign of James's love for and confidence in him, and to the chagrin of the Hamilton clan, for example, who feared a diminution of their status and who jealously guarded their own claim to the throne. Thomas Fowler reported back to England to William Cecil, Lord Burghley, a few years later on 28 March 1589 that the Duke 'is "so proper a youthe, so wy[se], stayed, actyve on horse and fote, cowrteows, of suche intertey[nment] and carryage of him selffe, so pleasynge to all men . . . [and] tr[uly] he is a parragon. The Kinge loves this Duke as him selffe".'[17] Bowes captures a striking image of the king's reliance when he wrote to Robert Cecil on 13 April 1594: 'The King is now determined to pass quietly to-morrow to Stirling, taking with him the Duke alone'.[18] This paragon of a phoenix had become confidant and trusted advisor to the king, who took refuge in his loving and pleasant company.[19]

POLITICS

In the procession to the opening of Parliament in May 1584 the young Ludovic, at James's order, carried the royal crown, the clearest symbol of monarchical power. By so doing, Lennox made a significant overt political statement, one of impressive royal favour and potential power. From that moment on, if it had not already been clear, Lennox would occupy important political or governmental posts, ones more given than sought. Knowing that this act of carrying the crown incited envy if not fear, Lennox nervously moved in the procession, hoping that he would not stumble or falter, that he would follow the expected procedures and protocol. Holding the crown, the young boy knew its importance, even if his limited experience did not allow him to understand fully the workings of the Scottish Parliament. But in a scant few months, Lennox had moved from a frightening yet hopeful arrival into a strange land to being near the centre of power, yet with much to learn and understand. Nothing in his life in France could have prepared him for such moments.

Lennox's first appointment that required all the skills that a fifteen-year-old could muster came in late 1589, when King James decided to leave Scotland (the first and only time that he left the British Isles) and sail to Denmark to collect Anne of Denmark, his intended bride. This was a potentially disruptive and challenging position for Scotland. James would need to make provisions for a smooth functioning government in his absence. Here Lennox makes an unforeseen appearance. James will essentially place the still young and relatively inexperienced Lennox in charge, a bold and daring move: a transplanted French youth, mastering the language and political landscape, will govern Scotland.

Since as early as 1582 James's counsellors had been urging marriage in order to bring additional stability to the kingdom with the possibility of a royal family, hence natural successors to James as rulers of Scotland. These advisers sensed a vulnerability in their sovereign without a supporting cast of immediate royal family – a problem readily discernible south of their border in England with its unmarried, childless queen. In 1587 James took some action by dispatching emissaries, one to Denmark and one to France, to seek a suitable marriage partner. By late spring 1589 James and his advisors had focused on two likely candidates: Catherine of Navarre and Anne of Denmark. Some favoured the Countess of Navarre because she was older than James and thus she might be able to guide and advise him. Finally, however, James chose the fourteen-year-old Princess Anne, daughter of King Frederick II and Queen Sophia of Mecklenburg. William Asheby, English ambassador, reported: 'He [James] is not hasty of marriage, but will match with the Danes to please his boroughs and merchants'.[20] Of course, James made certain to establish that Anne had an appropriately large dowry with which to enter the marriage. This dowry, among other things, ceded to Scotland control of the northern isles of Orkney and Shetland.

Thus, James sent George Keith, the Earl Marischal, to complete the negotiations and to serve as proxy at a wedding ceremony on 20 August 1589 in Denmark. By this time, James had convinced himself that he was in love with Anne. Asheby writes that James is 'now far in love with the princess of Denmark, hearing of her beauty and virtues and her affection towards him' (CSPS, 10:129). Having gazed on her picture and heard reports of her beauty, James knew that he loved Anne, whom, of course, he had yet to meet.[21]

On 1 September the youthful Anne set sail from Denmark on a ship named *Gideon* for the coast of Scotland. Unfortunately, nature did not cooperate. Violent tempests at sea banged her ship and the accompanying ships, knocking them out of commission. With good reason Anne feared for her safety, not to mention the insufferable seasickness that she experienced. On one occasion the fleet actually spotted the Scottish coastline but could not land. Eventually, they had to give up and return to Scandinavia. James suffered as well. William Asheby, in a letter to

Francis Walsingham on 24 September, commented: 'The King, as a true lover, wholly passionate, and half out of patience with the wind and weather, is troubled that he hath been so long without intelligence of the fleet' (CSPS, 10:157). What to do?

First, James decided in October to send a flotilla to fetch Anne and bring her to Scotland; but when he learned the likely cost of such an endeavour, he knew that he could not afford it. So he chose a scaled-down operation and determined to make the journey himself – of course with an appropriate retinue of followers, numbering around 300. After allegedly spending days of solitary, prayerful consideration, James decided to venture forth. He wrote John Maitland, the Lord Chancellor, on 19 October, reassuring him that he would 'set down a solid order to be followed in all times coming by the subjects. . . . And let this be proclaimed in Edinburgh the morn without fail'.[22] James produced two remarkable documents, the first of which he addresses to 'The People of Scotland'. The second indeed outlines the system of government that will prevail in his absence. Despite the boldness and seeming abruptness of his intended departure, he had given considerable thought to what he would be leaving behind.

In a revealing letter to the Scottish people, dated 22 October, James spells out the reasons for his action and offers rationales for it; in the process, he perhaps unwittingly offers considerable insight into himself. He confronts the seeming 'delay' of his getting around to marriage (he is now twenty-three years old). James writes: 'The reasons were that I was alone, without father or mother, brother or sister, king of this realm and heir apparent of England. This my nakedness made me to be weak and my enemies stark'.[23] The lack of a family permeates much of the king's thinking and underscores his sense of being alone in the world. Somewhat defensively, he argues that he has no sexual problem, objecting to those who think that he is 'a barren stock'. James sees no reason to rush into marriage: 'God is my witness I could have abstained longer'. He seems somewhat self-conscious about his virility and masculinity and seeks to put to rest that issue. Instead, he wants to assure all that he is neither hasty nor devoid of rational thinking. James goes into considerable detail about where (Craigmillar) and how he reached his decision, underscoring that he made this determination all by himself, without benefit of counselors. 'I have ever kept my intention of my going as close as possibly I could from all men' (p. 99), James writes. Interestingly, nowhere in the letter, focused on his marriage, does he mention his 'love' for Princess Anne, the presumed reason for this daring venture. The king closes by promising that he shall return, 'God willing, within the space of twenty days, wind and weather serving' (100). (He would not return for six months.)

The second document repeats some of the information found in the first, but it explicitly outlines how the country will be governed in the king's absence. Like the first, this one has the date of 22 October and would be released once James had left. The king here also insists that his decision derives from rational, considerate thought; and he reviews Anne's futile attempt to come to Scotland and his subsequent suffering. The final section focuses on government. James writes: 'the Privy Council shall reside continuously in Edinburgh under the Duke of Lennox as President, who shall have Bothwell continually associated with him'.[24] Further, 'all the officers of state shall give constant attendance upon the Council in Edinburgh' (111). James adds later that 'John, Lord Hamilton, shall have responsibility for the three Marches and sheriffdom of Lanark' (112). With additional names cited, James has established a kind of triumvirate with Lennox as the head. He writes: 'in case any matter should require united deliberation, Lennox and Hamilton together, along with their councillors, shall take steps to do whatever they consider needful for the King's service and the public welfare' (112). James closes by urging the ministers to pray for his safety and admonish the people also to pray for the king's well-being and success. The king then exits the kingdom, gets married in Norway, and moves on to Denmark, where he spends his time indulging in eat and much drink and occasional theological discussions. In other words, James had a great time, and he and Anne got along together surprisingly well – a successful beginning.

Surely the appointment of the fifteen-year-old Lennox as President of the Council and thereby quasi-leader of the country must have struck more than one Scot as strange, if not bizarre. A fair amount of envy also emerged. What had James been thinking? After six years of residence in this, for him, new country and not much assurance yet of his political skills, Lennox himself might rightly have wondered about the king's judgement. For better or worse, no way existed to challenge the king's order. Surrounding Lennox with Bothwell, Hamilton and others at least provided some seasoned veterans of Scottish politics who could advise him. Clearly, James saw something in Lennox that gave him confidence that the young man could handle the job, whatever others might think. He surely knew that Lennox would do nothing to undermine the king's authority; indeed, Lennox obviously owed everything to James for his status and welfare. Doubtless numerous conversations with the king gave Lennox knowledge of the personalities and political inclinations of many Scottish nobles. James must have heard in these conversations statements and questions that assured him of Lennox's trustworthiness and competence. Yet, the appointment of a fifteen-year-old, non-native to head the government must have taken some time to process and accept.

Queen Elizabeth, for one, had her doubts, which she did not hesitate to voice, as evident in letters, dated 29 October and 30 October, from William Cecil to William Asheby. The queen likes the idea that John Hamilton has charge of the southern part of Scotland. But, 'Her majesty disapproves of the Privy Council being directed by so young a person as the Duke of Lennox, "and he accompanied with noe more constant a person than the Erle Bothwell".'[25] Cecil reports Elizabeth's additional fear that the 'Spanish and Popish' factions might see an opening for mischief in James's absence. Asheby responds immediately to Burghley on 30 October with assurance: 'The Duke and Bothwell, being governors, endeavour to show their respect to their office, carrying themselves with seemly gravity, frequenting sermons, and ready to proffer all good [offices] toward her majesty and her realm' (CSPS, 10:183). Such reassurance seems to have mollified Elizabeth's worries for the moment. Frequenting sermons is always good. Thus, a few months later, 10 February 1590, the queen writes directly to Lennox, a tacit acknowledgment of her acceptance of his position. She has been reassured by Bowes, ambassador, of Lennox's 'good disposition to the performance of all good offices' that may strengthen the bond between England and Scotland (CSPS, 10:240). Elizabeth then offers this advice:

> that the more carefull you shall be for the King our good brothers good and of his relm, during the tyme of his absence, the more honour and reputation will redounde unto you thereby. And so we doubte not but you will contynue, according to the place you hold there, and the trust commyttid unto you by the King. (10:240)

Elizabeth's shrewd advice and judgement erase whatever lingering doubts she might have had. Such doubts would be fully understandable from her perspective and that of others; but three months into Lennox's tenure, he has passed muster at least with Queen Elizabeth. This provides solid evidence of Lennox's political acumen, no matter how unexpected that might have been.

Through effort and a good measure of luck, Scotland remained rather calm during James's absence. One potential problem did occur in March 1590: namely, the sighting of a Spanish bark off the coast of Scotland. This raised alarms, in part because of the presence of the Spanish Armada just two years earlier headed to England and fears remained that the Spaniards might try again. Bowes reports to Burghley and Walsingham on 20 March: 'The Spanish bark still lies off the coast at Whithorn, and not likely to be stayed, notwithstanding the King's letters to his Council'.[26] With more confidence Bowes reports on 24 March that Bothwell learned of this boat and informed Lennox; he found the duke 'very willing to send to the provost of this towne to staie the captaine' (10:260). The provost responded and tracked down the captain, who was staying in Leith, and kept him in custody. This action effectively ended whatever threat the boat might have posed. King James wrote to Bowes about the incident on 31 March, in which he commented on the 'relief' at the apprehension of the crew (10:260). End of possible crisis. Therefore, Bowes can indicate to Burghley that 'This estate contineweth in good quietnes . . . I trust this peace and quietnes shallbe preserved, or at least th'estate shalbe warned of the danger arising' (260). David Calderwood, no fan of Lennox, offers a sweeping evaluation: the country 'was never in greater peace than during his [James's] absence'.[27] Not all credit can rest on Lennox, of course; but he should receive a large portion of it, having kept the fractious country and its volatile clans in check. And at fifteen years old – quite an achievement.[28]

Finally King James returned to Scotland, accompanied by his bride, Princess Anne, and a retinue of nobles and servants. The royal party and the several ships arrived at Leith on 1 May and Anne began to lay eyes on Scotland for the first time. She, young and inexperienced and not knowing the Scots language, nevertheless smiled graciously; and the Scots found her beautiful and approachable. Because things were not quite ready in Edinburgh, the entourage lingered in Leith for five days before moving on towards Holyrood Palace in the city. As they entered Edinburgh, Anne travelled in a beautiful coach drawn by six white horses; the vehicle had been sent over by the Danes in justifiable concern that the Scots might not be able to present her in suitable style. Alongside the coach rode Lennox, Bothwell and Hamilton, the ruling trio in James's absence. The king also rode nearby on horseback. In a few days Anne's coronation would take place.

Lennox assisted in the plans and preparation for Anne's coronation as queen, including bearing her crown for the ceremony, an event resisted by some leaders of the Scottish Kirk because James wanted it to take place on a Sunday. But crowned she was in Holyrood Abbey on 17 May in an elaborate seven-hour-long ceremony that some ministers found 'popish', especially the act of anointing her body with oil. The minister Robert Bruce preached and did the actual anointing of Anne. Lennox actively participated in the service, escorting the queen on several occasions, especially as she withdrew into a private chamber to prepare herself for the actual coronation. As the coronation closed, Lennox, along with other nobles of the estates, knelt and pledged fidelity to Anne. Two days later, on 19 May, Queen Anne made an official royal entry through Edinburgh, experiencing a pageant resembling the one for James in 1579. Lennox helped to arrange the pageant. Escorted by Danish and Scottish lords on horseback, Anne moved again in the special Danish chariot through the excited city. She encountered an Angel who descended to welcome her, saw on one scaffold an array of the Nine Muses, and then the Four Cardinal Virtues who, emblematically costumed, greeted the queen. Several globes burst to reveal various characters. One scene included representations of all the previous rulers of Scotland. Another displayed the seven planets from which a box covered with purple velvet and embroidered with the letter 'A' appeared; this letter set about with diamonds and precious stones came as a gift from the city. At Nether Bow Anne saw a tableau that depicted her marriage to James, a scene that rounded out this day of celebration and adulation.[29] Like James, Anne came to rely on Lennox, whom she trusted; she also became a close friend with his sister Henrietta Stuart, Countess of Huntly.

After these heady days of celebration and having successfully governed Scotland in the king's absence, Lennox remained central in governmental positions, most not sought but granted. He, for example, continued to serve on the Privy Council for the rest of his time in Scotland.[30] Lennox used the Privy Council on occasion to lodge complaints against others. For example, a report on 8 September 1593 indicates that destruction has occurred on his wooded property in Methven. The account enumerates an impressive long list of miscreants. The accusation notes that the people 'daylie and nichtlie cuttis and distroyis the said Lordis wode of Methven, peillis [peals] the bark of the treis of the said wode, and hes almaist distroyit the same, contrair the tennour of divers Actis of Parliament'.[31] The report concludes that the persons named, 'having been charged to appear and answer to the complaint, and not appearing, while the Duke appears personally, are to be denounced as rebels' (97).

In January 1595, the Privy Council reports also include instructions that King James gave to the 'Octavians', a group that the king enlisted in a futile effort to manage his household and finances. Among the principles, James took note of Lennox's position as Lord Chamberlain, stating that he

> will cause my Lord Duke of Lenox, as chamerlane of Scotland, to hald hand to the keiping of gude ordour in the howse, and punissing [punishing]

transgressouris thairof, whan his Lordship may gudelie do the samin and sall
be requeistit to that effect. (*Reg*, 5:758)

In July 1591 Lennox became Lord Admiral of Scotland, having been
granted this office, which had been vacated by the disgraced Earl of
Bothwell. He held the first admiral court the day after his appointment.
After that, less intense involvement: 'Lennox afterward followed the pattern of like-minded peers, promoting his clients and kin to handle the
actual duties of office and exercise authority on his behalf'.[32] Eventually,
Lennox appointed several relatives of Sophia Ruthven, his wife, to positions of responsibility, which they fulfilled satisfactorily. The seventeen-
year-old Lennox seems to have learned the crucial skill of delegating
authority and responsibility. Doubtless presiding over the Privy Council
in James's absence helped him develop and nurture such talents.

In November 1591, James arranged for Lennox to be appointed to the
Court of Sessions so that he 'might obtain "better sight and knowledge
of the affairs of the country, and manner of proceeding in civil cases"'.[33]
The king hoped that this position would enable Lennox to perform his
duties better. Obviously, James is grooming Lennox for continued government service and this appointment signals another vote of approval
for the duke. Also, Lennox could easily report to James on the discussion
and actions of this body.

Lennox functioned as Sheriff of Edinburgh in 1601, demonstrated in
the records of the Privy Council. Lennox lodged a complaint against the
magistrates of Edinburgh for encroaching on his prerogatives as Sheriff.
The document records: 'By the privilege of his sheriffship, the taking and
trial of thieves and malefactors within the bounds of his office apper-
tains to him'.[34] The duke is annoyed that the city authorities failed to
turn over some thieves to his jurisdiction. These magistrates argue otherwise, namely, that the thief had been caught within the bounds of the
city's freedom. But Lennox observes that they failed to try him within
the required twenty-four hours after his apprehension. The Edinburgh
authorities argue that the thief had been taken '"reid hand and with a
fang" [spoils]', and therefore they should be in charge (*Reg*, 6:209). This
rather small matter nevertheless underscores Lennox's jealous concern
for his governmental privileges and responsibilities. James seems to have
taught him well.

In that same 1591 an Act of Parliament placed Lennox in administrative oversight of the city of Glasgow. The city sought to solidify its
relationship with the duke, made obvious especially during the period
of 1596–1601.[35] 'In 1599, the duke asked the burgh to lay on a banquet

for the Earl of Huntly and his wife Henrietta Stewart', Lennox's sister (p. 85). The city pled inadequate funds but instead provided 'two tuns of wine'. The following year the city offered Lennox a seat in the High Kirk, an unusual honour. When in 1600 Lennox handed over the daily administrative duties to one of his protégés, Sir George Elphinstone, he retained an interest in Glasgow that continued into the English period, only surrendering his right to make appointments in the city in 1605.

Lennox branched out further when, in November 1594, he received appointment to the Lieutenancy of the North. This office had been occupied by his brother-in-law Huntly but he lost the post after he murdered James Stewart, second Earl of Moray, and thus continued his on-again, off-again relationship with James and the court. For various reasons, several lords of the north turned down the request to fill this office and Lennox became an obvious choice. 'The king left 100 horsemen and 100 footmen at his [Lennox's] disposal'.[36] But Lennox's tenure as Lieutenant had mixed results. David Calderwood found much to fault in his service because he 'tooke up rigourouslie the penaliteis of the commoun people that obeyed not [his] proclamatiouns, but componned easily with the assisters of the rebeles'.[37] Others accused Lennox of fraternising with Huntly, which was forbidden by the terms of his commission. While this seems egregious behaviour, no less than King James himself seldom consistently dealt with Huntly. But Lennox succeeded in getting the Earls of Errol and Huntly to leave the country, thus solving a major problem in the north and for the court. Roger Aston, in a letter to Robert Bowes dated 14 February 1595, confirms the result: 'Huntly and Errol have been heard, and all matters agreed upon concerning their departing out of the country. They have given in surety under the pain of 40,000 *l.* to depart between this and 15th March'.[38] Aston adds: 'The Duke is on his journey out of the north'. George Nicolson, writing to Bowes on 19 February, concurs and notes that Errol and Huntly are 'not to return again without the King's licence, nor to practice in the meantime against the King, the religion or country, and without any promise by the Duke for respite, remission of favour' (11:536). Along the way, Nicolson notes, Lennox 'also held Justice Courts [Justices Ayres in Scots] in Aberdeen and Elgin for the punishment of the highland thieves and broken men'. Apparently one of the results appears in a report from Nicolson to Bowes on 13 January 1595: 'Highland thieves hanged by Lennox'.[39] King James and the Privy Council responded quite favourably to Lennox's actions: 'All this was found very thankful and dutiful service by the King and Council, and the same night an act of Council was made thereupon'. Nicolson closes: 'The north is in great quietness'

(CSPS, 11:536). Thus, whatever shortcomings Lennox may have manifested in the lieutenancy, he ended with considerable success. He managed adeptly, for the moment at least, to solve a thorny problem for the king; and he left the north in 'quietness'. All in all, a political success.

Another manifestation of his political involvement came in his diplomatic missions, especially ones to France, first in 1595 and then, most important, in 1601, which included a crucial stop in England. What better way to demonstrate his relationship with James and his political importance than to engage in diplomacy in the king's name. The trip to France included a visit with his mother for the first time in eighteen years. In late July 1601 Lennox went to France at James's bidding with no particular diplomatic agenda there except to strengthen ties between the two countries and 'for confirming the old amity and friendship'.[40] He had an audience with the King of France 'and was very kindly accepted'. An anonymous 'spy' report offers a somewhat different perspective: James 'had sent his kinsman, the duke of Lennox, to France, to beg the King to maintain the ancient friendship, and when the time came to aid him in his claim to the English throne'. But, 'when the Duke submitted this to the king of France, it appears that he did not reply a single word to this purpose, although it was the main object of the embassy'.[41] This seeming indifference annoyed both Lennox and James. A few days later, the king went to Fontainebleau, where the queen was to await childbirth. Lennox followed 'and was entertained with hunting and the like sports unto the queen's delivery', which occurred on 17 September (Spottiswood, 3:100). After visiting the king and queen Lennox then went to see his mother. According to Thomas Douglas in a letter to Robert Cecil (10 February 1601), Lennox's mother had objected to his official trip to France 'unless he has greater sums of money with him than Scotland can afford at this time'.[42] Douglas, presumably quoting the mother, reports her as saying: 'I rather ye should stay in Scotland with the title (only) of a duke than in France not to perform the part of an ambassador'. Somehow, she thought that her son would travel without sufficient money and recognition; perhaps she did not understand his superior position in the Scottish court. What she and her son discussed after many years' separation remains unknown. Doubtless he brought reports of Henrietta and Marie, his sisters, and their good political fortunes, as well as his own. In the intimacy of their conversation, did Lennox explain his relationship with King James and his prominence in Scotland?

Lennox then made his way to London, his most politically important stop, arriving at the beginning of November 1601. Spottiswood reports: 'his commission indeed was no other but to salute the queen in the king's name, and let her know the kind and filial affection he carried unto her, whereof he should be willing to give proof at all occasions'.[43] Robert Cecil, Elizabeth's chief counsellor, had written to Patrick Master of Gray in Scotland, acknowledging the preparations for Lennox's visit and the queen's willingness to accept him.[44] James Elphinstone, for example, had written to Cecil in June, indicating a possible visit by Lennox and asking for Elizabeth's permission: 'if it shall happen the Duke either compelled by storm or weather or wearied of the sea willingly to enter, pass or return through her Majesty's dominions he may have a passport and safe conduct'.[45] This seemingly random possibility had, of course, been carefully planned. On 21 June Queen Elizabeth indeed granted a 'passport' for Lennox, issued to all her Admirals, ordering them to 'suffer him and them quietly to land and to enter into any our ports and towns and there to abide as long as he or they shall have occasion' (13:837).

Lennox and the queen had carried on a correspondence for some time and she understood thoroughly his importance. Two reports from Bowes to Cecil underscore Lennox's solicitous regard for Elizabeth. Bowes writes on 1 February 1597: '[He] proffered devotion and good offices of the Duke of Lennox to her Majesty'; and a month later on 23 March: 'The Duke of Lennox's devotion to her Majesty'.[46] In the background of this 1601 visit lay many transactions and negotiations between Cecil and others with King James, such as the visit of the Earl of Mar and Edward Bruce in early 1601 to the English court. All such efforts paved the way for James's eventual succession to the English crown. These plans remained unknown to the queen but they resided very much in Lennox's mind as he met Cecil and other members of the English Privy Council. Spottiswood observes: 'The duke, after three weeks' stay, being feasted by the queen and entertained with all compliments of amity, returned home, and came to Edinburgh in the end of December' (3:101).

Elizabeth herself wrote to James on 2 December about her meeting with Lennox: 'your faithful and dear Duke has at large discoursed with me as of his own knowledge what faithful affection you bear me and has added the leave he has received from you to proffer himself for the performance of my service in Ireland'.[47] She confirmed James's high opinion of Lennox:

Sure, dear brother, in my judgment for this short acquaintance that I have had with him you do not prize with better cause any near unto you. For I protest without feigning or doubting I never gave ears to greater laud than such as I have heard him pronounce of you.

Did not Thomas Fowler call Lennox a 'paragon'? With great joy and eagerness, King James, with Christmas approaching, conversed with Lennox long into the night about impressions of Elizabeth, who retained supreme political importance for James. He had never met this renowned ruler but he would succeed her in England. Lennox responded with great accounts of his time in England, gamely answering James's endless questions, not slacking in his enthusiasm and, if possible, increasing the king's desire for the English crown.

Lennox's political experience and skills aided and strengthened the relationship with Elizabeth and, perhaps more important, with Cecil and others who, behind the scenes, plotted for her eventual successor and the emergence of King James as the new monarch of England. Lennox helped make such a development more plausible and desirable. In the process Lennox developed additional ties to Queen Elizabeth and enhanced the love and respect from James. In April 1602 Lennox wrote to Cecil about his visit, recording the pleasure of that earlier occasion and pledging his support of Elizabeth: 'I . . . both remember her favours and renew my former offer with further overtures for her Highness's service, which at all occasions I more heartily embrace that it so happily succeeded, that jointly as I serve her I satisfy him whom I must always serve' (CSPS,13:974). Cecil later responded with promises of his support for Lennox, who has perfectly understood the delicate situation of needing to reach out to Elizabeth while maintaining his support of James. By so doing, Lennox gained Cecil's crucial support for James's eventual succession. An anonymous analysis in July 1593, found in Spanish records, characterises Lennox thus:

> In the court and around Edinburgh the most powerful man is the duke of Lennox, a Frenchman and a relative of the King, a young fellow of 23, very well inclined in religion . . . The King loves him dearly and would like to make him his heir, if he could.[48]

The writer concludes: 'The power of the Duke centres in the court'. This exceptional praise comes a mere ten years after Lennox's arrival in Scotland as a child, a clear testament to his status.

SIBLINGS AND MARRIAGES

All of Lennox's siblings eventually followed him to Scotland, abandoning their mother in France. Their arrival in Scotland delighted Lennox and reassured him. In a sense, the siblings now follow the path of their father, who had come to Scotland in 1579. As early as 1581, George Gordon,

Earl of Huntly, had contracted a potential marriage with the nine-year-old Henrietta Stuart, Lennox's sister. By 1586, Henrietta had become of age and Huntly decided to begin marriage arrangements.[49] With this marriage Huntly would become related to King James. Despite resistance from the Scottish Kirk because of Henrietta's overt Catholicism and Huntly's barely hidden Catholicism, the two were married in Holyrood Chapel on 21 July 1588. Huntly actually subscribed to the Confession of Faith, although his enthusiasm for this could only be suspected. For the ceremony, James took on the role of father of the bride, arranged for and paid for the festivities, and even wrote a masque for the occasion, a fragment of which survives.[50] 'The marriage secured Huntly's position at Court, and cemented the already close relationship between James and Huntly' (p. 257). Henrietta also became a confidante of Queen Anne. Such a position of political strength enabled Henrietta repeatedly to defend her husband and help secure his return to James's favour after having been banished on more than one occasion. Bowes reports to Burghley on 10 March 1596 on a disagreement between Lennox and his sister as he sought to draw her away from Catholicism and made some threats about her children if she did not comply.[51] Exactly why Lennox undertook this challenge with his sister remains unclear. In any event, nothing came of the momentary conflict. Both Huntly and Henrietta became mainstays of the Scottish court and they enjoyed a long and apparently successful marriage. And they benefited from the support of the king and Lennox.

The sister Marie also married well, becoming the second wife of John Erskine, second Earl of Mar. Thus, both of these sisters married two of the most powerful Scottish lords. Mar had been James's childhood companion and his family retained custody of Scotland's future monarchs at Stirling Castle, including Prince Henry. Mar's mother, Annabella Murray, James's 'Lady Minny', opposed this marriage because of Marie's religion. Nevertheless, the wedding took place on 7 December 1592, although it had been arranged for the summer but postponed because of Mar's illness. Marie also brought with her a staunch Catholic faith, the opposite of her husband's Protestant religion. Mar often opposed Huntly, in part on religious grounds. Some challenging dynamics developed between the two households. Mar had also been part of the group that helped drive Marie's father from Scotland in 1582; this obviously did not deter the marriage. Marie and Mar did have an intense argument with Lennox, as reported by Sir James Sempill to Robert Cecil on 26 May 1602. Marie seems to have begun the conflict: 'A month ago the Duke got letters from his sister the Countess of Mar complaining that her husband should have no opposite [opponent] in this country but him, her brother'.[52] When Lennox came to Stirling, 'she entered more roundly with him'. Mar and Lennox eventually met and sorted out what was basically a misunderstanding. The whole episode underscores that families, bound together by many common interests, nevertheless have their disagreements; Lennox found himself in the middle of them. Marie and Mar produced seven sons and five daughters. They eventually followed James to England, as did Lennox, although they retained strong ties to Scotland. Mar faithfully served James in the English court.

The third sister, Gabrielle, was betrothed to Hugh Montgomery, Earl of Eglinton, in 1598; but she decided to return to France and there entered a convent. The brother Esmé, named for their father, arrived in Scotland later but in time to move to England in 1603. There, along with Lennox, he became an important figure in the Jacobean court and a notable patron of the arts, a passion shared with Lennox. They were arguably the two most important brothers in the court besides the famous William (Pembroke) and Philip Herbert (Montgomery). Through the family travails, Lennox retained strong connections to his sisters and brother.

Two things stand out about Lennox's own marriages: unlike his sisters, he did not seek to accrue power through marriage; and in his first marriage, he risked permanent damage to his relationship with King James, blatantly going against the king's wishes. As early as 1586, when Lennox was twelve years old, names of potential marriage partners began to be floated about. John Hamilton's daughter became the first to be mentioned in a letter from Walsingham to the Master of Gray, 14 September 1586. Walsingham writes: 'Has heard the rumour of an intended marriage between the Duke of Lennox and Lord Hamilton's daughter', which the writer considers possibly dangerous.[53] Even Queen Elizabeth weighed in, expressing her opposition to such a marriage: 'the Queen's dislike of the marriage pretended between the Duke of Lennox and the daughter and heir of Lord Hamilton, and that she prayed him [James] to attend some fitter match for the said Duke'.[54] James had other ideas, specifically his kinswoman Arbella Stuart. As such Thomas Fowler reported to Walsingham on 18 December 1588: 'His majesty would fain have the Lady Arbella for this young duke, his kinsman, whom he loves, and means to work for it'.[55] James's ongoing interest in such a match is apparent in documents from March 1589.

But Lennox had other ideas and passions. He desired Sophia Ruthven, daughter of the deceased Earl of Gowrie, who had been responsible in 1582 for the capture of the king and the separation of Esmé Stuart, the father. Lennox seemed undeterred by such history. Robert Bowes reports to Burghley on 24 October 1590: 'The love betwixt the Duke of Lennox and Mrs. Lylias [Sophia] Ruthven . . . is discovered to the King, who labours by all means to draw the Duke from that marriage'.[56] Indeed, Huntly and other lords also tried to dissuade Lennox from this rash action. The couple had apparently been having an affair prior to the attempt at marriage, underscoring Lennox's passion and desirability. James went so far as to have Sophia warded with the Laird of Wester Wemyss. But Lennox invaded the place and abducted her, and they eloped and married on 20 April 1591. Another contemporary source reports: 'the Duik of Lennox past over the watter at Leith and past to the Waster Wemes and tuik out thairof ane docheter of the Erle of gowries . . . and caryit hir away on his awin hors all the nicht'.[57] No extravagant royal wedding here. Not surprisingly, James was highly offended and immediately banned Lennox and Sophia from court. Within ten days, of course, he relented, and they appeared at court. Lennox was seventeen years old at the time; thus, his action might look like teenaged romantic impetuosity. Whatever it was, it risked the ire and displeasure of the king. The experience also reveals something about Lennox's passion. Fortunately, for his sake, his relationship with James rested on a solid foundation. Alas, the marriage lasted only to May 1592, when Sophia died.

In September 1598 Lennox married again, this time a more subdued event. Nicolson reported to Cecil on 2 September: 'To-morrow the Duke is to be married but with the company of his friends and wife's in quiet sort'.[58] Once again, Lennox does not enjoy the expected large wedding. Unlike the first marriage, however, Lennox had apparently given considerable thought to this one, as manifested in a lengthy, dense legal document that constitutes a pre-nuptial agreement between him and Jean Campbell, daughter of Sir Matthew Campbell of Loudon. This agreement focuses on property and, not surprisingly, especially land. Several curious items appear also, such as the promise to 'pay yeirlie to the said Ieane during her lyftyme twenty four chalddris victuall'.[59] ('Chalddris' or 'chaldron' refers to a measure of thirty-two bushels and 'victual' is the Scots term for grain or corn.) She is also due seven 'chalddris victualles aucht score great salmonne & aucht dussane of trouttis'. The fish presumably come from the rivers that dot Lennox's properties. Therefore, 'the said nobel lord with consent forsaid bindes and oblesses [obligates] him and his forsaides' to these terms. The document looks to the future: if it shall happen 'the said nobel Lord (as god forbid) to depart this lyfe within the space of year & day efter the compleitting of the said marriage That the said Ieane not withstanding the[ere] of salhaue sufficient ryt & tytill to the hail lands', including the woods and fish. Any children of this marriage shall also enjoy title to the properties. This careful document aside, little information emerges about the marriage. Jean did give birth to two children, but both died in early childhood.

In September 1607 Lennox filed a complaint with the Privy Council against his wife, arguing that the duchess was not taking proper care of their daughter, Elizabeth. (The son had presumably died by this point.) Lennox suggests that Elizabeth is now of an age at which she needs 'educatioun and upbringing'.[60] Further, Lennox complains that Jean 'violentlie detenis [detains] and withaldis' the daughter from him. The mother and daughter did not appear, as had been ordered; thus, Lennox now requests the Council issue an 'order to denounce dame Jeane Campbell rebel'. An entry in October 1607 from the Council orders her to 'deliver Lady Elizabeth Steuart, her daughter . . . to Ludovick, Duke of Lennox, or Waltir, Lord of Blantyr, or to any other having the Duke's commission to receive her' (*Reg*, 7:696). Declaring his wife a 'rebel' solidifies the demise of this marriage, which effectively collapsed through rancour and ended with Jean's death in 1610. Lennox might have heard in this marital experience the words of King James on the subject of marriage in his *Basilicon Doron*: 'First of all consider that Mariage is the greatest earthly felicitie or miserie that can come to a man'.[61] Lennox experienced that whole spectrum.

A different kind of wrinkle in Lennox's personal relationships comes with knowledge that he apparently had an illegitimate son, presumably born in Scotland, perhaps between the first two marriages, perhaps not, but in all likelihood sometime in the early 1590s. Confirmation of Lennox's paternity comes in three reports of the Privy Council in 1611. The first occurs in an account of 20 June of the conflict between Mungo Buchanan against John Deniston for the slaughter of Buchanan's cattle. The accuser Buchanan notes that the 'author of these barbarous acts was the defender, who indeed, that very night on which the last "insolence" was committed, was seen walking on the mure [moor] with a hagbut [small firearm] in his hand'.[62] Deniston had been called before the Justices of the Peace of Dumbarton and then taken into custody by the bailiffs. The accuser appeared before the authorities, and the 'Lords ordain the said baillies [bailiffs] to deliver the defender to Sir Johne Stewart, son of Ludovik, Duke of Lennox, who is commanded to bring him before the said Lords, to be examined concerning the crimes foresaid'. This simple statement makes two things clear: that this John Stewart was the son of Lennox, and that he had already in 1611 assumed important responsibilities. Stewart's name shows up again in a report of 31 August on the matter of a bond for the release of the Earl of Orkney from Edinburgh Castle: 'The band [bond] is subscribed this day at Edinburgh Castle by the principal and cautioner before Sir Johnne Steuart, son natural [illegitimate] of Ludovik, Duke of Lennox' and others (*Reg*, 9:245). This account acknowledges the way in which John is the son of Lennox, in what seems to have been an open secret. A final item in the Privy Council reports in 1611 comes on 11 October when John MacIntyre and John Lindsay lodge a complaint against Mungo Buchanan. In a hearing MacIntyre appears, 'but not the other pursuer, and all the defenders appearing by Sir Johnne Stewart base [illegitimate] son of Ludovick, Duke of Lennox, who confesses that he caused the defenders to intromit [interfere with] with the said timber, because, as he alleged, it was cut within the Duke of Lennox's bounds' (*Reg*, 9:261). Thus, John Stewart is himself caught up in this problem, even as he has been protectively looking out for Lennox's property. The Lords 'find that the said Sir Johnne has done wrong in the violent intromitting with the one half of the said timber belonging to McInteir without any process of law, and therefore ordain him to restore to the said complainer his half'.

Additional confirmation can be found in Privy Council records of 1620. By at least 1620 John Stewart had become Keeper of Dumbarton Castle, revealed in records in which John Stewart, 'knight, constable and keeper of the Castle of Dumbarton', files a complaint against William Middlemass.[63] The Council reports that 'the custody of that castle had been committed by his Majesty to Ludovick, Duke of Lennox, the complainer's father, who entrusted it to the complainer'. This information suggests that Lennox cared for this son, although the details of the relationship remain scarce. John Stewart's complaint against Middlemass comes about because, in Stewart's absence, Middlemass had seized the castle, making 'him selff maister and commander thairof'. The Council ruled in Stewart's behalf, ordering 'the defender to deliver up the castle to Sir John and remove from it before the 7th of March next' (*Reg*, 12:209). This son will survive his father.

CONFLICTS

Lennox did not always appear as the 'paragon' of virtue and restraint. He jealously guarded his privileges and fought to sustain them, and he lashed out at those who would do any kind of harm to King James. His conflicts range from physical to political and personal. Bowes reports to Burghley on a scuffle in Edinburgh on 7 January 1591:

> In the King's retourne the other day from the Tolbuthe, the yonge laird of
> Loggye [John Wemyss] – nowe in displeasure with the Duke of Lenox by his
> disobedynece shewed in the King's chamber – parted from the King and sod-
> denly mett the Duke in the streete and followynge the King.[64]

As head of the Bedchamber, Lennox exercised his responsibility to correct behaviour of those serving with him there. In the street, Lennox
'drewe his sword and stroke Loggye. And so many swords were drawn
and such concourse of people neare the King' that several of the noblemen hustled the king into a shop for his safety. Bowes adds: 'Loggy is
lightly hurt on the head, but the Duke is commanded from the court for
some tyme, and for his unseasonable attempt so neare the King's person'.
Calderwood also reports this event with a few additional details, such
as the response of the king: 'The king fled into a closse-head, and incon-
tinent [immediately] retired to a skinner's booth, where, it is said, he
fylled his breeches for feare'.[65] James probably did not want this story
to be repeated, but it underscores James's lifetime fear of being attacked
or assassinated. Calderwood adds information about the provocation:
'The querrell was, that Logie, a varlet [servant] of the king's chamber,
would not ishe [depart] at the duke's command . . . till he was putt out
by force, whereupon he upbraided the duke' (116–17). Wemyss would
not 'upbraid' the duke again. Lennox did not tolerate such perceived
insolence and did not hesitate to strike with physical force. Although
sent away from the court for his actions, Lennox returned in a few days
with no additional penalty.

Another skirmish in 1593 turned deadly. Nerves were on edge as
conflicts with Bothwell and Huntly caused major problems; thus, small
incidents could easily escalate into full-fledged assaults. Bothwell had
attempted to injure the king and Huntly had been declared a rebel. In
that context, Bowes reports to Burghley on 14 February 1593:

> Yesterday the Duke and Sir James Sandilands purposing, as it is said, to pass
> to Leith to play at the golf, overtook Mr. John Graham, one of the Lords
> of Session, who, thinking that Sir James would assail him in revenge of the
> quarrel betwixt them, turned with his company, exceeding far the number
> with the Duke and Sir James.[66]

A fight ensued, as the parties began to shoot at each other with pistols,
'wherein Graham was slain and sundry of his servants and party sore hurt.
Sir Alexander Stewart, being with the Duke, was shot through the head
and killed'. A proposed innocent game of golf turned violent. Lennox survived, although shaken by the experience. He was obviously no stranger

to physical violence, a somewhat regular occurrence in Scotland. His impulsive, passionate responses could lead to deadly results.

Lennox, an apparent enthusiast, enjoyed a more peaceful golf game later in October 1593, as noted in a letter from Bowes to Burghley on 19 October: 'the Duke of Lenox, and Huntleye played at the Goffe on the sandes at Leithe'.[67] While at Leith, they also reported to James a sighting of Bothwell. A document in the National Records of Scotland records Lennox's purchase of golf clubs and balls. This report dates from April 1599 carrying over to 1600; it is a report from a 'bower', who seems well-connected to the duke. For example, the bower sold Lennox 'four goulff clubs to his lordship quhene my ladie came with him'.[68] Presumably, the duke's second wife, Jean Campbell, joined him for the game. This same bower delivered 'thri dousing [dozens] of goulff balls yt same sounday to his L'. This report also indicates Lennox's interest in archery, shown in his purchase of bows and arrows. Not all work and politics for Lennox; nevertheless, such pleasures do not obscure his conflicts with others.

The rest of Lennox's disputes and conflicts involved struggles over property and favour with the king, and some concerned his relatives by marriage, all evidence of his aggressive ambitions. Lennox fought with the Earl of Mar over possession of Edinburgh Castle. Disappointed about the office of Treasurer, Lennox turned his attention to gaining control of Edinburgh Castle, obvious from correspondence from Bowes to Burghley dated 21 November 1591: Lennox 'seeks again the castle of Edinburgh, which will not be readily obtained without composition and favour of the captain thereof'.[69] In a letter from James Hudson to Burghley on 31 December 1591 the writer indicates that he has argued against turning the castle over to Lennox because of his inexperience in such matters, which rings a bit hollow given Lennox's recent experiences of leading the government. The king had been inclined to award the castle to Lennox but hesitated; in addition, Queen Anne advised against it.[70] But the conflict continued even after Mar's marriage to Marie, Lennox's sister. Bowes reports to Burghley, 13 May 1592:

> The Duke of Lennox and the Earl of Mar continue their suits for the keeping of the Castle at Edinburgh. The Chancellor [John Maitland] labours earnestly for Mar, but the Duke presses the King greatly for his grant, and albeit he once gave the goodwill thereof to Mar, now he seeks it for himself by all means.[71]

Bowes adds bluntly: 'The King's present want of money is thought to prevail against Mar'. Lennox eventually succeeded and gained control of the castle, victorious over his brother-in-law. The Mar family, however, retained its management of Stirling Castle.

Lennox and Mar would continue to interact in various ways and he even supported Mar to replace Maitland as Chancellor upon the latter's death in 1595. Both Mar and Lennox had skirmishes and disagreements with Maitland, as did many others. But James needed Maitland and depended on him for counsel and administrative skills. In June 1593 James summoned both Lennox and Mar and informed them that their 'younge yeares . . . did not suffice to carry the weight of this government in these troublesome storms' and therefore he had resolved to use the Chancellor's services.[72] Both young men surrendered their claims and laid aside their differences in deference to the king and his choice. Later, Mar would not hide his disagreements with Maitland. It seems somewhat odd that James should find Lennox too young to carry out responsible governmental duties having given him effective charge of the government in 1589–90 when he went to Denmark. Perhaps James found Lennox too fractious for this crucial position. When Maitland died in 1595 Lennox did not seek that position, possibly because it would involve intense, regular administrative duties, an involvement he did not prefer. Instead, he sought to become Keeper of the Seal, an office denied him by James. John Colville writes to Bowes that Lennox seeks the Seal position and honour and the Chancellor position seems likely to go to Mar.[73] Two weeks later, in October 1595, Roger Aston reports to Bowes that the 'Duke "commenses" this course and is altogether for Mar'.[74] Not even Lennox's support for Mar could prompt the king to decide about the important Chancellor position. Indeed, James waited until 18 January 1599 to name John Graham, third Earl of Montrose, as Chancellor; he had earlier served as guardian of the young Lennox. Not even family connections could always stifle conflict between ambitious young men.

Although they had worked together peacefully in governing Scotland during James's absence, Lennox and the much older Lord John Hamilton, eventually first Marquess of Hamilton, had serious disagreements and arguments involving status and property in the mid-1590s. The basis for enmity lay in the Hamiltons' claim to the Scottish throne. They descended from a daughter of King James II. Before Lennox's arrival and elevation as Duke of Lennox John Hamilton was the obvious heir to the throne. Lennox supplanted him, and the Hamiltons never lost sight of that development. Many recognised Lennox as being 'nearest' to the throne, a position he held until the birth of Prince Henry in 1594. The relationship between Hamilton and Lennox gains further complication because Hamilton is the uncle of Huntly, Lennox's other brother-in-law.

An anonymous report in March 1593 documents a struggle over Hamilton's determination to hold court at Linlithgow, a move that Lennox opposes.

> Since the Duke takes part with Sir James Sandilands, who claims that seigniory and purposes . . . with the assistance of the Duke and other friends, to stay Hamilton's progress herein, troubles are like to arise and the griefs smoking in the hearts of the Duke and Hamilton are like to burst hastily into flame unless speedy remedy be provided.[75]

Hamilton has additional worry because a friend of his had been killed in Edinburgh's streets by 'the King's guard discharging their pieces in their going to the watch'. Two months later Lennox finds himself the victim of scurrilous libels, brought against him by Chancellor Maitland and Hamilton that he, Lennox, had supported Bothwell's causes and intended to give him some revenue.[76] The 'Duke was warned that some of his enemies had conspired his death'. Bowes concludes: 'It is feared that out of these practices great dissension shall follow betwixt the Stewarts and Hamiltons, and in every corner quarrels arise so fast amongst persons of quality'. In June, Bowes reports that King James 'wishes good agreement betwixt the Duke and Hamilton. The Duke sent the Laird of Bogie to remove all suspicion of any unkindness towards Hamilton, who answered that he never gave any just cause of offence'.[77] Hamilton does let pass the opportunity to state his fundamental grievance, namely, that Lennox has 'defrauded him of his birthright, in that he endeavoured to have been declared the second person in succession of this crown'. There's the rub. The politics of late sixteenth-century Scotland remain fraught, to the king's dismay and fear. Potential harm lurks in these quarrels; no simple solution prevails, especially as Lennox gains more and more kingly favour and wealth. Griefs smoking in the hearts can easily burst into flame, endangering the country's welfare. Lennox is not immune nor free of blame.

The strife between Hamilton and Lennox continues into the latter part of the 1590s. The battle shifts to a struggle over Dumbarton Castle, which James had given to Hamilton in 1586 'for life'. As early as 16 September 1592 Bowes writes to Burghley of the 'Alarm of John Hamilton lest Dumbarton Castle shall be taken from him'.[78] Lennox intensifies his struggle against Hamilton to the point that, according to an anonymous source of 21 May 1593, 'A hunting between the King and Lord Hamilton prevented by Lennox'.[79] The fight over property becomes a kind of proxy for the contention about the relative position or proximity to the Scottish throne. Lennox now makes his move to secure

Dumbarton Castle for himself; if he succeeds, he will control two of the three principal castles associated with the king, having already wrested from Mar a claim to Edinburgh Castle. Bowes reports to Burghley on 8 September 1597 what may be the opening salvo. He writes: 'The Duke of Lennox (pretending [intending] title to the castle of Dumbarton by ancient grant made thereof by the King of Scots to the Earl of Lennox his ancestor) has made petition to the King to be restored to his right therein'.[80] James seeks the easy way out of this conundrum by trying to persuade Hamilton's bastard son to urge his father to surrender the castle to Lennox. But Hamilton insists and reminds the king that the castle was 'given by the King to him for term of his life and for his own security' (CSPS, 13:82). Further, Hamilton claims that such a potential surrender will add 'public and great dishonour' to his name. He also worries that Lennox might try to take the castle by force, and he promises a force of 10,000 men to defend it. For the moment James decides to lie low, but Hamilton continues to fear a surprise attack. Each side stands firmly against the other, but surely Hamilton makes a good point that, having been granted the castle 'for life', he should not be compelled to surrender it. Lennox seems to be trying to see what he can gain in his ongoing quarrel with Hamilton. Does he in fact need Dumbarton Castle?

Each succeeding month breathes more life and uncertainty into the struggle, whose outcome may seem foreordained, given Lennox's status and the king's regard. Lennox begins to believe that his honour is at stake, rather than trying to turn the tables on Hamilton's position, as he argues that Hamilton resists Lennox's legitimate claim to the castle. Hamilton digs in his heels and says that Lennox shall not have it 'but upon the swordpoint'.[81] Two intractable forces wage war. In late October 1597 James makes another move, trying to quell a potentially raging fire. He suggests some kind of commission to mediate the conflict. Hamilton resists, claiming that Parliament also gave him the castle, and he will not negotiate with Lennox about it. 'The King seems scarce satisfied herein and the Duke has heard . . . that Hamilton has been liberal in speech against him'.[82] These beginnings, as Bowes writes, 'are like to produce some storms'. Storms now join fire in the maelstrom. Bowes returns to the metaphor on 31 October: 'The contention betwixt the Duke and the Lord John Hamilton still continues and increases threatening some storm to arise thereby'.[83] Again, the idea of mediation appears with a report to be given to the 'umpirage of the King'. Hamilton remains intractable. But Bowes observes: 'Nevertheless it is looked that the Duke shall receive favour and contentment at the Parliament and otherwise in Court for recovery of the castle'. Bowes seems to have adopted Lennox's argument about the return of the castle being but a 'recovery' of his superior claim. The ambassador adds another point, namely that some people worry that 'the castles of Edinburgh, Stirling and Dumbarton, being the chief strengths in this realm, should be cast altogether in the hands of the Duke and the Earl of Mar so nearly allied to Huntly' (CSPS, 13:117). Bowes correctly senses the ultimate outcome of this struggle: Lennox will win. The king himself begins to hint at such a result.

On 9 December 1597 George Nicolson reports to Cecil that the matter between Lennox and Hamilton is 'of no small importance to the quietness' of the land and that all of this noise has moved James 'to use his authority to take Dumbarton from Lord Hamilton for the Duke'.[84] A few days later Lennox marched with forces to the town of Hamilton, angering Hamilton, who believed it 'some stratagem to be devised against him'.[85] Even though the officers pointed out that they were merely on 'retreat', Hamilton furiously responded, breaking the soldiers' drums, for example. Despite all the drama that has battened onto this conflict, on 20 January 1598 Aston calmly writes to James Hudson: 'The Duke and the Lord Hamilton are agreed and the castle of Dumbarton shall be delivered to the Duke on Saturday next'.[86] Aston, in his succinct statement, might have said more accurately that Hamilton agreed; Lennox surrendered nothing. The will of the king and the strength of Lennox have snuffed out the fires of rage. Dejected, Hamilton can no longer fight on this matter.

Bothwell, cousin of King James and Lennox, enjoyed considerable favour with the king in the 1580s but, through a series of disastrous choices, Bothwell destroyed the king's trust and support. Some of Bothwell's actions intersected Lennox's life and involved him and tarnished his reputation, at least for a while. But Bothwell, along with Hamilton, ably assisted Lennox in governing Scotland during James's trip to Denmark in 1589–90. This may have been the highpoint for Bothwell, following up on his admission to the king's bedchamber in 1582 and his appointment as Lord High Admiral in 1588. From this peak Bothwell descended rather precipitously. His attacks on James, including physical assaults, infected the court and touched Lennox. When James returned from Denmark he found that Lennox had joined with Bothwell in creating a kind of 'Stewart faction' at court, sometimes opposing the king's will. Somewhere on the outskirts of Bothwell's shenanigans Huntly lurks. Bothwell and Huntly succeed in creating enormous headaches for James, and not incidentally, for Lennox. Conundrums abound.

In the spring of 1591, Bothwell colluded with Huntly and others to march against the king's forces in what became known as the 'Brig o'

Dee rebellion', a rebellion that eventually came to naught because James had amassed sufficient troops and Huntly's forces retreated rather than fight. James made his way on to Aberdeen without opposition. Although Bothwell was on the outskirts of this event he was charged with treason, added to an earlier charge of witchcraft. James was not in a forgiving mood. Although imprisoned for a while, Bothwell escaped and roamed about freely, but he did not escape the king's stripping him of positions, giving Lennox, in fact, the position of Admiral. Bothwell had set in motion his ill fate. But he never seemed to learn, depending on audacity rather than good sense.

A daring feat in late December 1591 revealed Bothwell's poor judgement and implicated Lennox in its execution. On the evening of 27 December Bothwell brazenly attacked Holyrood Palace, where the king and queen resided. Calderwood records: 'He and his complices came to the king's doore, the queen's, and the chanceller's; at one tyme with fire for the king's doore, with hammers to the queen's doore'.[87] Bowes, writing to Burghley on 5 January 1592, provides potentially incriminating details, claiming that Bothwell gained entry into the palace through the duke's stable, where the horses had been tied that 'they should not hinder the passage, and also steel caps and weapons ready for such of Bothwell's fellowship as wanted, and a new ladder'.[88] Bowes adds that 'an especial servant of the Duke was in company with Bothwell in that action, together with sundry other circumstances noted in the behaviour and words of the Duke and his wife'. Calderwood concludes: 'It was suspected that the duke was upon the conspiracie, for the conspirators came through his stables, and he himself came not till all was ended' (5:141). Fortunately, the Provost of Edinburgh got word of what was happening and roused sufficient numbers of citizens to come to the palace, thereby assuring that Bothwell could not succeed. The following day, according to Calderwood, James went to the Kirk in Edinburgh for a service of thanksgiving. Patrick Galloway preached, using the text of Psalm 134, highlighting the king's deliverance from harm. Bothwell once again escaped and, despite charges against him and efforts to capture him, moved about the country without restraint. Suspicion and circumstantial evidence made Lennox look bad in this situation, but nothing came of it. James simply rejoiced in not being harmed, although unnerved by Bothwell's ill-conceived actions.

Such actions continued, Bothwell unable to let well enough alone. On at least two occasions the king sent Lennox to pursue Bothwell: first, with Huntly on 9 February 1592 and then with Home on 30 July that year.[89] Instead, on 27 June 1592, with three hundred men, Bothwell attacked

Falkland Palace, where James was residing. Bothwell used a battering ram, attempting to break down the door. James had been moved to a secure place in the palace. The assault continued at various levels of intensity for some six hours before Bothwell gave up and left. James had much reason to feel insecure and to worry about those around him. Treachery of some kind was afoot. This time no suspicion came Lennox's way.

But Lennox did participate in Bothwell's last disastrous attempt to harm King James, which may well have been in James's thoughts when he did not appoint him to the Chancellor position. On 24 July 1593 Bothwell gained entry into Holyrood Palace through the back gate, once again suggesting a measure of inside help. He, according to Calderwood, 'rapped rudelie at the king's chamber doore, which was opened by the Erle of Atholl . . . the king sitting in the meane tyme upon the privie, and William Murrey with him'.[90] This state of undress embarrassed and threatened the king. James would have gone to the queen's chamber, 'but the doore was locked, and the duke, Atholl, [and others] went between him and the doore, and interceded for him'. Now, Lennox appears fully involved with this escapade, but perhaps with good purpose. Bothwell brandished a sword and James thought his life was in danger. The king asked what they meant: 'Came they to seeke his life? lett them take it: they would not gett his soule'. But Bothwell, upon his knees, claimed that 'he sought not his life, but came to seeke his Hienesse' pardoun for the Road [raid] of the Abbey, and the Road of Falkland'. Cooler heads prevailed; James agreed to a compromise and Bothwell consented to withdraw from the court until his trial for witchcraft. Edinburgh, soon aware of some controversy, was in a state of 'great confusion' (Calderwood, 5:257). Hundreds of people came towards the palace. James shouted from a window that the 'Erle of Bothwell had come in upon him by [without] his expectatioun and foreknowledge; had promised faire'. Things calmed down; and Calderwood concludes his report: 'In the meane tyme, the duke keeped the backe gate, the Laird of Craigiehall the fore gate'.

Did Bothwell initially intend bodily harm to the king? Why were Lennox and others involved at all? Perhaps Lennox truly thought that a meeting between Bothwell and the king, no matter how fraught, would generate peace; but this event certainly seems a strange way to go about attaining peace. It offered only momentary respite. Bothwell's action, piled in on top of earlier ones, sealed his fate. By 1595 he went into permanent exile in France. Queen Elizabeth's overt and covert support of Bothwell further complicated matters for James. Even she, eventually, tired of him and abandoned him. In fact, James wrote to Elizabeth on 19 September to recount the July event and to explain his reaction to it, namely, to excuse his leniency towards Bothwell, which James does with complicated logic. The king writes somewhat hopefully: 'If he behave himself well hereafter, the better will it be for him; if otherwise, ye and all the Christian princes in the world shall be witnesses of my part'.[91] Exactly what James would have done remains unknown, as Bothwell's exile took care of the problem. Ironically, Queen Anne, unlike Elizabeth, remained in contact with Bothwell, whom she liked.

As troublesome as Bothwell proved to be, George Gordon, Earl of Huntly, offered stiff competition for that designation. No greater thorn in the royal side existed, in large measure because James adored him; thus, every slight, large or small, resonated with unusual pain. And Huntly presented many occasions for challenges and pain. Lennox fits sometimes uncomfortably in this relationship; after all, Huntly married Lennox's sister Henrietta in 1588. He had also supported and befriended their father Esmé during his time in Scotland. No matter the damage that Huntly caused, James could never bring himself to be harsh with him. Huntly's Catholicism, regularly denied, complicated these relationships. Henrietta's religious persuasion was obvious. All that aside, Huntly was probably the most powerful Scottish lord; at moments he seemed like a member of the royal family. Members of the ruling class needed a scorecard to know at any given moment if Huntly was in or out of royal favour.[92]

The full flush and excitement of the Huntly wedding had barely faded when in February 1589 James learned of Huntly's collusion with Spain. He had been part of a group of Scottish Catholic leaders who had written to King Philip II of Spain, offering their assistance should the Spanish decide to invade Scotland – all of this not long after the threat of the Spanish Armada. This revelation shocked James, Lennox and other supporters of the king. These Catholics had committed treason. But James could only muster enough outrage to sentence Huntly to imprisonment in Edinburgh Castle, a sentence that lasted one whole week, 27 February–7 March.

Instead of harsh punishment James wrote Huntly a solicitous letter, full of remonstrance and personal hurt. Even during Huntly's extremely brief imprisonment, James visited him regularly and dined with him. Lots of rhetorical flourishes in the letter, not uncommon to James, raise uncertainty about the seriousness of it. James comes across as a jilted lover, which may indeed be how he felt. James writes plaintively:

> how many million of times, and specially that night in the cabinet, after that suspicion among you in the abbey, did I not then, I say, amongst innumerable other times resolve you that ye could not both trow [trust] me and those busy

reporters about you, and assured I you not that I could not be your friend if ye trusted these practisers [plotters].[93]

'Millions of times' compounds with 'innumerable other times' to exaggerate the feeling. The 'night in the cabinet' presumably refers to a private meeting, perhaps in the king's closet. James asks rhetorically: 'As for me, what further trust can I have in your promises, confidence in your constancy, or estimation of your honest meaning?' (p. 91). By asking this question, James effectively answers it. He closes by urging Huntly 'never to trust hereafter but such as I trust' (91). This remarkable letter demonstrates James's anguish and sense of betrayal, but it also serves to discharge his outrage. One week in prison for treason.

In 1592, Huntly received a commission from James to track down Bothwell. These two sometimes functioned together; sometimes, they clashed as enemies. Keeping track of both must have cost James many sleepless nights. Lennox often felt caught in the middle; certainly, he cared deeply for his brother-in-law and sister but he could see Huntly's unreliability. In late 1592 Huntly crossed another dangerous boundary because authorities discovered yet another Spanish conspiracy, known as the 'Spanish Blanks' affair, supported by Huntly and other Catholic lords. Blank pages with Huntly's signature, and that of others, offered support for a proposed Spanish invasion. Someone would fill in the blanks with specific plans. The Scottish Kirk reacted in fear and demanded action from James, who did muster a force in February 1593 and marched to Aberdeen to encounter Huntly, who, of course, had escaped. No serious punishment ensued. Lennox, as noted earlier, did, as Lieutenant of the North, succeed in getting Huntly, Errol and others to agree to terms that spelled out the conditions for their departure from Scotland. Thus, in 1595, Huntly went into exile in France, only to return the following year, even though his time of exile had not expired. James readily welcomed Huntly and Henrietta to court, all apparently forgiven. Huntly would no longer exercise power, however. For this, Lennox could also be grateful: the threats of Bothwell and Huntly had subsided.

ROYAL FAMILY

Lennox's connections with the royal family centred, understandably, on the king with whom Lennox had, for the most part, a mutually loving relationship. James loved Lennox from the moment of his arrival, greeting him with kisses and taking personal care of him. Their mutual love did not resemble that shared between James and Esmé Stuart, which was more intense and more intimate with some level of homoerotic desire. Even though James was eight years older than Ludovic he initially regarded him as his child. Their love grew over time, and it never faltered, with a few exceptions, such as Lennox's first, impetuous marriage to Sophia Ruthven. But disfavour never lasted. Thomas Fowler in March 1589 outlined the fourteen-year-old Lennox's attributes, such as his skill as a horseman, courtesy and grace; he concluded by pronouncing Lennox a 'paragon'.[94] Fowler states simply: 'The King loves this Duke as him selfe'. Proof of that love Fowler finds in James's determination to find an appropriate match for Lennox: 'all the Kinges care was how he myght procuer the L[ady] Arbell for wyffe to the sayd Duke'. A headstrong teenager did not accede to James's choice for a suitable wife. Fowler also reports, 'for more proffe of love to the sayd Duke hys majestie dealt secretly I know, which was to disprove the tytell of the Hameltons to the crowne of Scotland and to approve the Duke's'. That would be a major sign of love; in this matter James, of course, succeeded, much to the dismay of the Hamiltons, who maintained a grudge against Lennox for this disruption of their claim.

The year 1594 became pivotal in the royal family and for Lennox, a year full of rejoicing, celebration and strife. On 19 February, at Stirling Castle, Prince Henry was born, now the heir apparent to the Scottish throne. The royal family would not be the same after this. Rejoicing and relief greeted Henry's birth. James had now fulfilled one of his major functions, namely to produce an heir. For the first time in nearly thirty years the Scottish people could focus on the significance and possibilities of a royal child. Henry's birth removed Lennox from immediate succession to the throne but he did not mind. Stability and an assured future for the country loomed as much more important. This birth also increased James's status as a likely successor to Queen Elizabeth. Necessary repairs and enlarging Stirling Castle caused Henry's baptism to be deferred until 30 August; this also allowed time to round up many foreign dignitaries for the ceremony. James hoped by this display to show the rest of Europe how a powerful monarch could function.

But a major problem sullied the celebration, namely, conflict between James and Queen Anne, an ongoing struggle in which Lennox sometimes found himself in the middle. Shortly after Henry's birth, James made an eminently sensible decision that nevertheless caused insuperable strife with Anne. James decided to place his son in the care of the Earl of Mar, Lennox's brother-in-law and James's childhood companion. The Earl and his mother, the Countess of Mar, at Stirling Castle would have major charge over this child. In an official act, the king notes that the

Mar family, including the countess, had taken care of him when he was a child, providing him with the only nurture that he experienced for several years.

> His Highness with advice of his Privy Council . . . makes, constitutes and ordains the said John Earl of Mar Keeper and Governor to the said Prince within the Castle of Stirling, with enjoyment of such honours, privileges and commodities as he, his father and grandfather enjoyed of before and with power to do all things needful for the execution of the premises.[95]

James only followed what had become common practice among royal and aristocratic families, the farming out of children. The fact of a royal child, and in this case heir apparent, necessitated special concern for his personal safety. Such an arrangement assured James ultimate control over the destiny of this child, and he eventually took similar action for all the royal children, although none of the others was secluded at Stirling. Although James followed tradition, he apparently had no other models or ideas about the nurturing of children. Anne, on the other hand, did possess different concepts of child-rearing, having herself experienced genuine family life. She and James fought over the issue of Henry's rearing for a decade. To be denied care and nurture of her child shocked and angered Anne.

Anne did not give up easily. In late February 1595 she made a 'motion' for the keeping of Prince Henry. Her action, Aston reports to Bowes on 4 March, results in 'the King these four days past very mightily, and he is highly offended with the plotlayers of this course'.[96] James apparently saw in these plans hints of his overthrow. Anne raised the topic again in June, compelling James in late July to write to Mar, confirming the arrangement. In this letter James wrote bluntly: 'you not to deliver him [Henry] out of your hands except I command you with my own mouth'.[97] James even writes that, should he prematurely die, Mar should not surrender the prince until Henry 'be eighteen years of age and that he command you himself'. Anne will bring this situation to a boiling point in 1603 and Lennox will have to intervene.

Expanding and enlarging the Chapel Royal at Stirling took much longer than expected and it cost money that James did not readily have. Thus, he struck a deal with merchants of Edinburgh, using the last of the money that Anne had brought as her dowry. This action hit a sensitive nerve in Anne. Bowes writes to Cecil on 21 April of this financial arrangement and Anne's displeasure. The Edinburgh merchants will use 'such part of the money received with her on their marriage and concredited to them for yearly profit'; the queen is 'little pleased', which ranks high in a list of understatements.[98] Anne apparently had not given her approval to this use of her dowry. Despite the joy of Henry's birth and the excitement of preparing for his baptism, the king and queen exist in uneasy tension.

But the conflict between them was not just financial; jealousy raises its ugly head. John Colville writes to Cecil on 26 July: 'It is certain that the King has conceived a great jealousy of the Queen, which burns the more the more he covers it'. This startling statement is compounded by Colville's next sentence: 'The Duke is the principal suspected. The Chancellor casts in materials to this fire. The Queen is forewarned, but with the like cunning will not excuse till she be accused'.[99] Colville worries that 'the end can be no less tragical than was betwixt his [James's] parents'. A few days later Colville added that James 'repents' all the plans for the elaborate baptism and that because of his jealousy 'he begins to doubt of the child . . . That matter takes deep root on both sides' (11:397). James begins to resemble Leontes in Shakespeare's *The Winter's Tale*, who irrationally and suddenly suspects his wife of adultery, thinks that his dear friend is responsible and doubts his son's paternity. Queen Anne obviously liked and trusted Lennox, but James had no serious reason to believe the patently absurd idea that Lennox should be blamed. The whole situation put Lennox in an untenable position. Jealousy, as Colville notes, takes 'deep root'. Tension has escalated and ensnared Lennox in its vortex. Records do not clarify exactly how or when passions subsided; but eventually James moved on, disgruntled and frustrated, but somehow surrendering the bizarre accusation against Anne and Lennox. The flame of jealousy smouldered and then burned out. The waters of baptism possibly helped.

This turmoil gets punctuated by two quite different moments. In a serene and revealing event, Bowes reports to Cecil on 13 April 1594: 'The King is now determined to pass quietly to-morrow to Stirling, taking with him the Duke alone'.[100] In that quietness and togetherness James and Lennox discussed the recent birth of Henry, the plans for the baptism and many other matters; and they enjoyed the journey away from the stress of Edinburgh. This wonderful image of the two together with no one else conveys simply the love that flowed between them, making all the more outrageous James's accusations a few months later. In a stark and anonymous message of 24 July, this news appears: 'The Duke of Lennox is deadly sick'.[101] No other reports comment on what must have been a frightening and monumental event. Surely James feared Lennox's illness and possible death; he would lose his most reliable and valuable confidant and advisor. From this threatening moment, Lennox finally emerged and remained in good health. The year 1594 contains a dazzling and, at times, baffling area of events. And then, finally, Henry's baptism in August.

No other occasion in late sixteenth-century Scotland surpasses the festive events associated with the baptism; no other occasion brought together such a wide swathe of European dignitaries, enabling King James to bask proudly in the excitement and celebration. In this late August Scotland seemed, for a fleeting moment, to play an out-sized role in European courts, a country and court to be reckoned with. The delayed baptism seemed well worth the wait. James had himself overseen the renovation and expansion of the Chapel Royal at Stirling. Queen Elizabeth, although not present, sent a gift and a special ambassador, Robert Radcliffe, Earl of Sussex. James shrewdly named her as godmother to the new prince. No one surpassed Lennox in importance in these events; he appeared to be everywhere, from the tournament to the sacred rites in the chapel to the great hall with its banquet and indoor pageant. Knowledge of these events comes from William Fowler's pamphlet, published in Edinburgh and London in 1594 and reprinted in London in 1603. Fowler served as Secretary to Queen Anne and he had participated in the marriage negotiations between her and James.[102]

The king, in consultation with Fowler and Patrick Leslie, Lord Lindores, determined that the festivities 'were to be deuided both in Feeld pastimes, with Martiall and heroicall exploites, and in houshold, with rare shewes and singular inventions' (Nichols, 3:747). Two days before the baptism itself the martial exploits took place in a valley below the castle and they involved running at the ring in a tournament. The participants included three 'Christians', led by James, Mar and Thomas Erskine; three 'Turks', led by Lennox, Alexander, sixth Lord Home and Robert Ker; three 'Amazons', 'in womens attyre, verie sumptuouslie clad' (748), led by Lord Lindores, Walter Scott of Buccleuch and John Bothwell, the Abbot of Holyrood Abbey. (Including the abbot in woman's attire as an Amazon must have been a source of considerable amusement.) The rules of the tournament, copious and thorough, governed this martial exercise. Queen Anne promised a reward of a 'riche Ring of Diamonds' (750) to the winner. 'The victorie fel to the Duke of *Lennox*, who bringing it to his side & pairtie, had the praise and prise adiudged to himself'. Thus ended the first day's celebration with Lennox as victor. The planned second day of martial games did not occur because everyone was just too busy with other functions.

The baptismal day arrived. King James processed first into the chapel with accompanying lords; then followed the many ambassadors, sent

first to the prince's chamber where the infant Henry 'was lying on his
bed of Estate, richly decored, and wrought with brodered work, containing the story of *Hercules* and his trauels' (Nichols, 3:752). The 'old
Countesse of Mar . . . took vp the Prince, and deliuered him to the Duke
of *Lennox*', who in turn passed Henry to the Earl of Sussex, Elizabeth's
personal representative, who then carried the baby into the chapel. In
the chapel 'the Princes Robe-royall, being of purple Veluote, very richelie
set with pearl, was deliuered to the Duke of *Lennox*, who put the
same about the prince' (752). Several other such transfers of the child
occurred, all involving Lennox, such as the approach to the pulpit for the
actual baptism when Lennox received Henry from the Countess of Mar
and again delivered him to Sussex. Henry has the distinction of being
the first Scottish royal baby to be baptised according to Protestant rites,
underscored by the choice of the preacher Patrick Galloway, Church of
Scotland minister, known for his strong anti-Catholic views. Galloway
used as his text Genesis 21, the story of Sarah. The choir then sang an
anthem from Psalm 21. The Bishop of Aberdeen, David Cunningham,
performed the rite of baptism, calling out the child's name, 'Frederick
Henry, Henry Frederick'. The crowd moved next to the King's Hall
where Lennox presented the baby to James who dubbed him a knight
and put a small ducal crown on his head.

And then the extraordinary feast and entertainment. After the assembled gathering of royal family and foreign dignitaries had feasted sumptuously, 'there came into sight of them all, a *Black-Moore*, drawing . . .
a triumphall Chariot . . . that it appeared to be drawen in, onely by
the strength of a *Moore*, which was very richly attyred, his traces were
great chaines of pure gold' (Nichols, 3:758). The chariot carried an
array of allegorical and mythological figures, all elaborately costumed
and bearing emblems and mottoes pertinent to them: Ceres, Fecundity,
Faith, Concord, Liberality and Perseverance (759–60). The chariot, the
writer reports, should have been drawn by a lion, but that might have
brought fear into the hall. Then followed a ship some 24ft long, containing Neptune, Thetis, Triton and Arion, all appropriately costumed. This
device refers to the king's own voyage to Denmark to fetch Anne: 'The
Kings Maiestie, hauing vndertaken in such a desperate time, to sayle to
Norway, and like a newe *Iason*, to bring his Queene our gracious Lady
to this Kingdome' (762). After the various figures on the ship distributed
gifts from the sea, a song followed, accompanied by viols. The song, sung
in Latin, not surprisingly praises James and cites the tokens 'of a loving
marriage. / Anna, I pray that you live happy and happily for many years'
(763). That 'loving marriage' has been sorely tested in the events leading

to the baptism. After more songs, the space cleared for the revels. Then, following a delicious light repast, guests began to leave: 'they departed about three of the clock in the morning, to their nights rest' (764). The prince has been safely asleep for several hours. Finally, James, Anne, Lennox and the various ambassadors straggled to their places in Stirling Castle, content, satisfied, knowing that they had participated in a historic and exceptional event. Scotland's star shone brightly on this day and night: an heir apparent has been duly baptised and recognised by world representatives. Lennox has helped burnish that star.

Royal births and baptisms occurred almost unabated for the next several years and Lennox appears at all of them. First, Anne gave birth to Princess Elizabeth in late November 1596; she was baptised at Holyroodhouse on 28 November. Bowes reports to Queen Elizabeth that the 'Duke of Lennox, three Earls, some ladies and the principal officers of Edinburgh shall attend'.[103] Bowes complains a few days later that presents from Queen Elizabeth have not yet arrived: 'it is high time that her gifts shall be speedily sent to me' (358). The ambassador then receives a terse letter from Cecil, who does not understand Bowes's apparent confusion about matters and observes the queen's displeasure: 'her Majesty wills you to proceed in her name, and thus to carry yourself: first, to let the King know that although she has not been by any letter of his invited or advertised who should accompany her at the christening as partner', she wishes to let the world know of her readiness to participate (373). Apparently some of the planning for this baptism has gone awry, underscored by Elizabeth's pointed comments. On 14 December, Bowes writes to George Nicolson about the baptism: 'On Sunday, 28 November last the Princess was baptised at Holyroodhouse. She was carried and presented to the baptism by myself supplying that office for and in the name of her Majesty, the only godmother, and she was named Elizabeth' (CSPS, 12:387). The queen may not have received an invitation in timely fashion, but surely being named godmother and giving the child her name must have settled the ruffled feathers. Bowes adds that the 'Duke of Lennox and the Earl of Mar helped to support me only for my ease in the carriage'. Bowes makes the point that since he had no gift from the queen to present, he simply avoided the subject, confident that in due time she would send a gift. (Perhaps when she received her invitation?!) Edinburgh officials, however, being invited to the feast, gave the princess 10,000 'marks Scots to be paid at her marriage'.

Not much in 1596 resembled the elaborate festivities associated with Henry's baptism. That remains true for the remaining baptisms. A brief report from Nicolson to Cecil, 20 April 1599, reports the birth of

Princess Margaret, who was on a Sunday 'baptised and named Margaret, second daughter of Scotland, the Duke [Lennox], Earl of Huntly, Lord Hamilton, and the rest of the noblemen and ladies being gossips [god-parents]'.[104] Feasting, dancing and running at the ring occupied the following Monday. On 19 November 1600 Prince Charles was born at Dunfermline Palace, Fife, and then baptised by David Lindsay, Bishop of Ross, on 23 December at Holyrood Palace. The records remain fairly silent about what festivities took place, perhaps few because of enmity between the king and queen. In fact, Anne believed that James did not care about the baby; and she, according to George Nicolson, therefore 'cared not with how little honour it should be baptised'.[105] She urged James to postpone the baptism so that her brother, King Christian IV of Denmark, could attend sometime in the spring. James refused.

Thus, Anne, as Nicolson notes, 'comes not to it [the baptism]' (CSPS, 13:749). Certainly the atmosphere does not lend itself to celebratory festivities. A fuller report accompanies the birth of Prince Robert, thanks to Thomas Douglas writing to Cecil on 6 May 1602. Douglas notes: 'the christening was kept with no great solemnity (God knows)'.[106] Douglas adds:

> The witnesses in the christening [at Dunfermline] were the Duke of Lennox, who was for the Marquess of Huntly his brother-in-law, who by reason of his late sickness could not be present . . . The Duke as nearest of blood carried the child to the church, and the Earl of Argyll held him up to the christening. (982)

Baptisms of royal children regularly took place with Lennox's understandable presence, underscoring, yet again, his prominence and importance for the royal family. (Sadly, neither Margaret nor Robert survived childhood.)

On 5 August 1600 a very strange episode took place that involved the king and Lennox, along with others. (To this day scholars remain puzzled about what exactly took place and why.) Apparently, Alexander Ruthven and his brother, the Earl of Gowrie, encouraged James to leave his hunting near Falkland and follow them to their castle because supposedly some curious treasure had been found. The king dismissed Lennox and went along with Alexander. (This same family had been involved with separating Esmé Stuart from James in 1582 and yet this somehow did not raise James's suspicions.) Lennox and Mar secretly followed anyway. After dinner with the Earl of Gowrie, the king followed Alexander to a remote upper part of the castle, Alexander locking every door behind him as they ascended. In a dark room James suddenly encountered an armed stranger, whose precise identity remains uncertain. James finally realised that he stood in danger of being killed; he struggled with the stranger and Alexander and finally cried out. After frantic effort, James's pages eventually found him and came to his aid, killing Alexander and the earl, who had ascended the steps for some unknown reason. Lennox and Mar had been misled by Gowrie, who told them that James had departed by another gate. They discovered what had happened and promptly went into the village to calm any possible uprising or disturbance. James had escaped without harm; he remained the only surviving eyewitness, which allowed him to construct a narrative of the event, his 'King James Version'.[107]

James insisted to one and all that the Ruthvens had wanted to murder him and so he gave out an official version of the story.[108] He also insisted that ministers of the Kirk should offer prayers for his deliverance. This idea received a frosty response. They did appear before the Privy Council where they heard James's letter, his version of things, and were admonished to ring church bells and give praise to God. But the ministers, Calderwood reports, 'answered all in one voice, they were not certain of the treasoun, and, therefore could make no mention of it; but would say, in general, that he [James] was delivered from a great danger' (6:45). They would not hide their incredulity. James sent all the recalcitrant ministers away from Edinburgh until they recanted. Robert Bruce, who played a crucial role in Anne's coronation, refused to relent and James banished him from Edinburgh on pain of death.

One document nicely sums up reactions to James's account: 'manie did not, nor doe not to this houre, beleeve the discourse of the conspiracie, and the depositiouns extant in print; yitt manie were not curious to examine or consider everie particular circumstance . . . and were content to be ignorant, or to beleeve'.[109] Lying low, if possible, seems to be the order of the day – ask Robert Bruce. Queen Anne did not hesitate to express her incredulity, and in this matter, she had plenty of company. Queen Elizabeth, on the other hand, sent a letter to James, dated 21 August 1600, congratulating him on his survival and his 'happy estate', reminding him that 'you are and one of whom since your cradle I have ever had tender care'.[110] Whatever Elizabeth may have thought about the story, she knew her duty to a fellow monarch.

Lennox seems to have adopted a rather silent approach, being wise enough to accept James's version of this frightening event, but never expressing any ringing endorsement of the received narrative. Of course, he had to be very grateful that James was not killed. After all, in a flash he could imagine a potentially bleak, if not dangerous, future for himself had James died. His life and welfare remained inextricably linked to the king and the royal family.

The whole story has many bizarre elements. Was it another attempted kidnapping of James, or was it James's plan to destroy the Ruthven descendants of those who had imprisoned him in 1582? Whatever had happened, James established 5 August as an ongoing day of celebration in honour of his escape from possible murder by the 'Gowrie Conspirators'. By the next day, 6 August, James sent word to Edinburgh, ordering the Privy Council to instigate general rejoicing for his divine deliverance, and so the commemoration of the king's deliverance continued every 5 August for decades; certainly it resonated in James's memory until his death in 1625.

Lennox will play a crucial role in the transition to rule in England in 1603. On 24 March the lives of King James, the royal family and Lennox changed forever. Queen Elizabeth died, and the path to the English crown opened for James finally and irrevocably. Two days later Robert Carey, in a surreptitious, frantic, exhausting and impressive journey, reached Edinburgh and entered Holyrood Palace, where servants awoke James and Carey told him of Elizabeth's death. Carey had brought no official documents with him from the Privy Council because it had not authorised the trip. But he had with him a blue ring that had belonged to Queen Elizabeth. James accepted the ring as proof of the validity of Carey's message. Everything that James had hoped for, dreamed about and angled for since childhood had now become a reality. In fact, as early as 1600, James had written to various Scottish lords about his plans to 'possess us in the crown of England according to our just and undoubted title'.[111] He also promised these lords that 'we shall, within the space of a year thereafter, thankfully pay and content every one of these persons that have advanced us at this time with such sums as the Duke of Lennox has in ticket'. Apparently Lennox had the job of keeping tabs on who had lent what to the king. In 1603 James would leave behind the stark, rough world of Scotland and enter the seemingly Promised Land, full of wealth and security. By the next day James received the official word from the English Privy Council that he had been proclaimed King of England, Scotland, Ireland and France. He would de facto unite Scotland and England. He thus anticipated the prophecy at the end of Shakespeare's and Fletcher's play *Henry VIII* by being the new phoenix from the north, succeeding Elizabeth, arising from her 'ashes of honor'. The bleakness of the Edinburgh sky gave way to the glittering hope of a new day and life that awaited him in the southern kingdom. James's thoughts also turned to the ponderous task of actually going to London.

One thing he knew for certain: he wanted Lennox to accompany him on the journey and to remain with him in the new kingdom. Thus, on 27 March he wrote to Lennox, informing him that Elizabeth had died and requesting that he prepare himself for service: we 'desire you to addresse yourself hither to us in your maist cumelie and decent maner, to attend upoun and accompany us . . . as you tender our plesour and service'.[112] Lennox responded affirmatively and enthusiastically. Unlike James, Lennox had, of course, visited England; but he had no way of anticipating what living there would entail. The chapter of his life that began as a nine-year-old arriving in Scotland and remaining for twenty years would now close, as a new, exciting chapter emerged.

King James also wrote to Prince Henry at Stirling Castle before leaving Scotland. The letter contains multiple instructions and admonitions. Thus, James writes, 'Let not this news make you proud or insolent, for a king's son and heir was ye before, and no more are ye yet'.[113] The king refers to the 'augmentation' that Henry will now experience. 'Be therefore merry but not insolent . . . Be resolute but not wilful'. James urges Henry to look upon all Englishmen as 'loving subjects'. The king also sends Henry a copy of *Basilicon Doron*, his conduct book, which the prince 'should study and profit in it'. And the king urges Henry to study: 'Be diligent and earnest in your studies, that at your meeting with me I may praise you for your progress in learning' (p. 212). James looks forward to their eventual rendezvous in the new kingdom.

On Sunday, 3 April 1603, the king went to St Giles' Church in Edinburgh where he addressed the people of Scotland, assuring them of his continuing devotion and promising to return for a visit at least every three years. (On the latter point, he made only one trip back to Scotland, that in 1617.) He was, he insisted, merely travelling to another part of his kingdom. His heartfelt sentiments moved some Scots to tears. On Tuesday, 5 April, he bade farewell to his queen in a public display of emotion as both shed tears. (Anne was pregnant and would follow later.) With Lennox, his brother Esmé Stuart, Mar, and others accompanying, James then began his arduous but exciting trip to England, moving along the Great North Road through places great and small, not reaching London until 7 May.[114]

This somewhat leisurely pace served several purposes. First, it enabled James to avoid London in the time of official mourning for Elizabeth and her funeral on 28 April (James never attended a funeral). Further, it

provided ample opportunity for him to see great stretches of the coun-
tryside and to meet his new English citizens, including those with political power, such as Robert Cecil. Crowds of people swarmed against the
king, to his chagrin, their enthusiasm unparalleled. Later he recounted
in his first speech to Parliament on 19 March 1604 something of his trip
southward: 'Shall it ever bee blotted out of my minde, how at my first
entrie into this Kingdome, the people of all sorts rid and ran, nay rather
flew to meet mee? their eyes flaming nothing but sparkles of affection'.[115]
In addressing Parliament in 1607, James likened his first three years of
English rule to 'Christmas'. On the 1603 journey he spent, for example, near the end of the trip, profitable time with Cecil at his house at
Theobalds, where they and members of the Privy Council discussed
major issues of transition and governing. About the latter, James made
two early decisions: to reconfigure the Privy Council with equal numbers
of Scots and English, and to elevate the importance of the Bedchamber.
Lennox became the honorific head of the Bedchamber, corresponding to
his political prominence in Scotland. This small group of men (at first
all Scots) had complete access to the king and therefore extraordinary
power, which diminished the importance of the Privy Council. Esmé
Stuart also joined this group.[116]

In early May, Anne made her move, only to be rebuffed by the old
Countess of Mar. The queen created such a scene that she had a mis-
carriage. As Calderwood reports: 'The queene went to bed in an anger,
and parted with childe the tenth of May'.[117] James first sent Mar to pla-
cate her, but, Calderwood adds, 'the queene would not looke upon him'.
Some rather fierce letters flew between Scotland and England. In response
to one of Anne's letters, James wrote and defended the Earl of Mar and
chastised Anne for her behaviour. James writes: 'And therefore I say over
again, leave these womanly apprehensions, for I thank God I carry that
love and respect unto you which, by the law of God and nature, I ought
to do to my wife and mother of my children'.[118] James adds: 'For the
respect of your honourable birth and descent I married you; but the love
and respect I now bear you is for that ye are my married wife and so
partaker of my honour, as of all my other fortunes'. James here strikes a
conciliatory note; but he observes that Anne had moved towards Stirling
with force, which would assist her 'by force to have assisted you in the
taking of my son out of his friends' hands'. (James regularly refers to
Henry as 'my' son.) He ends with hopeful anticipation: 'Praying God, my
heart, to preserve you and all the bairns, and to send me a blithe meeting
with you and a couple of them' (p. 215).

When James got word of Anne's efforts and her refusal even to speak to Mar, he decided to dispatch Lennox, who arrived on 19 May. After much negotiation, the Council concluded:

> It was thought good that the Erle of Marr sould deliver the prince to the duke, and that the duke again deliver him to the counsell. The counsell, to pleasure the queene, delivered him to her and the duke, to be transported, and to be delivered by them to the king.[119]

This sounds strangely reminiscent of the baptismal ceremony in 1594 in which Lennox passed the infant Henry to the English ambassador, only to have him returned. On 17 May, James had written the Earl of Mar: 'In all other thinges concerning the transporting of our sone yee shall dispose your selfe (according as our cousin the Duke of Lennox will particulariely acquaint yow) to that whiche is our plesour; and advise with him carefully upon our honour and his surety'.[120] Lennox had shrewdly brought with him four of Queen Elizabeth's jewels, which delighted Anne and helped lower the temperature of these encounters. Finally, in triumph, Anne appeared in Edinburgh on 28 May with Henry in tow. 'Upon Tuisday, the 31st of May, the queen and the prince came from the palace of Halyrudhous, to the Great Kirk of Edinburgh, ryding in a coache, and accompanied with manie English ladeis in coaches'.[121] Anne had won; it took Lennox to smooth out this very rough spot as he travelled with her and the prince towards London. Princess Elizabeth would join them in a few days; the sickly Prince Charles remained in Scotland until 1604. Once again, Lennox had proved indispensable to the royal family.

Settled into this new kingdom and now twenty-nine years old, Lennox had much reason to reflect on the twenty years since his arrival in Scotland in 1583 as a nine-year-old child. Little of what happened subsequently could he have foreseen. Even now, Lennox remained slightly incredulous, for example, at being placed in charge of the Scottish government in 1589 at the age of fifteen. The numerous honours, positions and gifts that greeted him on this twenty-year trajectory still astonished him. And he recognised his own impressive and at times aggressive ambitions as he fought, for example, to take control of Edinburgh Castle and then Dumbarton Castle. He had represented the king on diplomatic missions and he had met Queen Elizabeth. Political and personal scrapes could not be overlooked, but no reason for undue regret. Disappointed in marriage, Lennox nevertheless cherished the king's unstinted love and that of the ever-expanding royal family. He had done much good for Scotland

(and for himself), and that gave him satisfaction. He grew in confidence and stature from the innocent, frightened child to the mature, sophisticated courtier, indispensable to the king. Life now spread out in front of him and he faced it eagerly. He would embrace England, and England would embrace him. What the anonymous Spanish source said in 1593 that Lennox is 'the most powerful man', whose power 'centres in the court', remains vibrantly and vitally true in 1603 as he departs for England.[122]

Notes

1. Robert Johnston, *The Historie of Scotland during the Minority of King James*, p. 114.
2. David Harris Willson, *King James VI and I*, p. 47.
3. I discuss their relationship extensively in my *King James and Letters of Homoerotic Desire*, pp. 32–64.
4. *Calendar of State Papers Relating to Scotland and Mary, Queen of Scots 1547–1603*, 13 vols., 6:153. Hereafter cited as *Calendar of Scottish Papers*, or parenthetically as CSPS.
5. Bergeron, *King James and Letters*, p. 51.
6. Quoted in Bergeron, *King James and Letters*, p. 63, from an account in David Calderwood's *The History of the Kirk of Scotland*, Thomas Thomson (ed.), 8:243.
7. Quoted in Bergeron, *King James and Letters*, p. 63
8. Robert Bowes, *The Correspondence of Robert Bowes*, Joseph Stevenson (ed.), p. 456.
9. See my discussion of the poem in *King James and Letters*, pp. 53–64.
10. I quote from the edition of the poem included in my *King James and Letters*, p. 229.
11. *Calendar of Scottish Papers*, 6:660.
12. Quoted and modernised from William Fraser, *The Lennox*, p. 453.
13. *The Register of the Privy Council of Scotland*, David Masson (ed.), 3:614.
14. *Calendar of Scottish Papers*, 6:661.
15. *Calendar of Scottish Papers*, 7:271.
16. John Burel, [*Poems*], (sig. A2v). Jamie Reid-Baxter has written plausibly that Burel also intended his book to be an instructional guide for Lennox: see 'Politics, Passion and Poetry in the Circle of James VI' in *A Palace of the Wild*, L.A. J. R. Houwen, A.A. MacDonald and S. L. Mapstone (eds), pp. 199–248.
17. *Calendar of Scottish Papers*, 10:17.
18. *Calendar of Scottish Papers*, 11:310.
19. Some historians have taken a rather dim view of Lennox. Julian Goodare, *State and Society in Early Modern Scotland*, writes that Lennox's 'main duty was to eat several square meals daily in the king's presence' (p. 80).

Keith Brown, *Noble Power in Scotland from the Reformation to the Revolution*, refers to Lennox as 'dim and lazy' (p. 194). Obviously, I take a more benign view of him.

20. *Calendar of Scottish Papers*, 10:122.
21. For an excellent report of all the events associated with James's wedding, see Alan Stewart, *The Cradle King*, pp. 105–18. Stewart's biography has been most helpful in understanding James's life.
22. *Letters of King James VI & I*, G. P. V. Akrigg (ed.), p. 96.
23. Ibid., p. 98.
24. *The Warrender Papers*, Annie I. Cameron (ed.), 2:111.
25. *Calendar of Scottish Papers*, 10:182.
26. *Calendar of Scottish Papers*, 10:257.
27. David Calderwood, *The History of the Kirk of Scotland*, 5:67.
28. For an extended and helpful discussion of the role of Bothwell in this governing process and of the general success of this effort, see Robin G. Macpherson, 'Francis Stewart, 5th Earl of Bothwell, c. 1562–1612: Lordship and Politics in Jacobean Scotland', Ph.D thesis, University of Edinburgh, 1998, especially pp. 277–310.
29. For a discussion of this royal entry pageant, see my *English Civic Pageantry 1558–1642*, revised edition, pp. 69–70.
30. Adrienne McLaughlin has noted what seems to be Lennox's spotty attendance at meetings of the Council: 'In the seven-year period between 1592 and 1599 there were 228 total sederunts of council and Lennox only attended 36 per cent of meetings overall' (p. 141). Of course, one would have to study the attendance habits of the other Council members to determine if Lennox's pattern was in fact unusual. McLaughlin, 'Rise of a Courtier: The Second Duke of Lennox and Strategies of Noble Power under James VI', in *James VI and Noble Power in Scotland 1578–1603*, Miles Kerr-Peterson and Steven J. Reid (eds), pp. 136–54. I am grateful for the many insights that this important article has provided.
31. *Register of the Privy Council of Scotland*, 5:96. I use the abbreviation '*Reg.*' parenthetically to refer to this publication.
32. Adrienne McLaughlin, p. 141.
33. Ibid., p. 140.
34. *Register of the Privy Council of Scotland*, 6:209.
35. Information derives from Paul Goodman's article, 'James VI, Noble Power and the Burgh of Glasgow, c. 1580–1605', in *James VI and Noble Power*, pp. 81–97.
36. Adrienne McLaughlin, p. 142.
37. Calderwood, *History of the Kirk*, 5:357.
38. *Calendar of Scottish Papers*, 11:534.
39. *Calendar of State Papers Relating to Scotland*, Markham John Thorpe (ed.), 2:670. Not to be confused with the *Calendar of Scottish Papers*, which refers to the later 13-volume series.

40. John Spottiswood, *History of the Church of Scotland*, 3 vols., 3:100.
41. *Calendar of Letters and State Papers Relating to English Affairs Preserved in . . . the Archives of Simancas* [Spain], 4:688.
42. *Calendar of Scottish Papers*, 13:769.
43. Spottiswood, *History of the Church*, 3:101.
44. *Letters and Papers Relating to Patrick Master of Gray*, Thomas Thomson (ed.), pp. 192–3.
45. *Calendar of Scottish Papers*, 13:836.
46. *Calendar of State Papers Relating to Scotland*, 2:731, 734.
47. *Calendar of Scottish Papers*, 13:904.
48. *Calendar of Letters and State Papers . . . of Simancas*, 4:604.
49. I have gleaned much information from Ruth Grant's doctoral thesis, 'George Gordon, Sixth Earl of Huntly and the Politics of the Counter-Reformation in Scotland, 1581–1595', University of Edinburgh, 2010. Grant calls this marriage a 'political marriage made in heaven', p. 154.
50. Ibid., p. 257.
51. *Calendar of Scottish Papers*, 12:162.
52. Ibid., 13:993.
53. Ibid., 9:19.
54. Ibid., 9:661.
55. Ibid., 9:650.
56. Ibid., 10:410. Jamie Reid-Baxter has noted the confusion about the first wife's name. See his article, cited above, 'Politics, Passion and Poetry', p. 210.
57. From the Johnston manuscript history of Scotland, quoted in Jamie Reid-Baxter's article, p. 244.
58. *Calendar of Scottish Papers*, 13:276.
59. National Records of Scotland, GD 220/6/2003 (7). I am indebted to the considerable help of Nicole Winard and Amy Thompson in transcribing this difficult document.
60. *Register of the Privy Council of Scotland*, David Masson (ed.), 7:440.
61. *Basilicon Doron*, James Craigie (ed.), 2 vols., 1:121.
62. *Register of the Privy Council of Scotland*, 9:197.
63. Ibid., 12:208.
64. *Calendar of Scottish Papers*, 10:450.
65. Calderwood, *History*, 5:116.
66. *Calendar of Scottish Papers*, 11:49.
67. National Archives, SP 52/47. Neil Millar writes about the event in *Through the Green*, December 2018, pp. 38–9.
68. National Records of Scotland, GD 220/6/2006/1. I am indebted to Rob Maxtone-Graham for calling my attention to this document and for sharing his transcription of it.
69. *Calendar of Scottish Papers*, 10:591.
70. Ibid., 10:610.

71. Ibid., 10:674.
72. Letter of Bowes to Burghley, 21 June 1593, *Calendar of Scottish Papers,* 11:101.
73. Letter to Bowes, 15 October 1595, *Calendar of Scottish Papers,* 12:44.
74. *Calendar of Scottish Papers,* 12:50.
75. Ibid., 11:73.
76. Based on a letter from Bowes to Burghley, 20 May 1593, *Calendar of Scottish Papers,* 11:91.
77. Letter from Bowes to Burghley, 23 June 1593, *Calendar of Scottish Papers,* 11:107.
78. *Calendar of State Papers Relating to Scotland,* 2:613.
79. Ibid., 2:628.
80. *Calendar of Scottish Papers,* 13:81.
81. Letter from Bowes to Burghley, 7 October 1597, *Calendar of Scottish Papers,* 13:97.
82. Letter from Bowes to Burghley, 21 October 1597, *Calendar of Scottish Papers,* 13:108.
83. *Calendar of Scottish Papers,* 13:117.
84. Ibid., 13:128.
85. Letter from John Macartney to Robert Cecil, 17 December 1597, *Calendar of Scottish Papers,* 13:134.
86. *Calendar of Scottish Papers,* 13:155.
87. Calderwood, *History,* 5:140. Calderwood lists the names of Bothwell's accomplices.
88. *Calendar of Scottish Papers,* 10:617.
89. Reports found in *Calendar of State Papers Relating to Scotland,* 2:602, 610.
90. Calderwood, *History,* 5:256.
91. *Letters of King James VI & I,* p. 125.
92. For extensive discussion of Huntly's life and career, see Ruth Grant's doctoral thesis, cited above.
93. *Letters of King James VI & I,* p. 90. The letter to Huntly dates probably from the end of February.
94. *Calendar of Scottish Papers,* 10:17.
95. Ibid., 11:280.
96. Ibid., 11:545.
97. *Letters,* Akrigg, pp. 141–2.
98. *Calendar of Scottish Papers,* 11:319.
99. Ibid., 11:386–7.
100. Ibid., 11:310.
101. Ibid., 11:386.
102. I follow here and quote from the text edited by Michael Ullyot in *John Nichols's The Progresses and Public Processions of Queen Elizabeth I: A New Edition,* Elizabeth Goldring, Faith Eales, Elizabeth Clarke and Jayne Elisabeth Archer (eds), 5 vols. I quote from vol. 3.

103. *Calendar of Scottish Papers*, 12:356.
104. Ibid., 13:450.
105. Ibid., 13:748.
106. Ibid., 13:982. This is somewhat puzzling because the Treasurer's accounts indicate considerable expenditure. (This information supplied to me by Maureen Meikle in private communication.)
107. Ibid., 13:678–89, offers copious documentation, some of it contradictory. Likewise, David Calderwood, *History*, 6:28–96, provides extensive primary documents about the Gowrie affair. For a helpful summary and analysis, see Alan Stewart, *Cradle King*, pp. 150–9.
108. Calderwood, *History*, 6:28ff.
109. Ibid., 6:75.
110. *Calendar of Scottish Papers*, 13:689.
111. *Letters*, Akrigg, p. 166.
112. A slightly modernised version of the letter is found in the *Third Report of the Royal Commission on Historical Manuscripts*, p. 396.
113. *Letters*, Akrigg, p. 211.
114. For an excellent discussion of the whole period of transition from Scotland to England, see Leanda de Lisle, *After Elizabeth: The Rise of James of Scotland*. On p. xxvi she includes a helpful map of the actual route that James travelled with its sixteen-plus stops.
115. Quoted in my *Royal Family, Royal Lovers*, p. 68.
116. For a thorough discussion of this new development, see Neil Cuddy, 'The Revival of the Entourage: The Bedchamber of James I, 1603–1625', in *The English Court from the Wars of the Roses to the Civil War*, David Starkey (ed.), pp. 173–225.
117. Calderwood, *History*, 6:231.
118. *Letters,* Akrigg, p. 214.
119. Calderwood, *History*, 6:231.
120. *Report of the Manuscripts of the Earl of Mar and Kellie*, 1:51.
121. Calderwood, *History*, 6:231.
122. *Calendar of Letters and Papers . . . of Simancas*, 4:604.

2

England: A Courtier in a
New World of Joy and Sorrow

ARRIVAL AND CORONATION

James's leisurely but purposeful month-long journey from Edinburgh to London culminated with his arrival on the outskirts of London on 7 May 1603. The king left Theobalds and his visit with Robert Cecil and near Waltham he met a delegation from London, having previously mainly been surrounded by court officials. But now John Swinnerton, one of London's two sheriffs, met James; and Richard Martin, of the Middle Temple, offered an oration in which he provided customary words of greeting on behalf of the City of London.

Martin's brief speech contains a number of rich images, such as the idea of the 'phoenix'. Martin addresses James: 'Out of the Ashes of this *Phenix* [Elizabeth] wert thou King *Iames* borne for our good, the bright starre of the North',[1] which has 'dispersed those cloudes of feare'. The speaker also emphasises James's descent and 'royall bloud, drawn to this faire inheritance from the loynes of our ancient Kings' (A4). James connects to four kingdoms, according to Martin, including Scotland, which 'hath tried your prudence'; Ireland, which 'shall require your justice'; France, which 'shall prooue your fortitude'; and England, which may 'be the schoole, wherein your Maiesty will practize your temperance and moderation' (A4v). London's citizens know about their new king in part from information 'drawne out of the obseruation of your Maiesties forepast actions, and some bookes now fresh in euery mans hands' (B2). This reference to James's published works certainly flatters the king and acknowledges the recent publication of *Basilicon Doron* in London. James brings with him a new kingdom, Scotland, 'which warre could neuer subdue' (B2v). Therefore, London's citizens rejoice, laying at James's feet 'their goods and liues'. London awaits the opportunity to welcome the king within its walls; James, Lennox and the royal party depart from this speech and occasion enthusiastic for what lies ahead.

At Stamford Hill the Lord Mayor of London, Robert Lee, greeted James and offered him the sword and keys to the City, a logical conclusion to Martin's speech. The mayor did not travel alone: 'Aldermen in skartlet gownes and great chaines of golde about their neckes, with all the Chiefe Officers and Counsell of the Citie; besides five hundred Citizens, all very well mounted, clad in velvet coates and chaines of gold' also appeared.[2] With trumpets sounding, this grand procession proceeded, 'the Duke of Lennox bearing the sword of honour before his Majestie'. Bearing the sword proudly, Lennox recalled that fitful and nervous moment in early 1584 as a nine-year-old, recently arrived from France, when he carried the royal crown along Edinburgh's streets and into the Scottish Parliament. Now, twenty years later, Lennox still holds a place of highest honour with King James. Lennox had not experienced such rich and dazzling display in Scotland. Perhaps they were indeed entering the Promised Land. Also, in this new country, he noted, 'they call me Lennox'.

Having first entered London through Aldersgate, James eventually, on 11 May 1603, made his way to Whitehall from Charterhouse. There he took the royal barge down the Thames towards the Tower. A robust thunder of twenty pieces of ordnance sounded from the Tower as James neared. At the King's Stairs the Gentleman Usher of the Tower presented the sword to James, which he then gave to Lennox, who again served as sword bearer, a recognition of his prominence.

George Marcelline confirms Lennox's central position in James's life:

> You wise and prudent *Lodowicke*, honoured so many times with royall honors of *Lenox, Grace of Graces*, that have left *France* (your Native Country) to be always by and at the right hand of *Our King*, as not able to loose the sight of him; neither be further off from his Majesty, then the Sun from the Eccliptick line.[3]

The Venetian ambassador, Giovanni Carlo Scaramelli, reports to the Senate in late June 1603: 'Although it has been customary for your Serenity to send letters of credence to four or six principal ministers, it will be best on this occasion to address the Duke only'.[4] A few months later, on 22 October, the ambassador sent a dispatch which concluded: 'Lennox is the person deepest in the King's confidence, and has some time ago been named the nearest to the Crown' (CSPV, 10:106). Thus, even in the new surroundings of England, Lennox continued to enjoy the king's favour and confidence, sustaining an unusual closeness with James and remaining of exceptional value to him, underscoring what some had observed in Scotland, this 'paragon'.

King James eventually settled into Whitehall Palace in Westminster, the property acquired by King Henry VIII in 1529 from the fall of Cardinal Wolsey, who had lived in York Place, the precursor of the palace. This palace became the official residence of the monarch and the seat of government. James decided early on to place Lennox in the palace, putting him into its Holbein Gatehouse, originally built in 1531–2, to which Hans Holbein had no particular connection but the name stuck. This gatehouse, resembling the one at Cripplegate in London Wall, contained on its upper floor residential space, which Lennox began to occupy. What this location lacked in comfort it more than made up in prestige. This fortress-like structure on the west side of the palace complex recalled a chivalric tradition in its design. From this gatehouse Lennox could look out southwards to the large tiltyard, where he would spend much time in participating in tilts and tournaments. More important, this gatehouse gave Lennox relatively close proximity to the king and his private lodgings. Thus, the Holbein Gatehouse reinforced Lennox's exceptional position and the king's regard. Architecture thereby underscores political and personal position, should Lennox's status need additional evidence and confirmation.

Not only had James placed Lennox on the Privy Council and made him head of the Gentlemen of the Bedchamber but also, in an elaborate ceremony on 2 July, installed the duke into the Order of the Garter, along with Prince Henry. (James himself had been invested into the order by Queen Elizabeth in 1594 on the occasion of Henry's birth.) The Order of the Garter had been established in 1348 under the aegis of King Edward III with St George as its patron and it remained the highest English knightly order. This new honour reinforced Lennox's acceptance in the English court, a signal honour for this Frenchman and adopted Scot, now included into this august knightly order.

On 25 July, St James's Day, King James achieved formal, ceremonial recognition of that for which he had strived assiduously for decades: he was crowned King of England. Because of the plague's virulent outbreak in London, the ceremonies had to be greatly curtailed and crowds severely limited. On that rainy late July day the streets were desolate and Westminster Abbey half empty, but sufficient number of people had gathered in the Abbey church in order to witness the ceremony and give their sanction to the new king. The occasion also contained the coronation of Queen Anne, the first crowned consort since Anne Boleyn. Even though sickness raged, the weather foul and the crowd sparse, the ceremony went on with great splendour.

James, the queen, Lennox and other members of the Privy Council went by boat on the Thames to the Abbey. Robert Lee, London's mayor, who had greeted James a few months earlier outside of the city, formed part of the procession, along with other members of the City's elite. Sixty Knights of Bath, newly created and dressed in their finery, joined in, as did thirty barons and fifteen earls. James marched to the church 'under a canopy, supported by four rods'.[5] Gentlemen of the court followed, wearing 'vests of crimson velvet reaching to the knees'. The queen also

Figure 2.1   Ludovic Stuart, Duke of Lennox, miniature by Isaac Oliver, c. 1605. Courtesy of National Portrait Gallery.

moved under a canopy; she 'was dressed in a long robe of crimson velvet, lined with ermine' (10:75). The Archbishop of Canterbury, John Whitgift, along with other clergy greeted James at the Great West Door. The coronation proceeded according to tradition, including the anointing of the king's body. The people shouted for joy, according to Scaramelli (76). James took communion but Anne did not, as she had told him beforehand, reflecting her not so secret Catholicism. Lennox and other lords knelt before James, pledging their allegiance; some touched and kissed the crown. 'The Earl of Pembroke, a handsome youth, who is always

Figure 2.2 Portrait of King James after John de Critz the elder, early 17th century. Courtesy of National Portrait Gallery.

with the King, and always joking with him, actually kissed his Majesty's face', which James enjoyed (77). That gesture must have caused some consternation, but the ceremony continued and concluded with Anne's crowning. All finished, the king, queen, Lennox and others made their way to the Thames and there took a barge, 'royally furnished', back toward Whitehall. 'They made a show of themselves for a space on the river' (77) – a concession to the limitations of the day. Nevertheless, Lennox felt relief and contentment. The coronation had proceeded without problem and his patron and protector had cemented his claim to the English throne. Kneeling before James in obeisance filled Lennox with admiration, confidence and love.

ROYAL FAMILY: EARLY YEARS

The cordial, loving and respectful relationships that Lennox had developed with the royal family over the course of twenty years in Scotland continued now in England. Queen Anne trusted him and relied on him, epitomised in his successful handling of the transfer of Prince Henry to her in Scotland before their departure for England. No one but Lennox could have handled this delicate piece of domestic negotiation, made possible by Lennox's skills and the trust that all the relevant parties had in him. Having attended the baptisms of the royal children, Lennox developed strong connections to Prince Henry and Princess Elizabeth, less so with Prince Charles, who, because of illness, did not come to England until 1604. Henry and Elizabeth loved Lennox and depended on him on a number of occasions. Lennox also did not hesitate sometimes to correct Henry's behaviour, but with no bad repercussions.

England was itself enthusiastic and ecstatic to receive a royal family, James's 'hopeful seed', as some called the children. Not since the reign of Henry VIII had England experienced a royal family, for James's immediate predecessors, Edward, Mary and Elizabeth were all childless. Royal children assured a potentially peaceful succession; they thereby made James seem less vulnerable. Later developments, such as death and a marriage, will lessen that sense of security. For the moment, however, all seemed well and promising, rather like the opening moments of Shakespeare's *The Winter's Tale* in which King Leontes of Sicily has a thriving young son and the king's wife, Hermione, is pregnant, signalling impending birth of another royal child. Alas, that situation deteriorates: seeming stability remains subject to possible change. That fictional narrative will find a counterpoint in the life of James and his family.

No portrait exists of the Stuart family in its early years in England, but two Venetian ambassadors, Francesco Contarini and Marc' Antonio Correr capture the family in 1610 in a vivid account sent to the Doge and Senate in Venice. They write of going to Whitehall Palace and being led into the Great Chamber where they passed through rows of 'great ladies and gentlemen of the Court, all richly dressed and covered with jewels', on their approach to the king.[6] James took steps toward the ambassadors and embraced them. 'The Queen stood by him and with her the Princess, who, in common opinion, is held to be of a rare beauty'. On the king's right hand stood Henry, Prince of Wales 'and hard by the Queen the Duke of York [Charles], his father's and mother's joy'. Officers of the Crown, including Lennox and other courtiers, stood nearby in 'rank of preeminence and in seemly order'. This static but vibrant portrait of the royal family prompts the ambassadors to refer to it as 'a magnificent spectacle'. No one present or reading about this scene could possibly argue with that conclusion. This momentary 'snapshot' underscores the kingdom's orderliness and stability. Lennox adds to that assurance.

After the plague had finally subsided, the City of London readied itself again for a royal entry pageant in celebration of the new sovereign and his family, presented on 15 March 1604. London's guilds and the Dutch and Italian merchants living and working in the city provided the extensive financing for this unsurpassed theatrical spectacle. Under the direction of Stephen Harrison, architect, the city erected seven triumphal arches scattered throughout as the royal party made its way from the Tower to the City and eventually to Westminster. Harrison also prepared a beautiful book, *Arches of Triumph* (1604, reprinted in 1613), that includes engravings of the arches, the first such pictorial evidence of an English civic pageant. The planning authorities engaged the talents of two well-established dramatists, Ben Jonson and Thomas Dekker, to prepare the speeches and dramatic entertainment at each arch; a third, Thomas Middleton, wrote a speech for Zeal. For the first time, major professional dramatists crafted such an entertainment. Shakespeare and his fellow members of the King's Men, under the patronage of King James, lined the streets, along with thousands of spectators, dressed in their royal livery. Two professional actors, William Bourne and Edward Alleyn, renowned for his performances in Marlowe's plays, took part, as did two of the children's companies of actors. By every measure, this pageant entertainment ranks at the top of such pageants in the Jacobean era. (Later, King Charles I never made a royal entry into London, although several had been planned; he did enjoy such an entertainment in Edinburgh in 1633.) King James, Queen Anne, Prince Henry, Lennox

and James's cousin Arbella Stuart all formed part of the official procession, which began shortly before noon and took five hours to complete.[7]

Not everything was so elegant and refined. As the Venetian ambassador, Nicolò Molin, points out: 'There was bull-baiting and other sports'.[8]
Such helps define cultural life in greater London. Molin also notes that
many in the city expected the king to create a new duke, in honour of this
occasion: an English duke 'is exceedingly desired, for there is no English
Duke, though there is one Scottish, Lennox, and the English cannot bear
to see the first rank held by one of that nation'. James did not create
an English duke until a decade or more later. This ducal issue cannot
have been a high priority and may only reflect the Venetian's perspective.
Molin observes that 'None of the Ambassadors were present at any of
these festivities, owing to the quarrel for precedence between France and
Spain'. The quarrel among ambassadors over 'precedence' will regularly
affect entertainments in the period, especially in the court masques –
much jockeying for preferred position, considerable hard feelings, many
harsh words and refusal to participate.

Molin also offers a helpful report of the procession, noting that the
king had scores of people accompanying him, including all of London's
officers and dignitaries, along with bishops, earls, barons and sundry
knights. Prince Henry rode on horseback ten paces ahead of the king.
James proceeded under a canopy 'borne over his head by four-and-twenty
gentlemen, splendidly dressed' (CSPV, 10:139). Queen Anne followed
twenty paces behind, seated on a royal throne. Arbella Stuart followed
'in a richly furnished carriage drawn by two white mules'. Lennox followed with other gentlemen of the Bedchamber. Apart from the planned
dramatic entertainment, the procession itself produced a remarkable
spectacle of power and position, underscoring James's unquestioned
right to the English throne.

The first arch, located at Fenchurch Street and designed by Jonson,
included a representation of the City of London carved atop. A silk curtain, painted like a thick cloud, covered the arch until King James and
his party arrived; and then it vanished. Jonson explains that the city had
been shrouded in grief but now it rejoiced in the new king's appearance.
The Genius of the City greeted James in a part played by Alleyn. The city
both literally and symbolically welcomed the king as he passed through
the arch. James and the spectators could obviously see the city spread
out all around them but they could now also see it represented. Various
allegorical figures, richly and emblematically costumed, greeted the sovereign. The triumphal arch located at Gracious Street contained allusions
to James's *Basilicon Doron* and to his poem *Lepanto*, written about the

sixteenth-century battle between Turkish and Christian forces. On this arch a large square depicted Henry VII, dressed in imperial robes, and James approaching him and from whom he receives the kingly sceptre. The founder of the Tudor dynasty thus gives his blessing and kingdom to James. One of the final arches, located in Fleet Street, depicted a New World, complete with a spectacular globe that turned. *Astraea* (Justice) occupied a prominent place, as if newly descended from heaven. Seated beneath her, Virtue, in white garments, challenged the figure of Envy, all dressed in black. The moral allegories become clear as instruction for James.

London on this day certainly looked like a new creation to the royal family and Lennox with its rich spectacle and unvarnished adulation. All the pageant devices acclaimed James's rule over England and attested to his transforming power. This royal entry entertainment became a glorious piece of myth-making, forming an appropriate gift to James and the court. Elaborate arches with their mute visual arguments, live actors, speeches, exceptional costumes and architectural wonders conspire to offer entertainment and instructions to sovereign and audience alike. Lennox took it all in, dazzled by what he had seen, honoured by being included and confident about the future in this new kingdom. No other public entertainment in the Jacobean period surpassed this moment. Lennox would forever treasure this experience.

On 8 April 1605 the royal family, gathered at Greenwich, excitedly greeted the birth of Mary, so named for James's mother. Not only did Mary add additional stability to the family but also had the distinction of being the first royal child born in England since Jane Seymour gave birth in 1537 to the child who would become Edward VI. Few alive could remember Edward's birth; therefore, much scrambling about and scrutinising of archival records took place just to recall how the baptism should be done. With this birth, according to the prayers appointed to be used, people shall 'with comfort and joy daily behold . . . so shall the King rejoice and thy people be glad therof . . . for such an increase of the Kings royall issue'.[9] Edmund Lascelles in a letter to the Earl of Shrewsbury reports the reaction to Mary's birth: 'for joy whereof, the next day after, the Cittizens of London made bonefiers throughout London, and the bells continued ringing all the whole day'.[10] King James responded in part by writing to his brother-in-law, Christian IV of Denmark, observing that 'although this is not our first child, it may nevertheless seem to be the first since it is the first to have occurred for us after the most happy union of our kingdoms'.[11] Clearly, James understands the importance of this 'English' child.

Lennox had been present in Greenwich and he prepared to participate in the baptism, as he had others, on the afternoon of Sunday, 5 May. This royal baptism was the first to follow the Protestant rites of the firmly established Church of England. A contemporary account reports:

> First, the three Courts at Greenwich, were rayled in and hung about with broad cloth, where the proceeding should passe. The Childe was brought from the Queene's lodgings through both the Great chambers, and through the Presence, and downe the winding stayres into the Conduit-court. At the foote whereof attended a canopy borne by eight Barons.[12]

Under this canopy 'went the Countesse of Darby, bearing the Childe, and shee was supported by the Dukes of Holsteyne [Queen Anne's brother] and Lenox . . . then followed the godmothers, the Lady Arbella and the Countesse of Northumberland'. In the royal chapel the Archbishop of Canterbury waited, and he received Mary. In the chapel 'stoode a very rich and stately font of silver and gilt, most curiously wrought' (1:512). The service then proceeded with Mary surrounded by the royal family, Lennox and others. Not so much attention and splendour had accompanied a royal baptism since Prince Henry's in 1594.

Two Sundays later, on Whitsunday, 19 May, another event took place related to the baptism: namely, the 'churching' of Queen Anne. This not uncommon practice took place in order for the mother to express her gratitude and thanks for a safe birth. This ceremony also occurred in the chapel at Greenwich. The king entered first, accompanied by the peers of the realm; James went into 'the Closset, and there heard a Sermon', before moving to the chapel's altar.[13] The queen came from her lodging 'with a great trayne of Ladies', and went to the chapel, 'supported by the Dukes of Holsteyne and Lenox, and being come before the altar, shee made low reverence and offred her besant' (Nichols, 1:514). Prayers of thanksgiving for Anne's health and safe delivery followed and then much music. James and Anne met at the altar, 'imbracing each other with great kindnesse'; they then departed hand in hand. Lennox moves seamlessly among these royal events, occupying a place of great prominence and importance for the kingly family.

The following year offered another royal birth: Sophia, born on 22 June 1606 at Greenwich. (This would be the seventh child born of James and Anne.) Sophia, named for Anne's mother, unfortunately survived only a few hours and died on the day of her birth. Three days later a barge carried Sophia along the Thames to Westminster Abbey for burial. Her monument in the abbey showed her asleep in an alabaster cradle; and a Latin inscription refers to her as a 'royal rosebud, untimely plucked to death . . . Torn from her parents to bloom afresh in the rose garden of Christ'.[14] After seven births and three miscarriages, Anne would not attempt to give birth again. The sadness deepened on 16 September 1607 when Mary, after several weeks of high fever, died and joined Sophia in the tomb. These deaths dashed the royal family's spirits. Lennox shared that feeling of despair, having himself experienced the death of his two children. He understood the full measure of pain that permeated the royal family, their hopes for these 'English' daughters cruelly destroyed.

But, of course, Lennox enjoyed many pleasant activities in 1605, such as going on 3 June to the lion's den at the Tower. King James had been zealous in physical enhancements for the lions and their surroundings, including building trap doors to allow the lions to move freely under certain conditions. On this particular afternoon, Lennox accompanied the king, along with several earls, to watch the lions in action. Mainly, they saw them devouring all kinds of small animals, the exception being a lamb that was lowered into the den. Surprisingly, the lions treated the lamb gently and the keeper lifted it back out of the way, not wanting to test the lions' kindness. The lions returned to 'normal'; when some dogs entered, the lions mauled them. All in all, a pleasant outing for Lennox and the king – another example of the diversity of Jacobean culture.[15] This brutality seemingly contrasts sharply with the dinner on 15 July that the king hosted for Prince George Lodwick, Prince of the Holy Roman Empire. Lennox had the task of accompanying the prince and listening to the prince's oration. Queen Anne and Prince Henry also attended the dinner at Whitehall, which ended with watching bear-baiting and bull-baiting. Perhaps good that this concluding event followed the meal.

On 16 July 1605 King James began a lengthy progress tour towards Oxford; this trip lasted several weeks. At Oxford the king and his retinue, which included Lennox, enjoyed many theological disputations, lectures and play performances. On 27 August, the king, riding on horseback, along with the queen and Prince Henry, made a formal passage through Oxford, the Duke of Lennox going before them 'carrying the sword'.[16] Oxford's Chancellor greeted the royal party, and the Vice Chancellor spoke while on his knees. The university presented James with a Greek Testament, 'in folio, washed and ruled', and two pairs of Oxford gloves 'with a deep fringe of gold, the turneovers being wrought with pearles' (Nichols, 1:542). Lennox led the way as the royal family exited the event. That same evening the party saw a play, a 'comedy', in which five or six 'men almost naked' appeared, displeasing the queen and the ladies. This comedy included 'many rusticall songes and dances, which made it very tedious' (548). James had to be persuaded to remain. A few nights later, at Christ Church, during a performance of Samuel Daniel's *The Queenes Arcadia*, James 'distasted it, and fell asleep' (553). On 31 August, amid much pomp and circumstance, Lennox received the degree of Master of Arts from Oxford – another sign of his importance to the royal family and the court.

At the direction of King James, the Privy Council issued a list of 'proposed economies' for the royal family and household in October 1605. No one could escape this proposed relative austerity programme, which in all likelihood never got implemented. For example, the report recommended 'that the Prince's house should be dissolved, and he to remain in his Majesty's house'.[17] Lennox got caught in these proposals as well: 'that the Duke of Lennox's diet be reduced to a diet of 10 dishes, being as much as is served to the Lord Chamberlain or Earl of Worcester'. The document does not indicate the time frame for having only ten dishes, presumably per day. The Privy Council wondered 'whether the diet issued to himself [the king] and the Queen shall continue in as ample manner for number of dishes'. What the Privy Council proposed the court would dispose, in a court not noted for its restraint.

The year ended with the Catholic-inspired Gunpowder Plot on 5 November, a potentially devastating event. Fortunately a letter reached King James, brought by the Earl of Salisbury (Robert Cecil), which the king rightly interpreted as spelling imminent danger. The king would later celebrate his skills at interpretation, perhaps a bit exaggerated. Nevertheless, the catastrophe did not happen, thanks to discovering the plot and the gunpowder casks placed beneath Parliament with the intention of destroying the royal family and all those gathered for the opening of Parliament. They caught Guy Fawkes red-handed, indeed with the instruments of setting the powder ablaze. In a later speech to the legislative body, James outlined the likely outcome had the explosion occurred: 'not only . . . the destruction of my person, nor of my wife and posterity only, but of the whole body of the State in general . . . the whole nobility, the whole reverend clergy . . . the most part of the knights and gentry'.[18] Such a view would of necessity include Lennox, who would have been present, although not a member of Parliament yet, but who regularly accompanied the king to the opening of Parliament. In James's mind this event reminded him of the Gowrie Conspiracy in 1600 in Scotland, a rather more mysterious event. From both, James perceived divine intervention and deliverance. Henceforth, 'Guy Fawkes Day' would be celebrated as a day of deliverance of the king from danger and likely death.

Lennox had every reason to be grateful, given how closely his well-being and life remained inextricably linked to James and the royal family.

In summer 1606 the City of London hurriedly got ready for a pageant in honour of King Christian IV of Denmark, Queen Anne's brother, who arrived in England on 17 July 1606, partly to console his sister after Sophia's death. Having received word of his impending visit, the Council and Aldermen established committees to arrange entertainment for his formal passage through London. One entry in Corporation records includes an order that 'our Pageant should bee prepared and placed in some such meet and convenient place within this Cytie'.[19] Another item in the records indicates a sum of £1,000 levied on the companies for pageant expenses. King James sent the Duke of Lennox to Gravesend to welcome Christian to England. The next morning, 18 July, James, Prince Henry, Lennox and others went from Greenwich to Gravesend to visit Christian on his ship.[20] From there, the group returned to Greenwich where Christian visited Anne, who 'still keeps her rooms because of her recent confinement'.[21] His surprise visit lifted the queen's spirits. The Venetian ambassador sent his secretary to offer his services to the King of Denmark: 'The Duke of Lennox procured him an audience, and the King graciously said that on his arrival in London he would gladly receive me' (CSPV, 10:383). Lennox, the ever essential person of contact and arranger.

For nearly two weeks thereafter James and noblemen offered various kinds of entertainment for the visiting Christian, including hunting, a dinner at Theobalds hosted by Robert Cecil, and a production of the play *Abuses*, presented at Greenwich by the Children of Paul's. The entertainment at Theobalds on 24 July became notoriously well known, thanks to John Harrington's report of the festivities. The excessive indulgence in alcohol by the Danes affected the whole event. For example, the person representing the Queen of Sheba fell into the Danish king's lap; then James arose to dance with this queen, but he fell down and was carried out. The Theological Virtues, Hope, Faith and Charity, appeared. 'Hope did assay to speak, but wine rendered her endeavours so feeble that she withdrew'; Faith 'left the Court in a staggering condition'.[22] So the evening went. What should have been a masque became a perverse parody. James apparently did his best to match his brother-in-law drink for drink. Hardly an uplifting experience.

Finally, on 31 July, London had its opportunity to welcome the Danish king. An anonymous account, *The King of Denmarkes Welcome*, provides copious details about the procession, including an account of all who participated in the kings' entourage and their elaborate dress. After members of the English Privy Council and Bedchamber came the Lord Treasurer, London's Lord Mayor, 'then the Duke of *Lynox* all alone'.[23] The reference to Lennox and his position calls attention to his prominence. Immediately after him followed Prince Henry, surrounded on either side by James and Christian. Along the railed streets stood the 'whole Livereys of everie severall Companie through the Cittie of London, which companyes extended their length from Tower-streete to Temple Barre' (C3v). These guild members wore 'Satten, Velvet, and other Silke Doublets, and Hose, Golde Chaynes about their neckes, and some Pearle Chaynes' (C3v). Banners of all kinds flanked the streets and embraced the procession.

The route followed the well-established pattern of moving from the Tower westwards through the City, passing the Royal Exchange, for example, where the conduit ran with wine and the city trumpeters stood atop the Exchange, sounding their instruments. The top of the great conduit in Cheapside contained 'the modell of a faire Garden' (*Denmarkes,* C4). Within this garden resided a consort of musicians, 'signifying (as some imagined) the Bower of the nine Muses'. Here the Recorder presented a gift and a speech on behalf of the City. A triumphal arch also arose in Cheapside, covered with sea scenes. Over the right-hand arch Neptune appeared, dressed in blue and mounted on a seahorse; over the left side in a sea cave sat Mulciber, mounted on a dragon (C4v). At the kings' approach, Concord 'was by a quaint devise let downe in her throne' from which she delivered 'a long speech to the Kings'. And she showed them a 'modell of a faire citie, and much other treasures: there sate the genious of the citie of London, who delivered to the Kings a long speech in Latin; so did also *Neptune*' (D1). Clearly the deviser of this pageant recalls the 1604 royal entry pageant. The speeches of Concord, London and Neptune, all in Latin, offer conventional speeches of praise.[24] On the Fleet Street conduit the kings beheld 'a verie fine artificiall sommer bower of greene bowes' (D1v). Within this bower the kings saw 'a faire Shepheard courting a coy Shepherdesse' (D2), who had apparently said that she would not love him until she 'could behold two Sunnes at one time of equall brightnesse: when there were two Majesties of like splendor, or two Kings in one state'. This seeming impossibility gives way to the reality of the presence of two such kings. After speeches and songs, the kings' party moved on to Temple Bar, where the Lord Mayor took his farewell. The royal party eventually reached Whitehall, 'where dismounting about seaven of the clocke in the Evening, they feasted and reposed themselves there all that night' (D2) – the end of a rich day in which London offered fervent praise and adulation, enhanced by drama and spectacle. Lennox, 'all alone', relished the City's offering, as he once again intersected its entertainments. The Venetian ambassador, Giustinian, comments: 'The ceremony was a magnificent and noble one, both on account of the great gathering of personages, the richness of their robes, and the trappings of their horses'.[25] This ambassador also reports on the struggle for precedence among the ambassadorial corps in London (10:388–90).

Lennox headed a plan to honour Christian's visit by 'a challenge to be issued by certain knights of the Fortunate Island' throughout Europe.[26] John Ford in *Honor Triumphant* (1606) captures part of the design for this proposed event. But this ambitious plan got scaled back to England only, proclaimed 'in the royal presence and the public places of Greenwich on 1 June' (Chambers,1:147). The death of Sophia further dampened this project. But Christian did participate in a tilt on 1 August, absent the full romantic possibilities that Lennox had imagined. The Venetian ambassador observes in a dispatch on 6 August: 'On Monday last both Kings tilted at the ring, so did the Prince; and yesterday the King of Denmark had a private joust' (CSPV, 10:384). Such strenuous exercise might counter the debacle at Theobalds.

Christian IV finally departed on 11 August for Denmark, leaving behind many pleasant memories and also gifts. Giustinian reports: 'He left everybody well satisfied on account of his presents, which including those to the King, Queen and Prince amount, they say, to two hundred thousand crowns worth' (10:394). According to the ambassador, King James was somewhat less generous, although Queen Anne 'sent her mother some fine horses handsomely caparisoned'. On board the Danish ship, James, Anne, Henry and Lennox dined 'sumptuously' with Christian and bade him farewell, as he assured them of his country's respect for and alliance with England. The royal family and Lennox derived much pleasure from Christian's visit as they moved away from the sad experience of Sophia's death. Perhaps John Ford sums up the experience well in his 'The Monarchs Meeting': 'Two Kings in *England* have beene rarely seene, / Two Kings for singularitie renowned: / The like before hath hardly ever beene, / for never were two with more honour crowned'.[27]

At the intersection of court and city life, Lennox accompanied James twice in the summer of 1607 to celebratory events in the City of London that honoured the city's guilds. On 12 June they, along with others, went to the Clothworkers' Hall, where they dined with the Lord Mayor and members of the guild, who presented the king with a purse filled with gold. James also accepted membership in the guild, thereby becoming 'free' of the Clothworkers. John Watts, the mayor, 'humblie besought his Majestie, of his most especiall grace and favour to the Cittie in generall, and to that Societie in perticuler that hee would be pleased to be free of the Clothworkers'.[28] James accepted and generously promised: 'I doe here give unto this Company two brace of buckes yearely for ever'. The Master and Wardens of the guild humbly accepted the king into their brotherhood, thereby conferring on James the designation of 'citizen of London'. Ambassador Giustinian reports: 'The King returned a few days ago to the City. He went that same morning to dine with one of the Merchant Companies. He was sumptuously entertained, along with the Prince, his son, the Court and a great retinue of nobles'.[29]

A month later King James, Prince Henry and Lennox went together to the Merchant Taylors' Hall for a similar occasion on 16 July. The guild's records reveal that members instructed Sir John Swinnerton 'to conferr with Mr. Benjamyn Johnson, the Poet, about a Speech to be made to welcome his Majesty, and for Musique and other inventions'.[30] The records note further:

> At the upper end of the hall there was sett a chayer of estate where his Majesty sate and viewed the hall, and a very proper child well spoken being clothed like an Angell of gladnes, with a taper of francinnsence burning in his hand, delivered a shorte speech contanying xviii verses, devised by Mr Benjamn Johnson the Poet which pleased his Majestie marvelously well.[31]

John Rice (later a member of the King's Men) was the speaker, as the guild records indicate. Jonson, no stranger to the guilds, had prepared the first Lord Mayor's Show of the Jacobean era (1604), unfortunately lost, like the speech given here in 1607.[32] The renowned organist John Bull performed, and Nathaniel Giles led the Children of the Chapel in singing (both Bull and Giles were members of the Merchant Taylors). Seven lute players and other singers filled the hall with music. The banquet itself strains the imagination what with its 417 chickens, 1,300 eggs and 441 gallons of wine. Small wonder that the presentation 'pleased his Majestie marvelously well' (Nichols, 2:138). Finally, King James 'came downe into the greate hall, and sitting in his chayre of state, did heare a mellodious song of farwell song by the three men in the ship'.[33] The king noted that he was already a member of a London guild and he suggested that the Merchant Taylors offer such to Prince Henry, which they readily did. The guild also extended membership to Lennox, along with some other noblemen. Lennox gladly accepted and thus, like James and Henry, became a 'citizen of London'. At considerable expense, estimated at £1,000, the Merchant Taylors had demonstrated their love to the king, prince, Lennox and others, erasing for the moment boundaries between court and city. In the judgement of the Venetian ambassador 'by these popular arts the King goes winning the love of his people, and more especially of the City' (CSPV,11:20). The 'love' of the city would come in handy numerous times, especially when the king approached the city for a loan, which he did on more than one occasion.

The Venetian ambassador, Marc Antonio Correr, had an interview with Lennox in early February 1609, having been unable to approach James, who after only two days of dealing with government issues, retreated to hunting at Royston. Thus, Correr 'took the opportunity' to speak with Lennox, whom the ambassador describes as 'High Admiral of Scotland, relation and Councillor of the King and always near his person'.[34] Lennox's proximity to James made him especially valuable to diplomats and others who had business with the king. Being 'near his person' underscores one of the reasons that James had placed Lennox in the Holbein Gatehouse after all. Correr adds that when Lennox returns – he also readied to go to Royston – he will again speak with Lennox and transact business. But Lennox's visit to Royston was not without incident, as the ambassador subsequently reports: 'The Court has lately been in a buzz over a challenge sent by Viscount Haddington to the Duke of Lennox about some words exchanged between them at Royston' (CSPV, 11:234). James learned of this and 'stopped the duel; he also quieted the Council which wanted to proceed against Haddington' for his unprecedented action. Despite his status, Lennox on occasion became a relatively easy target for those with grievances of any kind. He also had some kind of verbal skirmish in 1609 with Christ College Cambridge, as documented in a letter that Lennox wrote to Cecil, 23 July 1609. The details of the quarrel remain, at best, fuzzy. Apparently, some letter has caused consternation, perhaps a petition from the college, as Lennox alludes to in another letter to Cecil, also from July. Lennox writes: 'The petition I sent you, I sent to eschew the presenting of it to his Majesty specially without your knowledge'.[35] Lennox knows that he should be solicitous of Cecil, whom he regards highly. The feeling is mutual, each having his reasons for not running foul of the other's prerogatives and office.

CELEBRATION AND DEATH (1610–12)

The next two years, 1610–12, focus on Prince Henry, who readies himself to become Prince of Wales. A melancholy note, however, enters the year 1610. In that year Lennox's second wife, Jean Campbell, died, bringing to a conclusion a fraught marriage, one permanently injured with struggles about the two children, who unfortunately died young. Lennox, in fact, had once sought a divorce from Jean. The records do not reveal if Lennox felt any particular grief about her death. Surely he at least experienced regret for the failure of this marriage, faults doubtless shared. His own responsibilities to the king and court and his regular absences from London limited his time for nurturing a marital relationship, should he have desired to do so. In all likelihood this situation suited him. The plans for Prince Henry's investiture occupied whatever empty space Lennox felt.

Lennox in fact remained at the centre of the plans and ceremonies, a tribute to his love of Prince Henry, whom he had watched from his birth and baptism in 1594 to his development as a young man full of promise and hope, the heir apparent to the throne. Lennox had served as the king's personal representative in the tense negotiations that allowed Queen Anne to lay claim to her son and secure his presence in 1603; and he in fact travelled with mother and son to England, where they joined King James. The duke observed approvingly as Henry established his own household at St James's Palace, a household noted for its orderliness, sobriety and discipline –qualities mainly lacking in the king's own household. And Lennox actively participated in the prince's *annus mirabilis* (1610); this year included the formal investiture as Prince of Wales, what commentators at the time referred to as the prince's 'creation'.

But first, English culture had to recuperate and even create the narrative and 'liturgy' of the actual investiture ceremony. No royal son had been created Prince of Wales since 1504, when Henry, son of Henry VII and later himself Henry VIII, at the age of thirteen experienced the official installation. While authorities began extensive research, Robert Cecil began the necessary quest for funding, first approaching Parliament in February 1610 and then later in April gratefully accepting the loan of £100,000 from the City of London, underscoring the reciprocal relationship of Whitehall and Guildhall.[36] A view of the year in terms of drama, experienced by Lennox and many others, shows it as bookended by two masque or tilting entertainments written by Ben Jonson: *Speeches at Prince Henry's Barriers* (6 January 1610) and *Oberon* (1 January 1611). These entertainments, full of romance elements, celebrate Henry in idealising, myth-making ways. They do not, however, specifically or immediately connect to the investiture, which takes place in mid-year, but they underscore several themes that run through the celebrations that acknowledge Henry's new status.

Prince Henry's challenge in late December preceded the actual barriers on 6 January. Under the name of Meliadus of Arthurian legend, presumed lover of the Lady of the Lake, Henry issued the challenge to all the knights of Great Britain, 'accompanied with Drummes and Trumpets in the Chamber of presence, before the King and Queene, and in presence of the whole Court'.[37] In a speech to the king, Henry hoped to present to him 'the first fruits of his chivalry at his Majestyes feete' (28). A short speech to the queen followed as the prince laid out the procedures of the barriers. Days of intense preparation followed as time drew nigh for Henry to make his first public mark as a chivalrous knight, full of valour and strength. Not surprisingly, he chose the Duke of Lennox as one of his six 'assistants' to ward off the fifty-six defendants. With the others, Lennox fulfilled the report of Marc Antonio Correr, the Venetian ambassador: 'All this week the Prince's six defenders have kept open table in the Prince's apartments; some of my suite have been invited more than once'.[38] Such hospitality graciously paved the way for the barriers on the day of Epiphany (see Chapter Four). Surrounded by Lennox and others and on full display to the court and ambassadors, Henry took a giant step in establishing his status as a true knight, wrapped in Arthurian mystique and confirmed by his physical strength in the barriers. Chivalry welcomes him, this prince who restores the decrepit House of Chivalry.

The loan from the City of London in late April, secured by Cecil, accelerated the pace for the official investiture of Henry. In late March 1610, Frederick Ulrich, Duke of Brunswick, Queen Anne's nephew, the son of her sister Elisabeth, arrived for an extended visit. Correr explains: 'He will remain many weeks in this city, as he is to assist at the ceremony of taking possession of his [Henry's] Principality which the Prince of Wales will celebrate a month hence'.[39] The ambassador reports later, James, Henry and Brunswick 'went down to dine at Greenwich, where the Queen is for change of air, as she has not been quite well. He [Brunswick] is lodged with the Prince and greatly honoured'(465). Apparently, no honoured visitor can complete an official visit without a trip to the Tower of London to see the lions, much as James and Lennox had done in 1603. According to a report, 'on the 20th of April, the two Princes [Henry and Frederick] accompanied by the Duke of Lenox, the Earle of Arundell, and others, came privatly to the Tower, and caused the great Lion to be put into the yard'.[40] The staff unleashed several dogs who attacked the lion, and so it went, with the lion fighting long and hard, to the apparent delight of the visitors. Lennox would surely have known how to explain to Brunswick the 'idea' behind such sport.

Two events helped determine the timing of the 'creation': the ongoing effects of the plague, which had begun in July 1608 and did not fully end until November 1610, resulting in part to the closing of the public theatres; and the startling and frightening assassination of Henri IV of France on 4 May 1610. Prince Henry had maintained a close alliance with King Henri; indeed, he thought of the French king as another father. The news of this murder devastated the young prince. The security and safety of the prince thus emerged as an important consideration for the public nature of the 'creation' festivities. Therefore, court authorities settled for a late-May beginning of the events, opting to have the main public pageant on the River Thames, possibly for security reasons. But perhaps something else lay behind not having an extravagant pageant through London's streets, as the Venetian ambassador implies:

> The King would not allow him on this occasion, nor yet on his going to Parliament, to be seen on horseback. The reason is the question of expense or, as some say, because they did not desire to exalt him too high.[41]

With considerable haste the City of London began to make its plans for a river pageant; and they hired Anthony Munday, already known as a writer of Lord Mayor's Shows, to put together a suitable entertainment. It took place on 31 May, the first of multiple events that unfolded over the next several days, including the formal investiture on 4 June.

Prince Henry, who had purposely gone to Richmond the day before, made his way from there downriver first to Chelsea and then to Whitehall, there to be received by his royal parents, Charles, Elizabeth and Lennox. Munday writes that by eight in the morning of 31 May 'all the wor-shipfull Companies of the Cittie, were readie in their Bardges upon the water'.[42] It seemed, Munday insists, that Neptune presided over the occasion and granted his favour to this pageant. Charles Cornwallis reports Henry moved along the river, encountering the barges 'with all the joy, love, and kindnesse possible, to the wonder of the World; all eyes were bent towards so joyfull and desired a sight'.[43]

Beyond such generalised spectacle, Munday arranged for two speakers: Corinea, Queen of Cornwall, on the back of a 'huge Whale', and Amphion, representing Wales, on a dolphin. Neptune's goodwill presumably prompted these figures and the sea creatures to appear on the Thames. At Chelsea, Corinea greeted and spoke to the prince. Appropriately costumed, she first identified herself as 'Queene to Brutes noble Companion *Corineus*' (Munday, 41), thus linking this occasion to the long-standing Trojan myth of British history. Corinea adds that she comes 'in honor of this generall rejoycing day, and to expresse the endeared affections of Londons Lord Maior, his Bretheren the Aldermen, and all these worthie Cittizens'. At Whitehall, the seat of royal power, Henry arrived, there to be greeted by Amphion, who insists that he represents Wales. He joins Corinea in expressing the devotion of London's citizens. With great noise, the river pageant ended. Henry had thus travelled from Richmond, a place long identified with his ancestor Henry VII, met with ancient figures and landed safely at Whitehall, with the full blessing of the City's authorities. Their commitment to this event can be underscored by Munday's choice of the renowned actor Richard Burbage to present Amphion and John Rice to represent Corinea; both served as members of the King's Men, Shakespeare's acting company.

Sunday, 3 June, focused on worship and the elaborate ceremony of the installation of the Knights of the Bath. Monday, 4 June, featured the actual investiture ceremony in the presence of assembled members of Parliament, nobility, Lennox and royalty in the Court of Requests. A contemporary letter describes the scene in which King James arrived in his royal robes; then 'After a good space of time the Prince entred at the lower end of the Great-chamber, having a surcote of purple velvet close girt unto him'.[44] Henry approached his father, who delivered the crown, staff and patent 'with the King's own hands. Which done, and the Prince with a low reverence offering to depart, the King stept to him, and, as it were by the way of welcome into that degree of greatness, took him by the hand, and then kissed him' (359). Marc Correr, the Venetian ambassador, adds that James 'displayed great affection, now saying that the Prince must not mind humbling himself to his father, now playfully patting his cheek and giving him other tokens of love'.[45] Henry received the patent that created him Prince of Wales, which had been read aloud by Cecil. Munday reports that Henry 'had his creation . . . with all the due ceremonies and vestures therto belonging, his Majestie himselfe girding on his Sworde' (Munday, 43).[46] On Tuesday night, 5 June, royalty and aristocrats gathered in the Banqueting House in Whitehall to watch and participate in Samuel Daniel's masque, *Tethys' Festival*, an opulent court entertainment that involved Inigo Jones's artistry as well.

Daniel represented several rivers, beginning with Tethys, Queen of the Ocean and wife of Neptune, attended by thirteen nymphs of the rivers. Aristocratic and royal women impersonated the rivers, such as Queen Anne as Tethys, Princess Elizabeth as Thames and Lady Arbella Stuart as the River Trent. These women as rivers controlled the masque, presiding and participating. Elizabeth as Thames may have reminded spectators of the recent river pageant. Prince Henry and King James served as the principal spectators, surrounded by a court of noblemen and women, including Lennox. The enclosed space of the court unleashed Jones's creative imagination, offering a fair return on his payment of £400. The opening scene, for example, contains an elaborate painted device of Neptune and Nereus. Daniel writes: 'On the Travers which served as a curtaine for the first Scene, was figured a darke cloude, interior with certaine sparkling stares, which, at the sound of a loud musick, being instantly drawne, the scene was discovered'.[47] This merely began the elaborate and convoluted display that Daniel and Jones arranged: painted scenes, replicas of classical figures or gods, devices inside of devices. This first scene itself represented a port or haven, by which Daniel had in mind Milford Haven in Wales, crucial to Henry VII's success.

Prince Charles, dressed 'in a short robe of greene satin imbrodered with golden flowers' (Daniel, 3:311) appeared as Zephyrus, celebrated in song. This song also refers to 'Meliades', the name for Henry in Jonson's *Barriers* six months earlier. The ladies, as the rivers, 'descended out of their Cavernes one after another, and so marched up with winding meanders like a River, till they came to the Tree of victory' (319). Soft music from twelve lutes and twelve voices identified this tree as Apollo's Tree, the tree of victory; it celebrates King James. Additional spectacular scenes, paintings and dancing followed, closing finally with Zephyrus, who conducted the queen and her ladies who 'march up to the King conducted by the Duke of Yorke' (323). This dazzling masque, commissioned by Queen Anne, celebrated Henry's life and looks forward to great achievements from him, dramatically realised in the court's private space, even as the open-air river pageant gave voice to Henry's connection to gods and goddesses, summoned by the goodwill of London's guilds and citizens. One last burst of entertainment on Wednesday: an afternoon of tilting, in which Lennox participated, and an evening of a sea battle on the Thames, closing with blazing fireworks. Thus, Henry's creation as Prince of Wales ended with a bang, a rousing close to this chapter and keen anticipation for the future. All the world seemed to open ever more brightly for his future. Lennox certainly thought so.

Already feted by city and court, Prince Henry commissioned his own masque and employed Jonson and Jones to produce *Oberon, the Fairy Prince*, performed on the first day of 1611. The court spared no expense and the elaborate quality of the performance gains confirmation from both court records and from the marvellous drawings by Jones that survive.[48] Lennox, among many others, gathered at the Whitehall Banqueting House, as they had twice in the past year for entertainments that honoured the prince. Members of the King's Men participated in performing the anti-masque. Out of the hall's stillness a scene opened displaying a rock and wilderness, from which emerged a satyr; and just as suddenly ten more satyrs appeared, '*running forth severally from divers parts of the rock, leaping and making antic action and gestures*'.[49] Then, another scene opened, revealing a '*glorious palace whose gates and walls were transparent*' (163). Silenus greets the two sylvans who lie before the gates; he speaks of the 'Fairly Land' in which Oberon and his knights live.

Out of songs and antic dancing the scene dissolved into a stunning spectacle: '*Then the whole palace opened, and the nation of fays were discovered, some with instruments, some bearing lights, others singing*' (167). This moment afforded the first glimpse of Oberon, danced by Prince Henry: '*At the further end of all, Oberon, in a chariot, which to a loud triumphant music began to move forward, drawn by two white bears, and on either side guarded by three sylvans*' (167–8). Everyone in the hall rejoiced to see Oberon in splendid costume, looking like an antique Roman, moving through the hall in a chariot drawn by white bears. The satyrs leapt for joy; and then the 'foremost Sylvan' began to speak: 'This is a night of greatness and of state . . . / A night of homage to the British court, / And ceremony due to Arthur's chair, / From our bright master, Oberon the fair' (168–9). After several dances and songs, Phosphorus, the day star, appeared and summoned the dancers to depart: '*the star vanished, and the whole machine closed*' (173). This insubstantial pageant faded; but memories continued to resonate about this prince, who brings credit and emerging renown to the royal family and honour to Arthur's chair. This vivid image lingered in Lennox's thoughts, seeming all the brighter in the darker days to come when a shining Oberon would be no more. The brightness of 1610–11 cannot be doubted as Henry seemed indeed to, according to Silenus in *Oberon*, 'fill with grace / Every season, every place' (p. 161).

The eighteen-year-old Henry cut a rather dashing and imposing figure. He exuded confidence and engendered hope. One contemporary described him:

> He was of a comely tall middle stature, about five foot and eight inches high, of a strong, streight well-made body (as if Nature in him had shewed all her cunning) with somewhat broad shoulders, and a small waste, of an amiable Majesticke Countenance, his haire of an Aborne collour, long faced, and broad forehead, a piercing grave eye, a most gracious smile, with a terrible frowne.[50]

Daniel Price, who entered Henry's service in 1608 as one of his chaplains, and who in 1610 preached the sermon on the day before the prince's investiture as Prince of Wales, refers to the prince's 'piercing *eye*, gratious *smile*, grave *frowne*, and divine *face* composed of *modesty* and *majestie*'.[51] Price also comments on Henry as being slow to anger, quick to apprehend and eager to pardon. Lennox could readily modify Price's judgement about Henry's anger. Ambassador Correr reports, on 4 May 1611, that at Royston Henry resented being 'reproved' by the king; 'this made the King so angry that he threatened the Prince with his cane, whereupon the Prince put spurs to his horse and rode off'.[52] Such insolence could not stand. Thus, Lennox urged Henry to apologise to his father, which he did in the king's chamber at Lennox's insistence; and the king 'cheerfully welcomed' Henry, forgiving him for his behaviour. This episode tempers the sometimes impossibly idealistic portraits of Henry and underscores Lennox's good favour with the royal children. Francis Bacon adds to Henry's portrait, noting, however, that something slightly inscrutable lingered in Henry: 'Many points there were indeed in this prince's nature which were obscure, and could not be discovered by any man's judgment'.[53] Henry's reticence, in contrast to his father's garrulous qualities, and modesty created mystery.

As Lennox knew first-hand, the prince was a dutiful son, obedient to his father and attentive to his mother. Even when his mother was busy and unable to see him, he waited patiently for her attention. Henry showed affection and concern for Prince Charles. But, as Bacon notes, 'his sister he especially loved; whom also he resembled in countenance, as far as a man's face can be compared with that of a very beautiful girl' (328). Their surviving letters reveal a close relationship between brother and sister. When Elizabeth finally arrived at court in 1608 from the Harrington household in Warwickshire their love for each other deepened; and Henry exhibited great care for her well-being, writing to her at one point: 'There is nothing I wish more then that we might be in one companie'.[54]

A competent student, especially under the tutelage of Adam Newton, Henry did not incline towards scholarship; in this he resembled Lennox. Nicolò Molin, the Venetian ambassador in 1607, notes the prince's response to studying: 'He studies, but not with much delight, and chiefly under his father's spur, not of his own desire, and for this he is often admonished and set down'.[55] In fact, the king admonished him on one particular occasion by suggesting that the crown might be left to Prince Charles, the earnest and careful student. Henry's tutor continued in this vein, prompting the prince to cry out: '"I know what becomes a Prince. It is not necessary for me to be a professor, but a soldier and a man of the world. If my brother is as learned as they say, we'll make him

Archbishop of Canterbury"' (CSPV, 10:513). Such a response did not amuse James, but probably appealed to Lennox.

But Henry did exhibit an interest in history. Cornwallis states that he 'read Histories, the knowledge of things passed conducing much to resolution in things present, and to prevention of those to come'.[56] In the epistle dedicatory to his *The Lives of the III. Normans*, published in 1613, John Hayward records an extraordinary conversation with Prince Henry about history in late summer 1612. In a second interview, which took place at St James's Palace, Henry began with a complaint about the quality of the published histories of England compared to other nations.[57] The prince explained his focus on history as deriving from an interest in his ancestors: 'he desired nothing more then to know the actions of his Ancestours; because hee did so farre esteeme his descent from them, as he approached neere them in honourable endeavours'(A3). Hayward's history of the Norman kings became the finished product of this exceptional conversation, and Hayward also presented a version of Queen Elizabeth's history when Henry returned from the progress.

Henry supported the arts generously, doubtless inspired by the example of his mother. Henry Peacham acknowledges the prince's patronage in the dedication to his 1612 emblem book, *Minerva Britanna*. Henry also served as patron to George Chapman, Ben Jonson, Michael Drayton and Inigo Jones, among others. Like Lennox, Henry had numerous books dedicated to him. For example, Jonson dedicated *The Masque of Queens* (1609) to the prince, underscoring the playwright's connections to the court. In the epistle dedicatory to Henry, Jonson makes clear that the prince has asked him to provide annotations to the holograph copy of the text, which he readily did, giving him a chance to demonstrate his scholarship. In Jonson's view, Henry was both 'born a Prince' and 'became' a prince. The playwright thus provides great praise for Henry's involvement with the arts. The prince also began, under the tutelage of Thomas Howard, Earl of Arundel, to build an impressive collection of paintings that eventually passed to Prince Charles. Henry collected sculpture, books and antique medals and had a purpose-built library constructed at St James's Palace. Increasingly, aristocrats and other foreign ambassadors presented Henry with art works for both Richmond Palace and St James's Palace.[58]

Cornwallis captures the prince's regard for the noblemen who regularly accompanied him and served him: 'Of the titular Nobility of this Kingdome upon occasion offered, he would expresse himselfe best to love and esteeme such as were most anciently descended, and most nobly and honestly disposed, when sometimes also he would not forbeare by name to particulate'.[59] Henry surely had in mind the Duke of Lennox, who had faithfully supported and nurtured him from his earliest days, even as Lennox occupied a special place in the king's confidence.

In the early months of 1612 the prince engaged in several festive activities. On Shrove Tuesday, for example, he with five others 'ran a match at the ring for a supper, against the Duke of Lennox' and his supporters.[60] Henry won, 'and the Supper and Plays were made at the Marquesse of Winchester's house on the Tuesday after'. During the summer he went on progress to, among other places, Coventry and Kenilworth Castle. He accompanied King James for part of this journey. Finally arriving at Woodstock on 26 August he hosted a sumptuous feast for his father, mother and sister. According to Cornwallis, Henry 'had given order to his Officers to provide a most magnifique Feast against their comming to the foresaid house'.[61] Cornwallis adds that the king and queen sat at a table by themselves at the upper end of the room, 'his Highnesse with his Sister accompanied with the Lords and Ladies sitting at another Table of thirty yards long and more, by themselves, there was to bee seene one of the greatest and best ordered feasts as ever was seene' (27). Admiring the whole scene and occasion and seeing the splendour, the king 'was forced to say, that he had never seen the like before all his lifetime, and that he could never doe so much in his owne house'.[62] The royal family would have much occasion to recall this convivial moment and all the goodwill that prevailed as they revelled in Henry's gracious hospitality: a fitting end to summer even as an uncertain future lay ahead.

One subject of conversation that August would have been a potential marriage for Henry. Having arrived at a marriageable age, Henry endured in fact considerable speculation about his future as husband. The court pursued various candidates, especially during the 1610–12 period, including Princess Christine, the nine-year-old second daughter of Marie de' Medici, and Maria, third daughter of the Duke of Savoy. About marriage Henry himself can best be described as willing but reticent, not unlike his father earlier. On the subject of marriage, Lennox could not offer much advice: as noted, he struggled in a most unpleasant marriage. Cornwallis reports: 'It is true, that to take a wife though hee shewed no vehement desire, yet he demonstrated a good inclination'.[63] Cornwallis adds that he had been present during several feasts hosted by the prince to which the most beautiful ladies had been invited, but Henry manifested no special interest. On another occasion, 'Mention being made of the mariage of some of his young Gentlemen, his Highnes said, I would not be so soone maried, and yet I wish to see my Father a grandfather'.[64] In a letter to James written from Richmond on 5 October 1612 Henry

Figure 2.3 Prince Henry from Michael Drayton's *Poly-Olbion*, 1612, STC 7226.
By permission of the Folger Shakespeare Library.

wished his father to resolve the marriage issue, to determine 'my part to play, which is to be in love with any of them'.[65] If not 'vehement desire', the prince at least registered a dutiful willingness to marry – inclined but not eager.

Two radically different events intervene and intersect Henry's story in October 1612: the reburial of his grandmother, Mary, Queen of Scots on 8 October and, a week later, the arrival of Frederick, Elector Palatine of Germany on 16 October, coming to marry Princess Elizabeth. These events affected the royal family and Lennox, producing reflection and introspection in the first case, and joy and excitement in the second. Lennox meets with things dying and things new-born: the past and the future converge within a week. Or, as the writer of Ecclesiastes observes: 'To every thing there is a season . . . A time to be born, and a time to die' (3:1–2).

The past entered the darkness that fell early on an October evening in London as a chill gripped the air. In the same month that Prince Henry became fatally ill in 1612, a strange procession of torches slowly moved from the north to Clerkenwell where the Archbishop of Canterbury, George Abbot, and other clergymen and noblemen waited on 8 October. The entourage stopped around 6pm before continuing its journey to Westminster Abbey. The Duke of Lennox, and others scattered through-out the streets, saw a coffin carrying the exhumed body of Mary, Queen of Scots, James's mother. With ample torches, the procession, which had begun seventy miles away at Peterborough Cathedral, wound its way to the abbey.

A grand monument awaited the queen's body in the abbey. This opu-lent tomb rested in the Henry VII Chapel, deliberately and directly oppo-site the one that James had commissioned for Queen Elizabeth. This torchlight movement, involving Mary's body, eerily recalls a similar procession that began late at night on 30 July 1587 from Fotheringhay Castle to Peterborough Cathedral, where it arrived at 2am, carrying the embalmed, heavy, lead-incased body of the executed queen. This bizarre night-time procedure attempted to prevent undue interest in her burial. After a stridently Protestant service, with only English men and women attending (apart from Mary's servants), Mary gained her resting place in the cathedral, not to be disturbed until 1612.

To answer the question of 'why now', Lennox would have to recall James's, at best, problematic relationship with his mother, one that Lennox knew about from his father and from his own observation. In the letter to the Scottish people, the one that complemented the other doc-ument that established Lennox as president of the Privy Council while

James went to Denmark to marry Anne in 1589, James had tellingly characterised his delay in marrying: 'The reasons were that I was alone, without father or mother, brother or sister, king of this realm and heir apparent of England'.[66] At the age of thirteen months, James in 1567 had become King of Scotland, his father having been murdered in February of that year and his mother driven into exile by the Scottish nobles and Kirk after her disastrous and ill-advised marriage to the Earl of Bothwell.

In fact, James never consciously knew his parents. This vulnerability governed many of his actions and offers a psychological base for understanding his search for family. James's knowledge of his mother he gained exclusively through her letters and reports from emissaries. Numerous Scots believed that Lennox's father, Esmé Stuart, had arrived in Scotland in 1579 to do the bidding of the Guise faction in France and to help Mary gain release from imprisonment. Esmé certainly participated in numerous attempts to resolve conflict and even to create an 'Association' by which James and Mary would share joint rule. Not long after the young Ludovic Stuart arrived in Scotland that idea died. By 1584, James had effectively given up on his mother; he saw a more promising potential future awaiting him in England.[67]

Mary's approval of the 'Babington Plot', a plan by insistent Catholics to assassinate Elizabeth and free Mary, determined her final destiny. On 3 August 1586 English forces arrested Mary for plotting against Elizabeth's life and a month later they moved her from Chartley to Fotheringhay Castle, twenty miles southwest of Peterborough in Northamptonshire. By 15 October she stood trial in the great hall at Fotheringhay Castle where a jury easily and readily found her guilty.

Nothing could now prevent Mary's execution. In a scene full of theatrical spectacle, Mary, dressed in black and carrying a crucifix and prayer book and wearing two rosaries on her waist, on the morning of 8 February 1587 made her way to the appointed scaffold (an elevated 'stage') and executioner's block in Fotheringhay Castle.[68] After speeches and prayers, some led by Richard Fletcher, Dean of Peterborough Cathedral and father of John Fletcher, eventually Shakespeare's fellow playwright and collaborator, the assistants stripped Mary's outer garment revealing a red petticoat. Blindfolded by her faithful servant Jane Kennedy, Mary then lowered her head on the block; and the blade fell against her with two blows, severing her head from the body. Servants burned all of Mary's clothes and the executioner's block, doing everything to make impossible the likelihood that something of hers could become a relic. Her imposing casket lay unattended and unburied in a secret place, underscoring her end and her isolation.

Finally, some five months later Mary's body made the journey in early
morning darkness to Peterborough Cathedral, where Dean Fletcher
welcomed it; and he presided over a service, ordered by Elizabeth, that
should give due respect to a monarch, a staunchly Protestant service that
Mary would have abhorred. The heavy coffin, bearing on its top her life-
like effigy befitting a royal funeral, moved slowly into the beautiful and
majestic Norman cathedral, sweeping up the grand nave toward its final
resting place in the south aisle of the choir. Mary would find her resting
place in an obscure, unmarked grave, directly across from Catherine of
Aragon, Henry VIII's first wife, who had lain in the north aisle since
January 1536: two foreign queens in an English cathedral.

James took a tangible step of remembering and honouring his mother
in 1603, shortly after becoming King of England. He sent a rich velvet
pall to Peterborough Cathedral to adorn Mary's gravesite. James never
visited the cathedral but being on English soil apparently prompted him
to make the gesture of honouring her grave. He thereby resembled the
dutiful son, an idea that could supplant less flattering ones regarding his
concern for Mary. Having secured the title of King of England, James
might now attempt to refashion and burnish his image as one full of filial
piety.

Then, in 1606, James ordered the construction of a marble tomb monument for his mother to be erected in Westminster Abbey, as he had done
for Elizabeth. Cornelius and William Cure, superb stone carvers and
master masons, carried out the project. In September 1612 they neared
completion; and thus, James sent a letter to the Dean of Peterborough
Cathedral requesting the exhuming of Mary's body. James wrote on
28 September:

> For that we remember it appertains to the duty we owe to our dearest mother
> that like honour should be done to her body and like monument be extant
> of her . . . And for that we think it inconvenient that the monument and her
> body should be in several [separate] places, we have ordered that her said
> body, remaining now interred in that our Cathedral Church of Peterborough,
> shall be removed to Westminster to her said monument, and have committed
> the care and charge of said translation of her body from Peterborough to
> Westminster to the reverend father in God, our right trusty and well-beloved
> servant, the Bishop of Coventry and Lichfield . . . to deliver the corpse of
> our said dearest mother, the same being taken up in as decent and respectful
> manner as is fitting.[69]

The letter emphasises her 'body' and that the king intends to honour
that body, of which he had little conscious awareness. James finds it

'inconvenient' that her body should remain in Peterborough and the monument be in Westminster; he intends, rather, to reconcile body and tomb. In his letter to the dean of the cathedral, James notes that monarchs 'of this realm are usually interred' in the abbey church. Mary, of course, derives from another realm, but he will make her central in England's recollection and commemoration. In a moment of unusual frugality, James also insisted that the velvet pall be sent along with the coffin.

Three things will bring about Mary's 'translation': the actual movement of the body, the velvet pall and the monument. In a little over a week, Mary's remains had been 'translated' from Peterborough to the outer precincts of London where Archbishop Abbot met the procession on that October night in 1612 on its way to the abbey. She will have been released from the obscure grave in Peterborough in order to take her place in a magnificent tomb in the symbolic heart of English political and religious life.

The translation of Mary also underscored a translation of James, a kind of expiation of whatever lingering guilt he felt about his mother. Her remains now moved to the Henry VII chapel where her corpse would occupy the largest and grandest monument. For the first time in English history a Scottish monarch would reside in the great Westminster church, a monarch executed by order of James's English predecessor. Now Elizabeth and Mary would lie across from each other in the chapel, seemingly equal, creating an unmistakable irony. As in the darkness that surrounded her initial stealthy burial in Peterborough, the body in October 1612 moved through dim London streets to the cold Westminster church where Lennox and others could pay their respects and confirm her 'translation', forever etched in their collective memory. October thus starts with a somewhat strange reburial, a confrontation with death and its commemoration bereft, however, of any outpouring of grief.

On 16 October a new possibility appeared that looked to the future: the arrival of Prince Frederick V, Count Palatine of the Rhine and Elector of the Holy Roman Empire. He came to England, eager to become the husband of King James's only daughter, Elizabeth. After a period of intense negotiation, James had finally settled on Frederick as being suitable, to the chagrin of Queen Anne but with the support of Henry, who longed for such a stalwart Protestant to marry into the Stuart royal family. In the negotiations, James offered a dowry of £40,000 and an allowance; the Germans responded with an offer of £1,500 per annum for Elizabeth and provided for the princess's retinue of thirty-six men and thirteen women. 'If she were widowed, Elizabeth would receive an income of £10,000 and be able to live where she chose'.[70] Although a somewhat minor German prince, Frederick found favour in James's eyes as the king envisioned some kind of pan-Protestant union across Europe. Frederick, not incidentally, offered attractive monetary terms.

In order for Frederick to be received correctly and with good taste, James entrusted the Duke of Lennox with the task, and he set out to retrieve the prince. As the Venetian ambassador Antonio Foscarini reports: 'The Duke of Lennox and other nobles have left in haste to receive him'.[71] The ambassador adds:

> The Elector will be received in great state. The arrival of the Palatine with so large a following, the fêtes which are being prepared, the expenditure in dresses and liveries, have attracted an extraordinary number of people to London and caused a great rise in the price of everything.

Lennox met Frederick at Gravesend and greeted him in French, the Duke's native tongue and one that the prince had learned (he did not know English). The young prince, like Elizabeth born in 1596, understood Lennox's importance and accepted this kingly gesture of confidence and compliment. From Gravesend, Lennox led the prince and his entourage towards London in a flotilla of at least 150 boats. According to the Venetian ambassador this group passed straight to Whitehall, and 'was saluted on [its] way by upwards of two hundred guns from the Tower of London, as well as by an infinity of salutes from the shipping, with which the river was full'.[72] The only disadvantage was the weather: 'the coldest day that came this winter, and yet he [the prince] caried himself with . . . assurance'.[73]

When Frederick arrived at Whitehall, he entered the great hall and found the king and queen seated on a dais, surrounded by Prince Henry, Prince Charles and Princess Elizabeth, the hall itself 'thronged with Lords and Ladies in the richest robes and laden with jewels'.[74] The ambassador adds: 'The Duke of Lennox walked with Prince Henry and all preceded the Palatine', who made his reverences to the king, who then embraced him: 'the King was extremely pleased . . . and tenderly embracing him he said he took him for his son'. Frederick next greeted the queen, 'who looked favourably on him'; then the prince approached Elizabeth 'and boldly kissed her'; she blushed at his assertiveness. In the days to come, Frederick focused his attention almost exclusively on the princess, ignoring opportunities for running at the ring, playing tennis or riding with Prince Henry.

Foscarini, the ambassador, notes Frederick's daily visits to Elizabeth 'with whom he is now very familiar' (CSPV, 12:444). He describes the prince as being 'very handsome [and] of pleasant speech'. Foscarini also notes Frederick's extravagant clothing and entourage: 'He changes his dress every day, and one is richer than another. All the gentlemen he has with him are covered with gold, chains and jewels'. In a fashion-conscious court, Frederick's appearance held much appeal. These two young people rivalled one another in dazzling array and satisfied everyone with their growing and comfortable intimacy. Chamberlain reports that Elizabeth invited Frederick to a supper and a play, 'and they meet often at meales without curiositie of bidding'.[75]

In response to Frederick's arrival, the Merchant Taylors invited Frederick and Prince Henry to the Lord Mayor's feast on 29 October, the day of the new mayor's inauguration; and 'great preparation was made for them'.[76] Chamberlain writes: 'the Count Palatine and his companie after they had seene the shew in Cheapside (which was somwhat extraordinarie with fowre or five pageants and other devises) went to Guild-hall, and were there plentifully feasted and welcomed by Sir John Swinerton the new Lord Mayor' (1:384). Lennox accompanied Frederick, along with other earls and barons, but not the ill Prince Henry.[77] The guild and the City of London presented Frederick a fair standing cup, a basin and ewer, with two large livery pots, valued at £500. Howes observes that the pots had the term *Civitatis London* engraved on them.[78] The merchants had sent the prince some wine a few days earlier. Clearly the city revelled in his presence.

Their 'great preparation' for the two noble kinsmen included Thomas Dekker's pageant, the Lord Mayor's Show *Troia-Nova Triumphans*, which Dekker wrote with assistance from John Heminge of the King's Men. This entertainment honoured John Swinnerton, Merchant Taylor, the new mayor. Lennox watched from a privileged place, along with other distinguished guests. Not even the lingering chill from yet another storm could dampen the crowd's enthusiasm. Dekker captured London's supposed link to ancient Troy, as he filled the pageant with drama, music, allegory and rich spectacle. The guild spent extravagantly, anticipating the appearance of Henry, Frederick and Lennox.

Dekker writes in the opening lines of his text: '*Tryumphes*, are the most choice and daintiest fruit that spring from *Peace* and *Abundance*; *Love* begets them; and *Much Cost* brings them forth'.[79] The entertainment will taste 'sweetly' for everyone, including 'the *Noblest strangers*', meaning Frederick, Lennox and others in his party. *Troia-Nova Triumphans* honours not only the new mayor this day, but also the visiting prince – hence the unusual expenditures. In the swirl of action and spectacle Dekker produced a show that rivalled royal welcomes, therefore worthy for two princes.

The procession of the mayor arrived at one of the allegorical pageant devices that included the 'house of Fame' where she sits 'crowned in rich attire, a Trumpet in her hand' and several places reserved for former kings and princes who have been free of the Merchant Taylors. 'A particular roome,' Dekker writes, 'being reserved for one that represents the person of *Henry* the now Prince of *Wales*' (3:240). (As noted earlier, Henry had gained the freedom of this guild in 1607.) In a lengthy speech Fame addresses the new mayor, reminding him that 'In this Court of *Fame* / None else but *Vertue* can enrole thy *Name*'. And Fame calls attention to Henry: 'A Sprig of which Branch, (Highest now but One) / Is *Henry Prince of Wales*, followed by none: / Who of this *Brotherhood*, last and best steps forth' (241). A particular room in the House of Fame contained a special place for Prince Henry, who, they expected, would be present to see this device, lending resonance for the concept of virtue's triumph. But his absence underscored the terrible fact that he remained ill in another particular room, one in St James's Palace.

Instead of a House of Fame for Prince Henry, Lennox saw and remembered an ominous rainbow, noted by Charles Cornwallis, writing about the events of 29 October 1612: 'This evening there appeared a fatall signe about two houres or more within the night, bearing the colours and shew of a *Rainbow*, which hung directly crosse and over Saint *Jameses* House'.[80] This strange rainbow had first appeared at seven o'clock. Lennox and many others saw it and pondered its meaning as it lingered over the palace where Henry lay critically ill. This rainbow contrasts with the mood earlier that day when the streets of London vibrated with thousands of spectators watching attentively and excitedly Dekker's Lord Mayor's Show. The mysterious rainbow puzzled those who saw it and disturbed the day's joy.

Shortly after the feast at Woodstock and the return from progress in late summer 1612 Henry began to show symptoms of some discomfort. Increasingly, he slept restlessly, he often felt listless and devoid of his usual energy, and occasionally he ran a fever. Just as often he would bounce back and engage in strenuous rounds of swimming and tennis. No one had any reason to be alarmed or worried about his health. By October, however, that changed, as his symptoms became more pronounced and persistent. Lennox and members of the prince's household began to notice. 'At the beginning of *October*,' Cornwallis writes, 'his continuall Head-ach, Lazinesse, and indisposition increasing, (which . . . he strove mightily to conceale) . . . he did lye a bed, almost every morning untill nine of the clocke, complayning of his lazinesse.'[81] Every morning he would ask the grooms of his bedchamber: 'How doe I looke this morning? . . . which they, fearing no danger, . . .would put off with one jest or other'. By mid-October his condition worsened and, looking pale, he moved from Richmond Palace to St James's Palace. No one suspected anything serious – possibly a fit of 'ague', a fever, a cold of some kind.

Henry alternated between being difficult in disposition and having a blank stare, to taking charge of matters regarding his sister's forth-coming marriage and even entertaining Frederick, Elector Palatine. On 24 October, paying no heed to his diminished health, Henry, in fact, played tennis with Frederick 'as though his body had been of brasse'; he even played 'in his shirt, as if it had been in the heate of Summer' (Cornwallis, 33). Even so, he looked pale and everyone noticed. He later went to bed, complaining of laziness and a headache. But on Sunday, 25 October, he emerged and readied himself to hear the sermon in his chapel, which he heard attentively, and then later went to Whitehall and heard another sermon with his father. Afterwards, he and his father dined. By three o'clock that afternoon, Henry became violently ill and made his way back to St James's Palace and took to his bed: 'This night hee rested ill' (38). And so he would for the remainder of his days, never leaving the palace again.

On 29 October, the fifth day of Henry's confinement and the day of the mayoral pageant and rainbow, Cornwallis reports: 'his Highnesse now being forced to keepe his bed continually, his head being so giddy, that he could not stand upright, his eyes also so dimme, that he could not indure the candle light' (Cornwallis, 46). And yet the doctors, who had begun to increase in number if not skill, kept hope and also greatly feared a wrong diagnosis or treatment and the consequences for them. Their treatments became more extreme, clear signs of despera-tion. Occasionally Henry felt well enough to put on his clothes and he did respond to visitors. Cornwallis writes: 'the whole World did almost every houre send unto Saint *Jameses* for newes; the better sort who were admitted to visit him; or acquainted with those neere unto him, knowing the danger' (51). Among the 'better sort', the Duke of Lennox came to visit Henry and sensed the impending disaster. On Sunday, 1 November, the regular course of bleeding had momentary beneficial effects; and that afternoon 'hee was visited by his Royall Father, Mother, Brother, Sister, the Palsgrave, with divers others of the Court' (53). All departed, Cornwallis says, 'reasonably cheerefull. Yet that night . . . hee passed unquietly'.

On Tuesday, 3 November, he became worse than before. Cordials and administered glisters provided temporary relief but for the extreme pain in his head the doctors decided to shave his hair, 'and Pigeons and cupping Glasses applyed to lessen and draw away the humour, and that superfluous blood from the Head' (Cornwallis, 57). Such treatments Henry endured with patience, but they had little positive effect. Hope of recovery had largely disappeared by Wednesday, 4 November. The various physicians, surgeons and apothecaries decided on a radical new treatment: 'This day a Cocke was cloven by the backe, and applyed unto the soles of his feet, but in vaine; the Cordials also were redoubled in number and quantitie, but without any profit' (59). That afternoon King James came to see Henry; but sensing the imminent danger, he left without visiting his son and gave an order that no one should see him except those who needed to tend upon him.

In desperation the doctors on 5 November doubled and tripled the cordials, opting not to bleed Henry more. Clearly the end was in sight; therefore, the Archbishop of Canterbury, George Abbot, came hurriedly and began his ministry of comfort and reassurance and prayers, even succeeding in getting Henry to repeat his confession of faith word by word after him. Finally, at last the archbishop confronted Henry frankly about his situation and sought to prepare him for death. This day Henry, in his state of confusion, began to cry out for his friend David Murray, who came immediately; but Henry could not articulate what he wanted to say. Later that same day Henry did manage to make a request of Murray 'for the burning of a number of *Letters* in a certaine cabinet in his closet, which presently after his death was done' (69).

Finally, on Friday, 6 November, Henry lay between life and death, experiencing extraordinary convulsions and loss of his senses. He did rally slightly when the archbishop called upon him to acknowledge his abiding faith by raising his fingers or hands, which Henry succeeded in doing. Daniel Price reports: Henry '*lifted up* his holy *hands* united, and afterwards his *eies bent* to *heaven*, from whence not long after appeared, in his deliverance, his *salvation*'.[82] Shortly after, the archbishop left, having 'with streames of teares, powred out at his bed side, a most exceeding powerfull passionate prayer' (Cornwallis, 73). At last, the cloudy night revealed the impending doom, as Henry surrendered life around eight o'clock that evening. The shipwright Phineas Pett, who had served Henry, had arrived shortly before Henry's death and reported: 'I came to St James about four of the clock, where I found a house turned to the very map of true sorrow, every man with the character of grief written in his dejected countenance, all places flowing with tears and bitter lamentations'.[83] John Hackett likened Henry's death to a light being extinguished so that 'a Thick Darkness, next to that of Hell, is upon our Land at this day'.[84] This once vibrant, active body could not fend off death. By the rivers of Thames, Trent, Avon and Humber people sat down and wept when they remembered Oberon, the fairy prince.

On the next day, by order of King James, members of the Privy Council, including Lennox, came 'to give order for the opening of his Body' (Cornwallis, 75), which began at five o'clock that evening in the presence of all the physicians who had been involved in the prince's care, including the Elector Palatine's physician. Thus began the official autopsy, in part to determine if Henry might have had some contagious disease. Cornwallis provides all the intricate details of this analysis. Modern medical science suggests that Henry died of typhoid fever, thus ruling out the possibility of poison.

On Monday, 9 November, the lords of the Privy Council returned to St James's Palace to offer directions about what needed to be done, starting with draping all the various chambers in black. Attendants brought in a coffin and they began their vigil. As the funeral day had been set for Monday, 7 December, the prince's servants moved the coffin into various chambers of the palace, finally taking it to the chapel, where it lay until the funeral, placed under a canopy set with the great arms of union. Servants had disembowelled, embalmed and enclosed Henry's body in lead. John Holles, the comptroller of the prince's household, reports in a letter to Sir Robert Mansfield, written shortly after the death:

> Since 12 of the clock of Saturday night that I attended my dear master's bowels to the grave, I have kept my chamber, was entering a hot ague for which I purged and let blood; but no mortal hand can cure the everlasting comfortless sickness of my soul.[85]

On Sunday night, 6 December, 'his representation was brought (made in so short warning, as like him as could be) and appareled with cloathes, having his creation robes above the same, his cap and crowne upon his head' (Cornwallis, 85). In brief, this 'representation' appeared clothed in the same manner as he was at the time of his creation (1610). This effigy 'was laid on the back on the Coffin, and fast bound to the same' (85). So it would remain as the coffin moved through the streets for the funeral. The garments of creation now served the purposes of death. The Lord Chamberlain's Records illustrate the procedure of creating the effigy: the figure was to be jointed so that it could be moved 'to sundrie actions first for the Carriage in the Chariot and then for the standinge and for setting uppe the same in the Abbye'.[86] The same records indicate a payment of £10 to 'Abraham Vanderdort for the face and hands of the Princes representation being very curiouslie wrought'. The coffin contained the actual body of the prince; but above a representation could remind everyone of

his physical likeness, a faint image of the one who in 1611 had seemed
to 'fill with grace / Every season, every place'. Sorrowfully, Lennox surrendered to the recognition that, in the words of the Third Queen in
Shakespeare and Fletcher's *Two Noble Kinsmen*, 'the world's a city full
of straying streets, / And death's the market place, where each one meets'
(Act I, scene v, lines 15–16).

Of the royal family's sorrow Chamberlain writes on 12 November
that the prince's death 'was exceeding grevous to them both [king and
queen], but specially to the King who takes yt with more impatience
then was expected'.[87] On Tuesday, 10 November, the family gathered in London to share their grief. Chamberlain notes particularly
Princess Elizabeth's reaction:

> The Lady Elizabeth is much afflicted with this losse, and not without goode
> cause, for he did extraordinarilie affect her, and during his sickness inquired
> still after her, and the last wordes he spake in good sense, (they say) were,
> Where is my deare sister? (1:390)

Antonio Foscarini, the Venetian ambassador, reported to the Doge and
Venetian Senate: 'The King received the news of the Prince's death at
Theobalds; it affected him greatly and made of the happiest the sad-
dest father in the world'.[88] He adds: 'The Queen's life has been in the
greatest danger owing to her grief. She will receive no visits nor allow
anyone in her room, from which she does not stir, nor does she cease
crying'. Elizabeth 'has gone two days without food and cries incessantly'.
Equally poignant, 'The Elector Palatine does not know what to do; he is
quite upset at finding himself here at such an unpropitious and lamentable juncture'. Unlike Hamlet who left Germany to go to Denmark for
his father's funeral, only to encounter his mother's wedding to Claudius,
Frederick has come from Germany for a wedding but has found a funeral.
Henry's death shattered the royal family's tranquillity and certainty. All
that seemed so bright and promising now lay in disarray. As Phosphorus,
the day star, at the end of *Oberon* vanishes and the machine closes, so
here.

And then the funeral. On 7 December, 'the representation was layd
upon the Corps, and both together put into an open Chariot, and so
proceeded'.[89] Spectators and participants saw Henry's closed coffin with
the lifelike effigy on top, this idealised representation seeming to blot out
the death that rested below, the creation garments serving death's reality.
The whole number of people in the procession reached about 2,000,
which took hours to move to Westminster Abbey from St James's Palace.
Untold thousands lined the streets.

The procession (Fig. 2.4) began with 140 poor men in gowns, followed by 300 servants of knights, barons and earls' sons. Sir John Win bore Henry's standard, which contained his motto, *Fax mentis honestae gloria* ('Glory in the light of a noble mind'). Henry's household servants numbered 306, accompanied by the Duke of Lennox's servants. Then followed 80 servants of the Archbishop of Canterbury, Prince Palatine and Prince Charles. The gentlemen and knights of Henry's Privy Chamber and Bedchamber processed, along with his Treasurer, Charles Cornwallis, and Sir Thomas Chaloner, the Chamberlain, who carried the white staff of office. The Archbishop, the preacher for the funeral, followed. Soon came 'the Corps of the Prince, lying in an open Chariot, with the Princes representation thereon, invested with his Robes of estate'; at the foot of the chariot sat Sir David Murray, Henry's close friend and Master of the Wardrobe.[90] The chariot, drawn by six horses, was covered with black velvet and plumes of black feathers; 'a Canopy of blacke Velvet borne over the representation by sixe Baronets' (B4v). Finally came '*Prince Charles* chiefe *Mourner*, supported by the Lord Privy-Seale, and the Duke of *Lenox*. His *Highnesse* Traine was borne by the Lord *Dawbney* [Esmé Stuart], Brother to the Duke of *Lenox*' (C1). Twelve earls served as assistants to the chief mourner. Prince Elector Palatine also moved in the procession, attended by noblemen from his own country. Out of the hundreds in the procession Lennox had a prominent position as supporter to Prince Charles, a certain sign of his long devotion to Henry and of the love and respect shown to him by the royal family.

After several hours the procession finally gathered in Westminster Abbey. After the opening music, which included anthems by Thomas Tomkins ('Know Ye Not') and an elegy by William Byrd ('Fair Britain'), the coffin, with Prince Charles and Lennox following, 'was set under a great stately Herse built *Quadrangle* wise with eight Pillars, shewing three to the view on each side foure square, Cannopy like, rising small on the top' and trimmed throughout with emblems associated with Henry, including the Order of the Garter and his personal motto.[91] As the crowd silenced, the Archbishop of Canterbury entered the pulpit to preach the sermon, using as his text Psalm 82: 6–7: 'I have said, Ye are gods; and all of you are children of the most High: But ye shall die like men, and fall like one of the princes'. The archbishop began by situating the text in terms of its occasion, scope and meaning. On the matter of princes dying, the bishop 'for ocular proofe and use of all, invit[ed] their eyes to the present dolefull spectacle of their late ever renowned *Prince*, who, not long agoe, was as fresh, brave, and gallant as the best of them' (Cornwallis, 88–9). The preacher offered consolation by referring to the 'exceeding measure of felicity, his Highnesse had attained unto by death'. Finally, 'with exceeding great passion and many teares, hee ended' (90). The sermon took two hours.

The great officers of Henry's household, such as Chaloner, Cornwallis and Holles, after the sounding of a trumpet, approached the coffin and broke their white staffs and rods across the coffin, 'thereby resigning their places' (Cornwallis, 92). And the service ended. The coffin, however, with its representation, remained under the hearse 'to be seene of all, until the 19. of the said Moneth of *December*' (92–3). For three days after this service, prayers, chants and psalms fulfilled the offices of the dead. Eventually, Henry's representation took its place among others in a chapel in Westminster. As he left the great abbey church, Lennox looked back at the hearse and its coffin and effigy and the spent candles and the now empty church and felt the pang of loss intensely. A mere two years earlier, he recalled, all the court had rejoiced in Henry's 'creation' as Prince of Wales and all the promise that he showed. Now a season with a time to die.

On 12 November, Holles wrote a letter to Lennox, responding to their loss. Holles writes: 'But he is gone, the glory of Christendom, the sole hope of this age, and the comfort of all virtues and worthy actions and men, is gone!'[92] Holles had served the king for eight years and in the past two years, Henry. During this time Holles's service focused on the prince, 'save those whom I knew he inwardly favoured, among whom your lordship was and deserved to be a principal' (33–4). He closes: 'be pleased to accept this testimony of my devotion to your service, which, while I live, the memory of my most worthy master shall cause me to be your's ever at commandment' (34). In this time of great distress, John Holles reaches out to Lennox, one of Prince Henry's 'principal' favourites, seeking mutual consolation. Scores of others responded similarly through letters, poetry and prose as each tried to capture and expunge the shared grief.[93] Indeed, England had probably never experienced such a response to a royal death in terms of published material. Writers such as John Donne, Thomas Heywood, John Webster, Cyril Tourneur and William Browne all wrote elegiac poems, celebrating Henry and commemorating his death. Musicians such as John Ward and Thomas Campion in his *Songs of Mourning* provide music in honour of Henry.[94]

Reading, pondering, and absorbing some of this elegiac outpouring, Lennox could relive the events of late 1612. He knew first-hand Prince Henry's virtues and could join in the poets' songs to his memory. Nothing, however, could erase his grief. Several images especially burned in Lennox's memory. He recalled that moment in mid-October as he

Figure 2.4   Funeral procession of Prince Henry from George Wither's *Prince Henries Obsequies*, title page, 1613. STC 25915. By permission of the Folger Shakespeare Library.

walked with Henry into the chamber in Whitehall, following Frederick, Elector Palatine who made his first entry in the English royal court. He also remembered the House of Fame device in Dekker's Lord Mayor's Show of 29 October and the representation of Henry there – and his absence because of illness. A few weeks later Lennox walked with Prince Charles in Henry's funeral procession, as he accompanied this chief mourner. Lennox thus walked in those city streets that end in the marketplace of death. On that December day, Lennox followed behind the coffin that bore Henry's body and the representation that lay on top. This representation may be very like Henry, as Gertrude in *Hamlet* would say, but it lacked the prince's vitality and life. Death had brought a period to life. Day-star, fairy prince and phoenix, now all shrouded in death and embraced by the quiet place of the grave, a noble kinsman dead.

'To every thing there is a season . . . A time to weep, and a time to laugh' (Ecclesiastes 3: 1–4). But how can Lennox, a royal family, or indeed a country move from weeping to joy? Lennox asked himself this question repeatedly. The tears had ceased to flow but the pangs of the heart remained. October, November and December became the cruellest months of 1612: a queen mother reburied; a royal prince and heir apparent sick, dead and buried. Even the harsh weather of those months reinforced grief. How does one recover? Lennox, of course, had experienced the painful death of his father in France in May 1583, the melancholy death of his second wife in 1610 and the deaths of friends in Scotland and now, England, such as Robert Cecil earlier in 1612 with whom Lennox enjoyed mutual respect and support. The death of George Home, Earl of Dunbar, on 20 January 1611, affected the duke greatly. Home, a Scot, had lent money to James for the trip south in 1603 and, along with many others, including Lennox, travelled with the king to England, where he remained, becoming a member of the Privy Council, inductee into the Order of the Garter and Exchequer of the Treasury. Dunbar served James faithfully and worked closely with Lennox in executing the king's will. This friendship Lennox recalled in a letter to the Laird of Kilsythe on 28 February 1611, in which he writes: 'it is trew that his deathe is ane infinitt lose for the King and his service and for priuatt. No man hes lost more then myself, bot in that and in all God's will be done'.[95] Death was thus no stranger to him. But to experience the death of a beloved teenager, an eighteen-year-old vital and vibrant prince, whom he had known since his birth in 1594 and been close to and helped nurture: this death was of another order. Lennox looked for some means of 'translation', of crossing over from death into renewal: things dying giving way to things newborn.

Figure 2.5 Portrait of Queen Anne in mourning, 1613, by unknown artist.
Courtesy of the National Portrait Gallery.

Lennox reacted in part by focusing on Prince Frederick, the sixteen-year-old recently arrived German prince who had come to marry Princess Elizabeth. Lennox not only welcomed Frederick to England, escorted him along the Thames to Whitehall and took him into the royal palace and into the presence of the royal family, but also had come to know him and enjoy his company. Indeed, Lennox felt an affinity with Frederick; for, he, too, had arrived as a young person into a foreign land, confused, perplexed by people whom he did not know and a language he did not understand. And Frederick had an unexpected death thrust upon him. As the Venetian ambassador reported, 'The Elector Palatine does not know what to do'. The loneliness and uncertainty in that statement capture Frederick's situation. Lennox sympathised with the young prince.

Notes

1. Richard Martin, *A Speech Delivered, to the Kings Most Excellent Maiestie*, sigs. A3v–A4. Another edition of Martin's speech appeared in 1603, and then two more in 1643.
2. Account found in John Nichols, *The Progresses, Processions, and Magnificent Festivities of King James*, 1:113.
3. George Marcelline, *The Triumphs of King James the First*, p. 75.
4. *Calendar of State Papers Venetian*, 10:56. Cited parenthetically as CSPV.
5. From a report by Carlo Scaramelli, the Venetian ambassador, in the *Calendar of State Papers Venetian*, 10:75. Nichols also includes a longish account from a manuscript in 1: 228–34.
6. Their account appears in the *Calendar of State Papers Venetian*, 11:423.
7. For an extended discussion of this pageant see my *English Civic Pageantry 1558–1642*, revised edition, pp. 72–87.
8. *Calendar of State Papers Venetian*, 10:139.
9. *Prayers appointed to be used in the Church . . . for the Queenes safe deliverance*, sig. A2v.
10. Nichols, *Progresses*, 1:505.
11. *The Letters of King James I to King Christian IV, 1603–1625*, Ronald M. Meldrum (ed.), p. 44.
12. Nichols, *Progresses*, 1:512.
13. Ibid., 1:514.
14. From Ethel Carleton Williams, *Anne of Denmark*, p. 112.
15. Account found in Nichols, *Progresses*, 1:515–16.
16. Nichols has an extensive account of all the events in Oxford, 1:530–62.
17. *Calendar of the Manuscripts of the Most Honourable the Marquess of Salisbury*, pt. 17:468.
18. Quoted from James's speech in Alan Stewart, *The Cradle King*, p. 219.
19. Corporation of London Records, *Journal*, XXVII, fol. 73. See *English Civic Pageantry*, pp. 90–1, for a discussion of this pageant.
20. Information comes from Howes's continuation of Stow's *Annales*, included in Nichols, *Progresses*, 2:85–6.

21. Report from the Venetian ambassador, Zorzi Giustinian, *Calendar of State Papers Venetian*, 10:383.

22. The account of Harrington's letter found in Nichols, *Progresses*, 2:73.

23. *King of Denmarkes Welcome*, sig. C2v. Quotations come from this pamphlet.

24. John Marston apparently prepared these speeches; at least he gets credit for them in British Library Royal MS. 18. A. A. H. Bullen includes them in his edition of Marston: *The Works of John Marston*, vol. 3.

25. *Calendar of State Papers Venetian*, 10:384.

26. Cited in E. K. Chambers, *The Elizabethan Stage*, 1:147.

27. This 'welcome' forms part of John Ford's *Honor Triumphant*, sig. F1v.

28. The report of Edmund Howes, reproduced in Nichols, *Progresses*, 2:132.

29. *Calendar of State Papers Venetian*, 11:19.

30. Information comes from Nichols, *Progresses*, 2:136.

31. *Collections III: A Calendar of Dramatic Records in the Books of the Livery Companies of London 1485–1640*, ed Jean Robertson and D. J. Gordon (eds), pp. 169–70. Nichols also includes a report of this entertainment, 2:136–43.

32. Recent research has unearthed what may be three songs, written by Jonson for this occasion. See Gabriel Heaton and James Knowles, '"Entertainment Perfect": Ben Jonson and Corporate Hospitality', *Review of English Studies*, 54 (2003): 587–600. They found the documents among the Cecil Papers at Hatfield House.

33. *Collections III*, p. 170.

34. *Calendar of State Papers Venetian*, 11:233.

35. *Calendar of the Manuscripts of the Marquess of Salisbury at Hatfield House*, Historical Manuscripts Commission 9, pt. 21:113. The other letter can be found on pp. 94–5.

36. See my discussion 'Creating Entertainments for Prince Henry's Creation (1610)', *Comparative Drama* 42 (2008–9): 433–49. In this I draw on the excellent research of Pauline Croft, 'The Parliamentary Installation of Henry, Prince of Wales', *Historical Research: Bulletin of the Institute of Historical Research* 65 (1992): 177–93. For an analysis of the entertainments offered to Henry see Martin Butler, *The Stuart Masque and Political Culture*, pp. 183–93.

37. W. H., *The True Picture and Relation of Prince Henry*, p. 27.

38. *Calendar of State Papers Venetian, 1607–1610*, 11:410.

39. Ibid., 11:461.

40. Account found in Nichols, *Progresses*, 2:307.

41. *Calendar of State Papers Venetian*, 11:507.

42. *London's Love to the Royal Prince Henry*, found in my edition, *Pageants and Entertainments of Anthony Munday: A Critical Edition*, p. 39. All quotations will be from this edition.

43. Charles Cornwallis, *The Life and Death of . . . Henry, Prince of Wales*, pp. 16–17.
44. Quoted in John Nichols, *Progresses*, 2:359. Nichols includes all the pertinent texts for the creation.
45. *Calendar of State Papers Venetian*, 11:507.
46. For a fuller account see *The Order and Solemnitie of the Creation of . . . Prince Henrie*. Nichols reprints this text, 2:324–41.
47. Samuel Daniel, *The Complete Works in Verse and Prose*, Alexander B. Grosart (ed.), 5 vols, 3:310. All quotations come from this edition.
48. See the drawings reproduced in Stephen Orgel and Roy Strong, *Inigo Jones*, 1:204–28. These drawings and many more concerning Prince Henry are reproduced in Catharine MacLeod's *The Lost Prince: The Life and Death of Henry Stuart*. This beautifully illustrated book served as the catalogue for the exhibit on Prince Henry at London's National Portrait Gallery that ran from 18 October 2012 to 13 January 2013, an exhibit that commemorated the 400th anniversary of Henry's death.
49. Quotations from *Oberon* come from *Ben Jonson: The Complete Masques*, Stephen Orgel (ed.), p. 160.
50. Cornwallis, *Life and Death*, p. 93.
51. Daniel Price, *Prince Henry His First Anniversary*, p. 5. This recollection of Henry, which Strong mistakenly refers to as a 'sermon' (p. 54), Price published on the anniversary of Henry's funeral. Price did preach a series of sermons about Henry immediately following his death and throughout 1613. His superb recollections of the prince have largely been ignored. The sermons preached on 10 and 15 November 1612 Price published as *Lamentations for the Death of the Late Illustrious Prince Henry* (London, 1613). The four sermons of 1613 were published as *Spiritual Odours to the Memory of Prince Henry* (Oxford, 1613). Price returned to the topic with his *Prince Henry His Second Anniversary* (Oxford, 1614).
52. *Calendar of State Papers Venetian*, 12:142.
53. Francis Bacon, 'Memorial of Henry Prince of Wales', translated from the Latin, *In Henricum Principem Walliae Elogium*, in *The Works of Francis Bacon*, James Spedding, Robert Ellis and Douglas Heath (eds), 6:329.
54. British Library, Harleian MS. 7007, f. 21.
55. *Calendar of State Papers Venetian, 1603–1607*, 10:513.
56. Charles Cornwallis, *A Discourse of the Most Illustrious Prince Henry*, p. 15.
57. John Hayward, *The Lives of the III. Normans, Kings of England*, sig. A2. This is probably the most extensive conversation with Prince Henry that has been preserved.
58. See Roy Strong, *Henry, Prince of Wales and England's Lost Renaissance*, especially the chapter 'The Prince's Collections', pp. 184–219. See also Timothy Wilks' discussion, 'Princely Collecting', in Catharine MacLeod, *The Lost Prince*, p. 118–20, the exhibition catalogue from the National Portrait Gallery's exhibit in 2012–13.

59. Cornwallis, *A Discourse*, p. 23.

60. Nichols, *Progresses*, 2:438.

61. Cornwallis, *Life and Death*, p. 26.

62. W. H., *True Picture*, p. 9.

63. Cornwallis, *A Discourse*, p. 19.

64. W. H., *True Picture*, p. 24.

65. British Library, Harleian MS. 6986, f. 180b. I have slightly modernised the quotation. Cited in my *Royal Family, Royal Lovers: King James of England and Scotland*, p. 106. In this book I discuss all the members of James's family.

66. *Letters of King James VI & I*, G. P. V. Akrigg (ed.), p. 98. The letter dates from 29 October 1589.

67. For a discussion of the relationship of James and Mary, see my *Royal Family, Royal Lovers*, pp. 35–46.

68. Antonia Fraser offers a superb account of the final moments in Mary's life: *Mary Queen of Scots*, pp. 531–42.

69. *Letters of King James*, pp. 326–7.

70. Information comes from Alan Stewart, *The Cradle King*, pp. 246–7.

71. *Calendar of State Papers Venetian, 1610–1613*, 12:439.

72. *Calendar of State Papers Venetian*, 12:443.

73. *The Letters of John Chamberlain*, Norman E. McClure (ed.), 2 vols, 1:381.

74. *Calendar of State Papers Venetian*, 12:443.

75. *Letters of John Chamberlain*, 1:384.

76. Ibid.

77. Reported by Edmund Howes in his continuation of John Stow, *The Annales or Generall Chronicle of England*, p. 915.

78. Ibid.

79. Thomas Dekker, *The Dramatic Works of Thomas Dekker*, Fredson Bowers (ed.), 3:230. All quotations from the pageant come from this edition.

80. Cornwallis, *The Life and Death*, p. 47. Cornwallis had served as Treasurer of Prince Henry's household.

81. Cornwallis, *Life and Death*, p. 30. This account is by far the fullest version about Henry's illness and death, offering specific and sometimes gruesome information. I depend on Cornwallis considerably. W. H., *True Life*, offers a similar account but much abbreviated. See also the modern account by J. W. Williamson, *The Myth of the Conqueror: Prince Henry Stuart, a Study in 17th Century Personation*, pp. 152–66. For additional information about Henry's death and funeral, as well as several other subjects, see the collection of essays edited by Timothy Wilks: *Prince Henry Revived: Image and Exemplarity in Early Modern England*.

82. Price, *Prince Henry*, p. 27.

83. Phineas Pett, *Autobiography of Phineas Pett*, p. 100.

84. John Hacket, *Scrinia Reserata* (London, 1692), p. 27.

85. Historical Manuscripts Commission, *Report of the Manuscripts of the Duke of Portland*, 9:35.
86. Quoted in W. H. St John Hope, 'On the Funeral Effigies of the Kings and Queens of England, with special reference to those in the Abbey Church of Westminster', *Archaeologia* 60, pt 2 (1907): 555.
87. *Letters of John Chamberlain*, 1:390.
88. *Calendar of State Papers Venetian*, 12:449.
89. *The Funerals of the High and Mightie Prince Henry*, sig. A4. Details about the procession come from this edition, which itself rather resembles a procession as it lists the hundreds of participants. Nichols reprints this tract, 2:493–9.
90. Ibid., sig. B4v.
91. Cornwallis, *Life and Death*, pp. 86–7. A drawing of this 'hearse', or catafalque, accompanies the text of George Chapman's *An Epicede* (London, 1613) in some copies.
92. *Report of the Manuscripts of the Duke of Portland*, 9:33.
93. For a survey of the elegiac material, see J. W. Williamson, *The Myth of the Conqueror*, pp. 171–92. See also Ruth Wallerstein, *Studies in Seventeenth-Century Poetic*, chapter 3, 'The Death of Prince Henry', pp. 59–95, for an analysis of this material. More recently Michael Ullyot has explored much of this material in his 'The Fall of Troynovant: Exemplarity after the Death of Henry, Prince of Wales', in *Fantasies of Troy: Classical Tales and the Social Imaginary in Medieval and Early Modern Europe*, Alan Shepard and Stephen D. Powell (eds), pp. 269–90. Ullyot says succinctly and accurately: 'The literary impact of Henry's death was both immediate and unprecedented' (p. 279). Even after Henry's death, Jonathan Lamb argues, Jonson's 1616 Folio responds to his death: 'Ben Jonson's Dead Body: Henry, Prince of Wales, and the 1616 Folio', *Huntington Library Quarterly*, 79.1 (2016): 63–92.
94. For a brief discussion of the responses to Henry's death, see my *Shakespeare's London 1613*, pp. 80–6.
95. *Report on the Laing Manuscripts Preserved in the University of Edinburgh*, 1:124.

3

Celebration, Dutiful Service, Favourites

ROYAL WEDDING

Two events began the transformation that led towards Princess Elizabeth's wedding: the official contract between her and Frederick on 27 December and the outpouring of dramatic performances at court, beginning in the Christmas season and spilling over into 1613. On Christmas Sunday, the Duke of Lennox, the royal family and others gathered in Whitehall for the official contractual engagement of Elizabeth and Frederick, a sure sign that the wedding plans were advancing. On that morning, according to Antonio Foscarini, Frederick went 'to the Princess's Chamber, gave her his right hand and led her to the King's Chamber, surrounded by her ladies. There they kneeled to receive the blessing which his Majesty gave. They then went to the Great Hall, where all their festivities are held'.[1] In this hall, the couple found Prince Charles and the king. One report adds: 'The Nobilitie and Prince Charles brought him [Frederick] in appaireled in a black velvet cloake caped with gold lace. Then followed she in a black velvet gown seemè of crosletts or quatrefoiles sylver, and a small white feather on her head'.[2] After the ceremony, everyone returned to mourning garments.

Sir Thomas Lake, serving temporarily as Secretary (in place of the deceased Robert Cecil), read the marriage words from the Book of Common Prayer. Foscarini reports:

> Then the Palatine said, 'I Frederick, Elector of the Holy Roman Empire, Count Palatine of the Rhine, Duke of both Bavarias, take you Madame Elizabeth, daughter of the most powerful, high and glorious King of Great Britain, for rich or poor, for well or ill, to be my wife while life me lasts.' (CSPV,12:474)

(Frederick had learned enough English to participate in the wedding.)
Elizabeth responded accordingly with the same promise. The Archbishop
of Canterbury gave them a blessing and added a few words. Chamberlain,
writing to Dudley Carleton on 31 December, adds some pertinent details,
such as the cumbersome and amusing French translation that Lake had
made of the ceremony from the prayer book. Chamberlain writes: 'But
they say he [Lake] had translated the wordes of our communion booke
into French so badly, and pronounced them worse, that yt moved an
unseasonable laughter as well in the contractors as the standers by'
(1:399). The archbishop interposed himself and restored dignity, adding
this blessing: 'The God of Abraham, Isaacke and Jacob blesse these nuptials, and make them prosperous to these kingdoms and to his church'.

Chamberlain adds: 'This affiancing was solemnised in the great banketting roome on Sunday before dinner, in the presence of the King
and great store of nobilitie; but the Quene was absent, being troubled
(as they say) with the gowte' (1:399). Lennox would have understood
Chamberlain's parenthetical statement well, for he knew of Anne's reluctance about this marriage, a reluctance that he did not share, having
spent considerable time with Frederick. Anne disapproved of Frederick,
believing him a minor prince and insufficiently powerful for her daughter; further, Anne truly desired a Catholic prince for Elizabeth. Eventually
Anne would come round, accepting Frederick, at least on some level. The
Scots had also hoped that Elizabeth would marry one of their nobles,
especially in light of Henry's death. But after 27 December only the official extravagant wedding ceremony remained to secure the political,
legal and religious link between Elizabeth and Frederick and the two
countries.

Drama at the Jacobean court stood between Henry's funeral and
Elizabeth's impending wedding; it constructed a bridge, a translation,
a confrontation with raw feelings. These performances underscored the
efficacy of art, which provides an aesthetic distancing, making it possible
to experience fictional death, comedy and history in the plays performed
by the King's Men and other acting companies. The season of 1612–13,
from Christmas through to mid-April when Elizabeth and Frederick left
England, saw twenty court performances by the King's Men alone. This
exceptional number reflected the court's need to shift from mourning
garments to festive wedding clothes.

George Buc, Master of the Revels, chose some nineteen different plays
to be performed from Christmas 1612 to Shrovetide 1613, not count-
ing the masques performed for the wedding of Elizabeth and Frederick.
Information about their titles – the most extensive of any group of plays

performed at court during the Jacobean court's first ten years – comes from payments recorded in the Revels Accounts and in the Chamber Accounts.[3] Several entries spell out the names of the plays and cite the payments, most of them coming in summer 1613. The King's Men performed eight plays by Shakespeare: *Much Ado about Nothing* (comedy, performed twice), *1 and 2 Henry IV* (history), *The Winter's Tale* (tragicomedy), *Othello* (tragedy), *Julius Caesar* (tragedy), *The Tempest* (tragicomedy) and the lost *Cardenio*, presumably written with the assistance of John Fletcher. Francis Beaumont and Fletcher had five plays presented: *The Captain* (comedy), *The Maid's Tragedy* (tragedy), *A King and No King* (tragicomedy), *Philaster* (tragicomedy, performed twice), all acted by the King's Men, and *Cupid's Revenge* (tragedy), performed by the Children of the Queen's Revels twice, on 1 and 9 January. Buc chose Jonson's *The Alchemist* (comedy), *The Twins' Tragedy* by Niccols (lost), *The Nobleman* by Tourneur (lost), *The Merry Devil of Edmonton* by Dekker and others (comedy), plus two anonymous plays: *A Bad Beginning Makes a Good Ending* (lost) and *The Knot of Fools* (lost).[4] Buc's apparent criterion was his familiarity with the plays. For example, *Cupid's Revenge*, *The Winter's Tale*, *The Tempest*, *A King and No King* and *The Twins' Tragedy* had all been performed at court within the previous year or so (others may have been, but the records are silent).[5]

During the performances and later on reflection, Lennox thought about the subjects, images, ideas and spectacle of the plays of this exceptionally rich Christmas season. From the frivolous high jinks of, say, *The Merry Devil of Edmonton* to the tragic consequences of *Othello*, spectators could seize on the multiple variations on marriage, which, at least theoretically, would have been a particularly suitable subject at court. Royal children, as in *The Winter's Tale* and some of the Beaumont and Fletcher plays, highlight the current situation in the Jacobean court and the importance of these children for the kingdom's future, in part because they raise the question of succession. A recurrent theme focuses on politics, the nature of kingship, power and the need for loyalty, as in the *Henry IV* plays. Betrayal may come in matters of love or in politics, witness *Much Ado* and *Julius Caesar*. Mystical, supernatural power emerges in *The Tempest* and in a parodic form in *The Alchemist*. The subject of magical power would certainly have interested King James. The gods manifest another dimension of power, particularly and cruelly compelling in *Cupid's Revenge*. This partial list reveals the infinite variety of these plays and suggests the likely impact they would have had on spectators.

Out of the comfort of Whitehall and the excitement of the performances, Lennox moved into the darkness of London, as the city continued to endure one of the coldest winters in years. These plays, creating a
spectacularly diverse and challenging landscape of emotions and experiences, wrenched Lennox and probably the court away from despair and
towards the renewal that certainly characterises *The Winter's Tale* with
its glorious answer to human suffering. A comic end that responds to a
tragic beginning prompted Lennox to recall the way in which King James
back in Scotland had envisioned that Lennox would be the new phoenix, replacing his father and thus bringing about a comic end. Dramatic
performances provide not merely entertainment but solace for the court's
dismay and suffering. The plays point to a transformed court, readying
itself for the glories of a royal wedding.

The path away from the court's dramatic entertainment leads to the
much-anticipated wedding, the occasion of a new beginning, full of
excitement and joy. Even the weather brightened. Lennox took delight
in all the festivities, including the installation of Prince Frederick into
the Order of the Garter, the group in which Lennox himself, along with
Prince Henry, had been inaugurated in summer 1603. The Garter ceremonies for Frederick took place at Windsor on Sunday, 7 February
1613, also the final Sunday at which clergy read the wedding banns for
Elizabeth and Frederick. The Order of the Garter, the highest English
knightly order, began in 1348 under the aegis of King Edward III with
St George as the patron saint. Of French birth and Scottish residence,
Lennox knew the exceptional privilege of a non-native being inducted;
and now Frederick would join the ranks, a grand compliment and a
sign of King James's determination to have the prince fully recognised
with an English pedigree. From the happy October arrival, Frederick
had enjoyed the Lord Mayor's Show but without the ill Prince Henry
and had experienced Henry's death, leaving him, in the judgement of the
Venetian ambassador, not knowing what to do. But Christmas, the abundance of plays presented at court, the ongoing planning for the wedding,
Elizabeth's regard for him and now the granting of knighthood in the
Order of the Garter had indeed transformed Frederick, as these events
changed the royal court.

Chamberlain went to court to meet the wedding couple and, on
4 February 1613, wrote to Alice Carleton, giving his assessment of the
teenaged pair:

> On Tewsday I tooke occasion to go to court because I had never seen the
> Palsgrave, nor the Lady Elizabeth (neere hand) of a long time: I had my full

view of them both, but will not tell you all I thincke, but only this, that he owes his mistress nothing yf he were a Kings sonne as she is a Kings daughter. The worst is mee thincks he is much too young and small timbred to undertake such a taske.[6]

Whatever Chamberlain means precisely, and it may be no more than their obvious youth, Queen Anne, as noted, had been at best lukewarm about this marriage, failing to appear at the official exchange of vows on 27 December. She had openly mocked Frederick, but even she had begun to change. Thus, Chamberlain can report on 10 February, 'The Quene growes every day more favorable, and there is hope she will grace yt [wedding] with her presence' (1:418). As Lennox well knew, some of the residue of resentment or uncertainty grew out of the court's wrestling still with the overwhelming reality of Henry's death. But in the final outburst of wedding festivities Queen Anne participated fully.[7]

Considering Henry's death, determining the date when the wedding should take place became problematic: wanting to move ahead but not with unseemly haste. Early on, James suggested holding off until May 1613. That idea did not last long because of political and economic pressures. Much of this resistance came from Frederick, who certainly had economic reasons for not wanting to wait around in the Jacobean court for several more months. Foscarini, the Venetian ambassador, reported in early January: 'The request of the Palatine that the marriage should take place at once has proved efficacious with the King, who has given orders that every one is to go out of mourning on March the 14th and to don gala dress'.[8] James, sometimes sensible, declared, according to Foscarini: 'mourning should be mourning, and marriage rejoicings rejoicings' (474). Weeping should give way to joy; blacks should defer to colourful, joyful clothing. The court finally settled on Sunday, 14 February, as the wedding day. But no royal wedding can exist in isolation; numerous activities should batten onto it. And, of course, there had been in England no wedding of a teenaged royal child in decades – indeed, not since the eighteen-year-old Henry VIII married Catherine of Aragon in 1509. (Henry experienced a few more weddings after this.) Thus, Elizabeth's wedding should be spectacular. It did not disappoint.

John Taylor, the Water Poet, having written an elegy for Prince Henry, now captures effectively what spectators experienced in the wedding celebrations: 'Gunnes, Drums, and Trumpets, Fire-works, Bonfires, Bells, / With acclamations, and applausefull noyse; / Tilts, Turneyes, Barriers, all in mirth excells, / The ayre reverberates our earthly joys'.[9] Taylor acknowledges how these events respond to or overcome Henry's death:

Figure 3.1 Engraving of Princess Elizabeth by Crispin van de Passe, 1613.
D226.7.P3 Cage. By permission of Folger Shakespeare Library.

'And when we all were drench'd in black dispaire, / Joy conquered griefe,
and comfort vanquish'd care'. So everyone hoped. Having barely had
time to catch their breath after all the play performances, the court
swung into full gear to ready Whitehall Palace for the wedding and its
associated activities. Many noted the stir, expense and decorations produced by the court staff under the guidance of the Office of the Revels

and the Office of the Works, whose Surveyor provided for the stage and seating in the Banqueting House. The Office of the Wardrobe outdid itself in preparing costumes and garments for the royal household. The Treasurer of the Chamber kept a ready, but inadequate, eye on expenses. Ushers, grooms, porters and artificers of all kinds flooded the palace's hallways, bustling about to prepare for the most important royal wedding. With both wistfulness and excitement Lennox, leaving the Holbein Gatehouse, wandered further into Whitehall's premises, checking on the arrangements in the Great Hall, the royal chapel and the somewhat new Banqueting House. He moved silently and sometimes noisily through this space certain that he and the royal family were approaching a monumental occasion of things newborn.

Festivities began on Thursday, 11 February, with exceptional fireworks along the Thames. One source highlights the setting: in the evening the king, queen, Prince Charles, Prince Frederick, Princess Elizabeth 'with the rest of the nobilitie of England' had gathered 'in the galleries and windowes about his highnes Court of Whitehall, and in the sight of thousands of people, many artisticall conclusions in Fire Workes were upon the *Thames* performed'.[10] This anonymous writer found the displays to be 'pleasurable'. So many bursts of light and noise resembled a kind of rainbow as the fireballs 'in their falling dispersed into divers streams like ranebowes in many innumerable fires'. In case the thousands of spectators had not seen enough fireworks, William Fishenden adds in Taylor's book the report of a pyramid 'in the forme of a triangled spire, with a globe fixed on the top thereof', which for a half hour set off countless fireworks, to 'the great delight and contentment of the King, the Queene, the Prince, the Princesse Elizabeth, the Prince Palatine, and divers others, the Nobilitie, the Gentry, and Commons of this Kingdome' (Taylor, C2v). Who could possibly disagree, even if everything did not work exactly as planned? In one evening of spectacular fireworks along the Thames spectators saw the Amazonian Queen, her nemesis and her saviour St George (not incidentally patron saint of the Order of the Garter). For good measure they got to witness the destruction of the Castle of Envy and countless fiery explosions, blanketing the sky.

Two days later on the Thames, Lennox, the royal family and numerous spectators gathered at Whitehall near the river between two and three o'clock in order to witness the sea fight between supposed Christian ships and Turkish galleys.[11] Great swathes of the river had been cordoned off in order for this show to take place. Sounds of ordnance filled the air. According to Taylor, the warring fleet included sixteen ships, sixteen galleys and six frigates, all 'artificially rigged and trimmed, well manned and

Figure 3.2   Engraving of Prince Frederick by Crispin van de Passe, 1613.
D226.7.P3 Cage. By permission of the Folger Shakespeare Library.

furnished with great ordinance and musquettiers' (A3v). Altogether a flotilla of 250 boats filled the river, stretching from Southwark to Lambeth Bridge. The Turkish galleys lay in wait and at anchor near Westminster in a harbour. Lots of noise and shots filled the air as the Christian ships approached. The curious predication of a battle between Christians and

Turks recalls, Taylor insists, 'the manner of the happy and famous battell of Lepanto, fought betwixt the Turks and the Christians in the yeare of grace 1571'. Such recognition points, of course, to King James's poem *Lepanto*, which celebrated the great Christian victory. This 1613 theatrical spectacle might also provoke an analogy to the Spanish Armada of 1588. The battle lasted some three hours 'to the great contentment of all the beholders' (A4v), Taylor says.

Sunday morning, 14 February, arrived fresh, cold and full of hope. After all the noise and stir of the fireworks and sea fight, tranquillity permeated the early hours of Sunday. Or, as Antonio Foscarini, the Venetian ambassador, wrote to the Doge and Senate: 'For many days we have heard nothing in this City but the noise of a crowd, salvoes of artillery, blare of trumpets, nor seen aught but a crush of nobles and gorgeous dresses and all the signs of rejoicing'.[12] Everything since late December had led to this moment, occasion and ceremony. At last, a royal child would be marrying. In the words of Anthony Nixon, '*England* hath put a face of gladnesse on'; young and old alike celebrate 'This Nuptiall day, wherein we all enjoy / Such perfect comfort throughout *Brutes* new *Troy*'.[13]

Whitehall Palace began to stir in anticipation. Lennox readied himself for the event and his part in the ceremony, remembering with fondness his participation in the baptism of Henry in 1594 and creation as Prince of Wales in 1610, and Princess Elizabeth's baptism in 1596. Memories flooded his mind, as he recalled the many occasions involving the royal family in which he had been key. What a particularly enchanting day this would be, Lennox thought, the culmination of planning and diplomatic negotiation, the results stretching far into the future. Chamberlain rushed from St Paul's to catch a glimpse of the wedding party, the Venetian ambassador enjoyed a privileged place from which to watch the spectacle unfold and hundreds of others crowded into Whitehall for a chance to see and be seen. King James made a point of processing from his Privy chamber through the palace so that many could see him, especially those not invited to witness the actual ceremony in the Chapel Royal.

As the great organ sounded, the procession began with Prince Frederick, accompanied by Lennox and Charles Howard, Earl of Nottingham, and other young courtiers. Frederick appeared attired in a white suit, 'richly beset with pearle and gold'.[14] Princess Elizabeth followed, preceded by her guardian Lord Harington; she wore a gown of white satin, 'upon her head a crown of refined golde, made Imperiall by the pearles and diamonds thereupon placed, which were so thicke beset that they stood like shining pinnacles upon her amber-coloured haire' (542–3). Pearls, diamonds and rich stones filled her hair, which she wore hanging down, a sign of virginity. Elizabeth's brother Prince Charles and Henry Howard, Earl of Northampton, led her into the chapel. Members of the king's Privy Council, bishops and Thomas Howard, Earl of Arundel, the bearer of the king's sword, followed. King James, 'himselfe in a most sumptuous blacke suit, with a diamond in his hatte of a wonderful great value' (544) then appeared, along with Queen Anne, 'attired in white satin, beautified with much enbrothery and many diamonds'. Chamberlain complained of the excess and 'braverie' that did dazzle so that 'I could not observe the tenth part of that I wisht' (1:423).[15]

Inside the Chapel Royal in the middle stood a stage or scaffold about five feet high and about twenty feet long, having several steps to ascend or descend at each end. On this 'stage' sat King James on the right hand, with the Earl of Arundel nearby; below the sword sat Frederick on a stool, and after him Prince Charles on another stool. On the other side sat the Queen 'in a chair most gloriously attired' and near her Princess Elizabeth (Nichols, 2:546). Upon a stage for all to see sat the royal performers.

The organ ceased and the choir of the Chapel Royal sang an anthem. Then the Bishop of Bath and Wells, James Montagu, ascended the pulpit and preached a sermon, based on St John's gospel account in the second chapter of the wedding miracle performed by Jesus at Cana in Galilee.[16] While the choir sang another anthem, the Archbishop of Canterbury, George Abbot, and the Bishop of Bath and Wells withdrew. They soon returned and ascended the stage as the archbishop led the marriage service. Prince Frederick's scant English enabled him, however, to respond to the royal wedding ceremony, which followed the service in the Book of Common Prayer. King James presented the bride. When the marriage vows ended, the choir sang another anthem and Frederick and Elizabeth knelt before the communion table.

As the service ended, Lennox and Charles Howard escorted the Princess Elizabeth out of the chapel towards the Banqueting House. Thus, Lennox had the privilege of accompanying Frederick into the chapel and leading Elizabeth out. He joined the hundreds who cheered 'God give them joy, God give them joy' (Nichols, 2:548). At last a royal child had married, solidifying for the moment an order of succession. The joys of the day 'were declared in manie places, as well City and Court; for the bells of London rung generally in every Church, and in every street bonfires blazed abundantly' (2:552). Small wonder that celebrations filled several more days. Lennox could join in the statement of the Abbess, in Shakespeare's *Comedy of Errors*, who, having been reunited with her husband and long-lost twin sons, cried out: 'After so long grief such Nativity' (Act V, scene i, line 409).

The court passed through sphere after sphere of masque entertainment, beginning on the wedding night with Thomas Campion's *The Lords' Masque*.[17] 'Masques were central to the ritual world in which early modern court life took place. They were staged at the very heart of Whitehall, at key moments in the court calendar'.[18] No moment could have been more 'key' in this court's calendar than this royal wedding; hence, the overflow of masques, with all of their excesses and extravagant expense. Such entertainments heightened the importance of the Stuart court in European eyes. King James himself had arranged this masque in honour of Elizabeth and Frederick. Several drawings by Inigo Jones, who worked with Campion, survive, showing the elaborate costumes of the masquers.[19] The text, not published until summer 1613, the accounts, reactions to the performance and Jones's drawings enable readers to capture a partial version of what Lennox and others experienced on that charmed evening of 14 February, after the wedding ceremony and after the banquet.

In the Banqueting House at Whitehall Campion's masque began by revealing a painted scene of a thicket and a cave from which emerged Orpheus, who confronts Mania, the goddess of madness. Her change marked the first of several 'transformations', forming the major themes and activities of the masque. Released from the stigma of madness, Entheus will assist Orpheus to 'create / Inventions rare, this night to celebrate, / Such as become a nuptial' (Campion, 107).[20] As the masquers woo transformed ladies, four more statues appeared, '*transformed into women*' (113). The chorus sang brightly: 'Live with thy bridegroom happy, sacred bride; / How blest is he that is for love envied' (114). With this and a dance Elizabeth and Frederick joined in the revels. The masque also represented the royal couple as statues, standing on pedestals near an obelisk and bringing in Sibylla, who after a song uttered her prophecies. A final dance concluded the masque. For Lennox and others, the masque seemed like a continuation of the wedding ceremony itself, especially in its reminder through various strategies, representations and speeches of the idea of 'transformation'. Has not the court and England been transformed this day by this hopeful marriage? If statues can be transformed, why not lives, ideas and countries? Fresh from seeing a new performance of *The Winter's Tale*, courtiers could see in these statues coming to life a recollection of Hermione at the end of that play, which also contains hopeful desires for the royal children. A young prince may die, in life and in fiction, but another prince and princess overcome that grief and point to a resilient future. New day-stars replace the night.

Just a few hours after running at the ring on Monday, the tiltyard once again functioned as the assembling point for entertainment, this time for George Chapman's masque that evening, *The Memorable Masque of the two Honourable Houses*.[21] This masque, sponsored by two Inns of Court (Middle Temple and Lincoln's), took place in the Great Hall in Whitehall Palace. But it began in London's streets, not far from the Guildhall, moving from the Inns and the home of Sir Edward Phelips, Master of the Rolls, in Chancery Lane and making its way to Whitehall. This outdoor procession is unique in masques to this point in 1613. The Temple of Honour functions as one of the essential features of the masque. In a way, the masque will be another expression of chivalry, complementing what the court had seen that afternoon in the tiltyard. Chapman, with the help of Inigo Jones, suggests that one arrives at Honour by means of the law, in keeping with the sponsorship of the Inns of Court.[22] Chapman's rich description of the street procession captures the dazzling spectacle, and it reinforces the intertwined relationship of London and the court. The performance in Whitehall includes the elements of the procession and adds others. Here Phoebus represents King James, and all the participants do obeisance to the king. The chorus even recognises his 'blest' mother, whose reburial in October the court recalled.

The masque closes with a focus on Love and Beauty, namely, the bride and bridegroom. The Great Hall at the palace has become just such a fair temple, honouring the king and the royal wedded couple. Foscarini, the Venetian ambassador, sums up the evening appropriately: 'after great eulogies of the couple, pronounced by Riches and Honour, all the Masque began to dance a ballet, with such finish that it left nothing to be desired'.[23]

Originally planned for 16 February, Francis Beaumont's *The Masque of the Inner Temple and Gray's Inn* got delayed until the following Saturday, 20 February – but not before it had moved from Winchester House in Southwark to Westminster by river on the original date. Chamberlain describes the river voyage, paralleling the other Inns of Court who had moved through London's streets on Monday:

> they made choise to come by water from Winchester Place in Southwarke: which suted well enough with theyre devise, which was the mariage of the river of Thames to the Rhine: and theyre shew by water was very gallant by reason of infinite store of lights very curiously set and placed: and many boats and barges with devises of light and lampes.[24]

The elegant movement on the Thames provided a stunning spectacle; Beaumont writes: 'This voyage by water was performed in great triumph. The gentlemen masquers being placed by themselves in the King's royal barge'.[25] In such array the entourage arrived at the privy stairs at Whitehall where the royal family and others waited.

But the expected performance in the Great Hall did not occur. Beaumont says simply: the hall was full; lack of space sent the masquers away. According to Chamberlain, space was not the only issue: 'but the worst of all was that the King was so wearied and sleepie with sitting up almost two whole nights before, that he had no edge to yt' (1:426). But the anticipated audience had thus already seen their stunning costumes, diminishing the impact of that spectacle. By Saturday the performance space had been moved to the Banqueting House and the masque went on then as planned, presumably with a now rested and alert king.

When King James entered the hall for the masque, he and the other spectators saw a mountain with four delicate fountains. The masque proper called for Olympian knights and Priests, located on the upper reaches of the mountain where they reside in 'pavilions', which *were to sight as a cloth of gold*' (Beaumont,140). At the uppermost reach of the mountain stood Jupiter's altar. The knights dance and the priests sing. Their second song suggests: 'at the wedding such a pair, / Each dance is taken for a prayer, / Each song a sacrifice' (141). The knights call out the ladies of the court to dance, which they do in several different forms. The masquers bestow their blessing on the newlyweds and endow the evening with wonder – deferred but no less powerful.

The ten-day trajectory of spectacle and theatre produced an exhausting but thrilling experience – from fireworks to sea battles to the wedding itself to the three masques to the tiltyard. God, goddesses, Indian masquers, allegorical figures, country folk, Olympian knights and priests filled the masques, enriching the courtly experience and engendering spectacle, dance and music. The splendour of the wedding itself rivalled the subsequent masques. Journeys of masquers through London's streets or at night along the Thames with lights blazing stirred wonder, as city and court converge. Themes of transformation, chivalry, honour, celebration, sanction for marriage and praise of sovereign power permeated the entertainment. Looking back over this February experience and acknowledging its occasional imperfection, Lennox might well have agreed with the Venetian ambassador's judgement: 'it left nothing to be desired'. A royal daughter had found a princely husband and the country rejoiced beyond a common joy.

The court had not finished celebrating. At the urging of the princess and Prince Charles they witnessed subsequent performances, starting on 27 February, of George Chapman's *The Widow's Tears* and John Marston's *The Dutch Courtesan*, plus three anonymous (and lost) plays. In early March, Prince Charles, Frederick and Lennox travelled to Oxford and Cambridge where, at the respective universities, they saw more performances, heard disputations and feasted. But in early April the royal family began its journey with Elizabeth and Frederick to send them on their way to Germany; the long festivity had ended and now the reality of departure loomed. Lennox travelled with the royal party because James had appointed him to accompany the princess to her new home; the king also included the Earl of Arundel, Viscount Lisle, and Lord Harrington (Elizabeth's former guardian) to travel with her. The week after Easter, on Saturday, 10 April, the entourage began its movement from Whitehall to Greenwich, but not before the Venetian ambassador, Antonio Foscarini, had a chance to bid the newlyweds farewell. At Whitehall he first met Frederick, who then escorted him to the Princess' room. 'The Princess then in familiar fashion and smiling talked of her going to a fair country as she understood, but she did not know if it was as fair as this'.[26] Foscarini went on to meet with King James, who asked the ambassador if he had seen the children. 'He seemed to feel their departure keenly, and said he hoped to see them soon again and with offspring' (526). (In fact, he would never see them again.)

On Tuesday, 13 April, the royal party journeyed on to Rochester; here the king and queen said their farewells to Elizabeth and her husband. The royal parents left, but Charles went on with his sister to Canterbury where he bade farewell. Elizabeth now rested in Canterbury, separated for the last time from her parents and brother. From there she wrote a profoundly personal letter to King James on 16 April. It put into perspective the effects of those glittering masques, fireworks displays and play performances that surrounded her opulent wedding. Elizabeth wrote:

> Sire, It is at this time that I feel the disagreeable effects of the separation and distance from Your Majesty, my heart which was oppressed with grief and dismayed at my parting now gives leave to my eyes to weep at being deprived of the view of the most precious object that they have ever knowingly contemplated in this world. I shall possibly never, as long as I live, again see the flower of princes, the King of fathers, the best and most gracious father under the sun. But the most humble respect and devotion with which I shall unceasingly honour You Majesty will never wipe from the memory of the one who waits here for a favourable wind and who would wish to return once more to kiss the hands of Your Majesty.[27]

This remarkable letter, as effusive and affectionate as any that James received from his children, underscores a separation that Elizabeth had begun to feel. She would never write quite so warm a letter to her father again. She would never see her father or any other member of her immediate family again. Happy with her new husband but saddened at leaving England, the youthful Elizabeth went to face the unknown in a strange land: more than an ocean would separate her from her parents and brother Charles.

At Margate, Elizabeth and Frederick readied to make their departure on 23 April, a day on which Lennox and other members of the Order of the Garter were to engage in activities associated with the feast of St George, but bad weather prevented this and thwarted their journey. Finally, on Sunday, 25 April, they set sail, reaching Flushing on 29 April. Elizabeth and Frederick sailed on the *Prince Royal*, built under the leadership of Phineas Pett, who also made the journey, as he reports. Pett accompanied the Lord Admiral and they travelled with the royal party as far as Flushing. On 2 May, he and the Lord Admiral took leave of Elizabeth and began the return journey to England. Frederick had left Elizabeth on 30 April in order to go to the Palatinate. Elizabeth began a journey of several weeks, receiving marvellous entertainment and hospitality everywhere, accompanied by Lennox and the entire entourage.

The leisurely, circuitous journey to Germany included a tour through part of the Low Countries with entertainment in Amsterdam, Haarlem and Utrecht. A few days later, the party reached Germany where, for example, at Oppenheim four elaborate triumphal arches lined the streets, presenting such allegorical figures as Fortitude, Virtue, Fortune, Hope, Concord and Faith, indicated by their emblematic properties. Lennox recognised these figures from various pageants and entertainments that he had seen in Scotland and England.

On 6 June, Elizabeth entered Franckendal where the city offered two pageant arches, one presenting several German kings and the virtues that each represented, and the second depicting Fame at the top of the arch with the qualities Constancy, Justice, Wisdom and Magnanimity located across the scaffold. On the first evening, the royal party saw a 'Regall Throne', illuminated by 100 lamps, representing a 'figure of that *Throne of Salomon*, when he entertained the *Queene* of *Sheba*' (B4v).[28] And the next night they witnessed a spectacular re-enactment of the Siege of Troy, including a castle representing Troy and the army of Greeks outside the walls. After being initially repulsed, the Greeks 'subtilly sounded a *Retreat*, and seeming to retire, lay hidden in Ambush, leaving a Horse of extreame proportion and greatnesse before the wals'

(B4v–C1). Unwittingly, the Trojans drew the horse into their walls and then the Greeks attacked.

On 8 June the entourage reached Heidelberg, the final destination of this part of Elizabeth's experience. Many shots of ordnance greeted the royal couple, a sign of the citizens' 'love, joy, and dutie' (*Magnificent*, C1). The throngs had come 'especially to behold *Her*, upon whom all their eyes were fixed with love and admiration' (C1v). The city had erected several arches, each containing its mute argument of visual meaning. Near the university, for example, the faculties of medicine, philosophy, theology and law each had prepared a scaffold saluting its particular art and the royal couple. After this procession Elizabeth arrived at the castle, where she met for the first time Frederick's mother and received gracious entertainment there.

During the next three days the tiltyard became the focus of activity. Frederick, dressed to represent Jason, entered the tiltyard first, along with Lennox and others. A stunning visual spectacle unfolded, including a procession of allegorical and mythological figures. For example, Jupiter appeared in a chariot, 'drawne by two *Griffons*, and those *Griffons* guided by *Mercury*, who sate as Coach-man' (*Magnificent*, C2). Next came Juno in a chariot, drawn by peacocks and guided by Iris. Arion, playing his lute and sitting on a seahorse, soon followed; and behind him came the Seven Deadly Sins, chained and driven forward by a dragon, spitting fire all the way. Frederick then appeared as Jason in a ship, which contained the Golden Fleece. Astounded by the spectacle, the spectators readied themselves for another day in the tiltyard.

On the next bright day, Frederick once again appeared as Jason, this time on horseback, surrounded by many supporters. Mythological figures arrived, such as Apollo and Bacchus. The Nine Muses, seated on Mount Parnassus, followed, and after them the Three Graces, accompanied by Hercules and Mercury. Elizabeth, Lennox and other members of the English party might well have thought of these tiltyard experiences as a glorious extension of the prolonged wedding festivities. They certainly would have been familiar with what they saw.

But on 14 June this all came to an end. On this day Lennox and other English members of the entourage took their leave of Princess Elizabeth and Frederick. For Lennox it had to be especially poignant: not only had the exceptional festivities concluded but also he was separating himself from this person whom he had known since her birth. As her father had left her at Rochester, so now Lennox, her father's representative, left her at Heidelberg. Alone now, but obviously with her husband, this teenaged royal princess would have to make her life in a new country, one still very strange to her, and she would have to make it without her faithful supporter Lennox. Elizabeth felt Lennox's departure keenly, as evident in her letter to James on 15 June. She writes that Lennox 'acquitted himself most worthily of the task it pleased Your Majesty to give him of escorting me into Germany, whose actions succeeded to the honour of Your Majesty and my unutterable pleasure'.[29] The princess adds that Lennox 'is the most able to inform Your Majesty of all that has happened on my journey, since he was the principal actor and spectator'. As she had written to her father from Canterbury earlier, she could now also say of the departing Lennox: she felt 'the disagreeable effects of the separation and distance'. All the events, festivities and pageants in Holland and Germany pointed to a new future for Elizabeth and Frederick, but they also looked to a past that would be no more. Lennox, meanwhile, made his way to France before continuing on to England.

FAVOURITES, PRINCE CHARLES

The end of 1613 involved the relationship of Robert Carr, Earl of Somerset and Frances Howard, who eventually married at Whitehall under James's auspices on 26 December, thus rounding out this year with another major wedding of political importance. In this development Lennox plays a minor role, although he surely understood how important Carr had become to King James. Carr, Viscount Rochester, a Scot, had come south with James in 1603, serving in a minor capacity as royal page. But at the Accession Day Tilt in 1607 at Whitehall, Carr fully captured the king's attention. Appearing under the aegis of Sir James Hay, another transplanted Scot, Carr entered the tilt. Despite his skill as a horseman, Carr fell from his horse and broke his leg. James immediately took notice of this attractive young man and became solicitous of his welfare, insisting that the king's own physicians take care of him. The king visited Carr regularly and even began to try to teach him Latin. This eventually led Thomas Howard, Earl of Suffolk, to write to John Harrington in 1611, describing Carr as 'straight-limbed, well-favoured, strong-shouldered, and smooth-faced, with some sort of cunning and show of modesty; tho, God wot, he well knoweth when to shew his impudence'.[30] Just the sort of young man to attract the king's attention and favour.[31]

As a sign of Carr's emerging prominence, Chamberlain wrote to his friend Dudley Carleton on 30 December 1607: 'Sir Robert Carre, a younge Scot and new favorite is lately sworne gentleman of the bedchamber'.[32] Two things stand out about Chamberlain's simple observation: how quickly Carr had become a 'favorite' and what an important position he had gained, Gentleman of the Bedchamber. Early in James's English reign the King's Bedchamber essentially supplanted the Privy Council as the political centre of government. With one exception, Philip Herbert, Earl of Montgomery, all the Gentlemen of the Bedchamber were Scots, starting with Lennox; and they basically controlled access to the king, having the most intimate contact with the king's person.[33]

In March 1611 James created Carr Viscount of Rochester, which carried with it a seat in the English House of Lords; he thus became the first Scot to sit in the English Parliament. Carr became a Knight of the Garter in April that same year and in 1612 he gained a seat on the Privy Council. James also made him Lord Treasurer of Scotland in 1613 and he served as a kind of personal secretary to the king. This led the Venetian ambassador, Antonio Foscarini, to observe that Carr 'holds the privy seal, with whom the king decides everything and in whom His Majesty confides above all others'.[34] The death of Cecil, James's chief political and government advisor, in May 1612 enlarged Carr's prospects by removing a major obstacle: Cecil's disfavour, which Queen Anne and Prince Henry shared intensely. Carr thus began to fan out across the political landscape, gathering titles, offices and considerable power, all the product of the king's generosity.

Lennox certainly understood Carr's status, and so did the powerful Howard family. Therefore, not surprisingly, Frances Howard, although married, began to move her affections in Carr's direction, no doubt encouraged especially by her great-uncle the Earl of Northampton. A potential alliance or even marriage with Carr would strengthen the Howards' political position. With the family's knowledge if not support Frances made overtures towards Carr and captured his attention. A letter from John Holles places Lennox curiously in at least one scene of an encounter between them. Apparently she had written to Carr asking him to meet her at Chesterford Park. 'When he had arrived he had found her sitting with the Duke of Lennox. Seconded by Lennox, Frances had then urged him to marry her, saying that there was nothing to stop them'.[35] According to Holles, Carr was not ready for this possibility: 'Your Lordship replied that you had yet made no fortune that you were at the King's bestowing. . . . nevertheless, she pressing you still, and my Lord of Lennox in her behalf, your Lordship said you would try the King' (Somerset, 103). Clearly Frances Howard wanted to dissolve her marriage with the Earl of Essex. That process would not be simple, as the events of 1613 bear out. First, she had to find a way to divorce her husband. For this purpose the king appointed a commission to consider the case; this took months of deliberation. Finally, on 25 September, she gained the divorce.[36] Two weeks before its granting a strange death occurred in the Tower, that of Thomas Overbury, a close friend of Carr. Frances Howard, Carr and even King James wanted Overbury out of the way for differing reasons. The cause of his suspicious death would not be uncovered for two more years.[37] For the moment, the pathway had cleared for the wedding of Carr and Howard, made even more likely by James granting Carr the title of Earl of Somerset on 4 November, in a ceremony that surpassed that for Lennox's gaining the title of Earl of Richmond on 6 October.

After Lennox had returned in August 1613, following the trip to Germany and then France, he had a momentary falling out with Somerset; this conflict Thomas, Viscount Fenton, reports in a letter to Mar on 18 August:

> Efter the Deukes returne . . . there was sume apperance of sume discontentment betuyx Lenoxx and Rotchester, in soe far as thaye war almost past speking kyndnes, and I can assure you wold have cummed to noe good, if it had not bein prevented be the industurye of my Lord Haye [James Hay] that did take exceiding great pains in it and did bring it to a verrye good end.[38]

Lennox's desire to be made Earl of Richmond was, according to Fenton, 'the cawss of the quarrell, but I praye your Lordshipe let noe thing be spokin of this erlldom, for it is keeped secret will [till?] it be done'. Striving for the king's favour regularly caused conflict among ambitious lords. As one who had served James for decades, Lennox would be less than human if he did not feel some chagrin and displeasure at Carr's meteoric rise. Then, the elaborate wedding.

At first, the wedding was to be a somewhat simple affair, as Chamberlain reports on 11 November to Dudley Carleton: 'The mariage was thought shold be celebrated at Audley-end [home of Frances' father] the next weeke . . . but I heare that the Queene beeing won and having promised to be present, yt is put of till Christmas and then to be performed at White-hall' (1:485). The change in plans, thanks in no small part to the change in Anne's attitude, led James to assume the cost of the whole endeavour, an expense that he could ill afford. Giovanni Battista Gabaleone, the newly arrived ambassador from the Duchy of Savoy, reported on the preparations in early December: 'At court they are working day and night on shows for the Earl of Somerset's wedding; the dancing festivals will be held in the royal hall as they were for the Prince Palatine, and there will be masques of great moment'.[39]

On St Stephen's Day, 26 December, Lennox and many other noblemen and court officials gathered with the king and queen at the Chapel Royal in Whitehall for the marriage of James's favourite and the newly divorced Frances Howard. Her great-uncle, the Earl of Northampton, led her into the chapel. 'She was maried in her haire,' Chamberlain reports (1:495), a sign of her virginity. The Dean of Westminster, George Montaigne, preached, and the Dean of the Chapel Royal, James Montagu, Bishop of Bath and Wells, led the service and officially joined the couple in marriage. Chamberlain cannot resist observing that Montagu had performed Frances' wedding to Essex in 1606; this 'fell out somwhat straungely that the same man, shold marie the same person, in the same place, upon the self-same day (after sixe or seven yeares I know not whether) the former partie yet living' (1:495). Few could pass up the irony. Ten days of festivities followed, stretching to 6 January 1614, rivalling anything seen at court since the February wedding and not to be equalled again in the Jacobean period.

After the wedding ceremony a little later in the evening, the court gathered in the Banqueting Hall within Whitehall Palace; there they saw Thomas Campion's masque, generally known as *The Somerset Masque* or *Masque of Squires*. Campion had had pride of place at Princess Elizabeth's wedding with the presentation of his *Lords' Masque* on the evening of the wedding and he had provided a progress entertainment in April for Queen Anne. Clearly, 1613 was a great year for this poet, musician, playwright and physician. As with his masque for the earlier royal wedding, Campion emphasises the theme of transformation. One can certainly note the seeming 'transformation' of Queen Anne, who had surrendered, at least in public, her antipathy to Carr, having appeared at his investiture as Earl of Somerset and having allowed the wedding to take place in Whitehall. Accordingly, Campion makes her a central figure in the masque, displacing, as it were, the usual prominence of King James.[40]

In an unusual move, Campion constructed two diverse worlds in the masque: an allegorical world, allied with the court, and the more realistic world of London, explicitly linking Whitehall and Guildhall. The entertainment stands between these often competing worlds. In terms of design, Campion created '*an Arch Tryumphall, passing beautifull, which enclosed the whole Worke*'.[41] In such an arch, Campion may be recalling the stunning triumphal arches that dominated London on the occasion of James's royal entry into the city on 15 March 1604. The first movement of the narrative involves knights who had attempted to make their journey to London for this wedding. Four squires emerge from the setting of woods and a sea scene and express their grief for the knights who have been changed into pillars of gold. Their imprisonment has come about because of the work of Error and Rumour. The masquers, previously charmed, come forward to dance, included among them Lennox, the earls of Pembroke and Montgomery and three of Frances' brothers.

Just as suddenly the scene changed to London and the Thames, all *'very arteficially presented in their place'* (273). In this scene, four barges appear as on the Thames; and the 'skippers' in them sing, followed by dancing. The squires, who had begun the masque, return at the end to extend their wishes and blessings to the newly married couple, 'The honour'd Bride-groome and the honourd Bride' (276). The masque closes, sending all off to sleep. London and court sing with one voice of rejoicing and the queen had enabled transformation, helping ratify this marriage as the celebratory mode seeks to wipe out resistance and rumour.

Catching their breath, Lennox and others of the court got ready for Ben Jonson's *A Challenge at Tilt, At a Marriage*, the first part of which took place on 27 December, followed by the tilt on 1 January. Jonson had earlier written *Hymenaei* for the 1606 wedding of Frances Howard and Essex. The *Challenge* involved the appearance of two Cupids, each vying for supremacy, one representing the bride and the other, the bridegroom. First Cupid lays down the challenge: a group of knights 'by their virtue shall maintain me to be the right Cupid, and the true issue of valor and beauty' – hence the tilt on 1 January.[42] The Italian Gabaleone reports: 'there was a tilt run on New Year's Day (their style), face to face, with very rich clothing and liveries, and triumphal chariots that were a most lovely sight and a great expense to the lords'.[43] Chamberlain cannot recall the names of all the challengers; but he does remember Lennox and the earls of Pembroke, Montgomery, Dorset and Rutland. Ten knights favoured First Cupid and ten, Second Cupid. Finally, the trumpets sound and the tilting began. After the tilting, each side claimed victory, only to be interrupted by the appearance of Hymen, who says that they both must yield. Hymen insists on the equality of both Cupids and redefines love's contention, asking who loves most. Hymen bids the knights depart as 'honorable friends and servants of love' (Orgel, 205).

On 29 December, the King's Men performed Jonson's *The Irish Masque at Court*; at the king's request they performed it again on 3 January.[44] Chamberlain writes to Carleton: 'The loftie maskers were so well liked at court the last weeke that they were appointed to performe yt again on Monday' (1:498). This strange entertainment, complete with rather bizarre Irish dialect, comes across as comical. The well nigh incomprehensibility of their language must have been part of the fun. Like the knights in Campion's masque, four Irishmen have landed on England's shores but without proper garments fit for a wedding. Amusingly, they

seem to have trouble even recognising King James. Such confusion, bor-
derline heretical, apparently caused much amusement, even for James. A
grand sort of dislocation, defamiliarisation goes on here, as Jonson pokes
fun at the typical masque. Given the centrality of the king's physical location for such performances, how could one not recognise him? While
Ireland had recently undergone considerable turmoil under oppressive
English rule, these Irishmen in the masque present no coherent political
message. They have merely come for a wedding, about which they have
heard even in Ireland. Much dancing ensues, as the speakers refer to
James's success in bringing peace and harmony to Britain. The masque
closes with two songs by the bard, who notes how quickly spring may
overcome winter by the king's presence. James had commissioned Jonson
to write this masque, so we cannot be surprised at its focus on the king.
The choice of Irish characters, however, comes unexpectedly.[45]

But the celebration of this wedding had not yet ended. Two more
events in early January 1614 extended the festivities: a procession into
the City of London and a masque presented there (discussed below), and
the performance on 6 January of *Masque of Flowers*, financed by Francis
Bacon, who, with Somerset's support, had become Attorney General in
1613. Small wonder that he felt obligated to provide entertainment for
the newly married couple. Bacon had tried to round up the help of the
various Inns of Court, who had assisted in Princess Elizabeth's wedding;
but only the Gray's Inn group could participate here at the beginning
of the year. And, of course, Bacon had been involved with Beaumont's
masque for the February wedding; indeed, Beaumont had dedicated his
text to Bacon.

An unidentified trio, 'I.G., W.D., and T.', dedicated the *Masque of
Flowers* to Bacon on behalf of the Gentlemen of Gray's Inn. They offer
the text to those who were present because the entertainment received
such approbation and 'represented to those that were absent, by commit-
ting the same to the press'.[46] Like the authorities in London, the Gray's
Inn people had precious little time to prepare. But on Twelfth Night,
Lennox, the royal family and others gathered in the Banqueting House in
Whitehall for the show, an exclamation point on several days of wedding
celebration. Like Campion and others, the author(s) of this masque chose
to emphasise 'transformation', in this case, changing flowers into men,
who had previously been transformed from men to flowers. The planners
present a perspective of a city from which emerges Winter, '*attired like
an old man, in a short gown of silk shag*' (161), who relishes his season.
But Primavera, Spring, enters and counters this view, covered as she is
in flowers. After, Gallus enters, '*in post, attired like a post*' (162). He

comes as Sun's messenger and he brings with him a letter addressed to both Winter and Spring. Winter reads aloud Sun's letter, which orders Winter to present winter sports and Spring 'sports of a more delicate nature' (163). Sun, by analogy King James, orders Primavera to return the flowers to men and present a dance at this marriage.

The main masque appears as the curtain opens to reveal a magnificent garden, complete with fountain, a globe and a golden statue of Neptune. In the midst of twelve gods sat Primavera; the whole group moved towards the king and began to sing about the charm that had changed men into flowers. A group of masquers, presumably courtiers, has received gifts from the newlyweds, and they wear the appropriate favours. A fourth song comments on the king: 'This isle was Britain in times past, / But then was Britain rude and waste; / But now is Britain fit to be / A seat for a fifth monarchy' (170). A note at the end of the text indicates that James asked for the first antimasque again; then the masquers removed their masks and approached the royal family – king, queen and prince – and kissed their hands. Not only have flowers been transformed into men but also the once unruly kingdom has been changed into a glorious garden.

In this same early January word arrived in England from Germany of the birth of Elizabeth and Frederick's son, the first royal grandson. Much rejoicing ensued; bonfires appeared throughout England in celebration. This royal birth afforded another measure of security for succession to the British throne. This birth seemed a punctuation mark following all the festivities of 1613. But the court could not remain forever in a celebratory mode. James thus turned his attention to political realities. His thoughts began to focus on the possibility of convening the Houses of Parliament. Understandably wary after the abysmal failure of the 'Great Contract' of the 1610 Parliament and its refusal to establish a rational plan for financing the monarchy and government, James received conflicting advice, largely pitted along the fault line of the Howard vs. anti-Howard factions. Northampton thought that such a session would be disastrous, while Francis Bacon and Henry Neville, among others, argued that it would be worth the risk, given the king's desperate need for funds. James finally decided to bring Parliament into session; thus, on 5 April, he made his way from Whitehall Palace to Westminster's parliament house in a procession that included Lennox.

Don Diego Saramiento de Acuña, Count Gondomar, the recently arrived Spanish ambassador, had been invited by James to attend the sessions. He left behind a vivid account of at least the early parts of the two-month-long session. Gondomar described the elegant royal procession thus: 'the King left the palace at noon with a large retinue on horseback. The trumpets preceded all, and after them came the King's guard on horseback, fifty persons strong; and after them came the supreme magistrates of the kingdom'.[47] Prince Charles followed, dressed 'with a large cape of crimson velvet trimmed with ermine; his breeches and vest were made of white satin'. The Earl of Shrewsbury came after him, carrying the cap of estate; then came Lennox, who 'rode on his left side carrying the sceptre, as Earl of Richmond', his relatively new title. Others followed, such as Nottingham and Lord Admiral, 'appointed High Steward by the King for this occasion' (5). Next to him rode his kinsman Suffolk, Chamberlain to the king. James wore a 'gold crown with pearls, diamonds, and rubies, trimmed with ermine, and a very large crimson cape made of velvet trimmed with ermine'. His shoes, stockings, vest and breeches were all white; he held in his hand a sword, 'unshielded and pointing upwards'. Somerset rode alone behind the king, acting as Master of the King's Horse, followed by the remaining members of the Privy Council. This dazzling array of colour and statement of prestige clearly intended to impress all spectators and to construct an image of royal power. Although James was in effect going to Parliament to ask for money, he clearly wanted to give a different kind of impression: not so much a supplicant as a powerful ruler.

Because of recent parliamentary elections, a disproportionate number of members of the Commons were new; this increased the difficulties of successfully completing legislation. Just a few days before Parliament opened, James appointed Sir Ralph Winwood as Secretary, whose job included representing the king to Parliament. Alas, he was totally inexperienced in parliamentary matters. Ineptitude, incompetence and ignorance governed much that went on in what became forever thereafter known as the 'Addled Parliament'. Battles over royal and parliamentary prerogatives broke out regularly. Entrenched forces wanted to grant the king nothing. In order to make his case, James addressed Parliament three times, on 5 April, 9 April and 4 May, the last two speeches mainly reiterating his earlier points and probably a sign of increasing desperation. Parliament could not even succeed in acknowledging Elizabeth and Frederick's son as having a legitimate place in the line of succession, much less solve financial problems. A magnificent procession became meaningless in the face of an intransigent Parliament.

By 1614, Somerset had reached the apogee of his political status, having become Secretary of State after Cecil's death and then Lord Chamberlain. Through him most affairs of state passed. But he began to make a fatal mistake: he seemed to be ever so slightly withdrawing from the king. Into that possible vacuum others moved to create a space for George Villiers, eventually the Duke of Buckingham, who had caught James's attention for the usual reasons, starting with Villiers's handsome features. Queen Anne and others began to champion his cause, to the detriment and displeasure of Somerset. James himself started to put some distance between the two. A potential rift exploded in September 1615, when the world first learned of the cause of Thomas Overbury's mysterious death in the Tower in September 1613. Little by little the court discovered that Frances Howard, now married to Somerset, had arranged for Overbury to be poisoned. Evidence included Somerset in some measure. To his credit, the king did not seek to protect him but instead set up a commission to investigate. Things went from bad to worse for the married couple. Eventually, in 1616, they faced trial for murder.[48]

Lennox, as happened occasionally, came under some kind of attack in mid-1615, as reported by Chamberlain in a letter to Dudley Carleton dated 15 June. Chamberlain writes:

> This day sevenight Sir John Kenneday and Sir George Belgrave were committed to the Gate-house from the counsaille table, for accusing a gentleman of fowle and scandalous speaches against the Duke of Lennoxe and generally all the Scottes, but fayling in theyre proofe, this was thought a speciall goode peece of justice. (1: 602)

James will not allow aspersions to be cast on Lennox's character; but, of course, Lennox remained an obvious target for frivolous and serious accusations. But such accusers risked the displeasure of the king and their efforts usually came to a bad end.

After an unpleasant spring of tawdry evidence, salacious accusations, trials and guilty convictions, the end of 1616 embraced the 'creation' of Prince Charles, who became Prince of Wales. Like his brother before him in 1610, Charles enjoyed a pageant along the Thames in his honour on 31 October. Indeed, the whole several days of ceremony quite consciously imitated what had been done for Henry. The river pageant, *Civitatis Amor*, written by Thomas Middleton, playwright, took place just two days after the Lord Mayor's Show, written by Anthony Munday, who had written the river pageant for Henry. The royal family and Lennox gathered at Whitehall for the conclusion of the pageant, but Queen Anne did not attend. Chamberlain writes to Carleton: 'The Quene wold not be present at the creation, lest she shold renew her griefe by the memorie of the last Prince who runs still so much in mens mind' (2:32).

Like the 1610 pageant this one included stops at Chelsea and Whitehall. Middleton created an imaginative poetic encounter between allegorical figures and Prince Charles. At Chelsea, for example, a figure representing London, 'sitting upon a sea-unicorn with six Tritons sounding before her', greeted Charles, as did the mythological figure Neptune.[49] London acknowledges the London authorities who have accompanied the barges along the Thames and who have arranged for and financed the show. London refers to Charles as 'Treasure of hope, and jewel of mankind'; 'Live long and happy, glory of our days' (p. 1205). Arriving at Whitehall, Charles encountered not only London but also Hope and Peace. Hope leans upon a silver anchor, 'attended by four virgins all in white'. Hope in a sonnet begins: 'Fair and most famous city, thou hast waked me / From the sad slumber of disconsolate fear' (p. 1205). But Hope rests assured that she has come to a place wherein she may plant her anchor. In a song, Peace greets Charles as 'spring of joy and peace, / Born to be honoured' and prays that the prince shall have all 'fair joys attend thee, / Glory of life' (p. 1205). Stuart political ideology and mythology appear in London's speech in the emphasis on the peaceful succession and peaceful reign of King James.

The installation of young men into the Order of the Bath took place on 2 November, followed on Monday, 4 November, with the actual inauguration of Charles as Prince of Wales. The account in Middleton's text follows almost verbatim the report in 1610. It remains unclear whether Middleton actually wrote this part of the text; someone, at least, only slightly modified the earlier one. Various lords of the realm, including Lennox, participated in the ceremony in which Charles knelt before his father, received the patent creating him prince and had the king place the robes on him and the other signs of his creation. Afterwards, Prince Charles hosted a dinner for Lennox and the other attending lords. The text reports that on Wednesday, 6 November, 'to give greater lustre and honour to the triumph and solemnity . . . fourteen right honourable and noble personages. . . graced this day's magnificence with running at the ring' (p. 1206). Lennox led the way. How fitting to have Lennox play a prominent role in the events; he had known Charles since his birth in 1600 and understood how much the kingdom now relied on him as the obvious successor to the crown.

In the midst of a turbulent and also joyous year, King James began in 1616 (the year of his fiftieth birthday) to think about and plan for a much desired trip to his native Scotland. Probably nostalgia prompted these thoughts more than anything else, although he talked about meeting with the Scottish Parliament and he certainly wanted to impose the Anglican Church's liturgical practices on the Scottish Kirk. He had little success with either, as things turned out. The enormous expense and

Figure 3.3   Engraving of Prince Charles by Crispin van de Passe, 1616. Courtesy of the National Portrait Gallery.

arduous nature of the proposed journey left only James enthusiastic for the experience. Most of the Scots serving in the English court in fact chose to remain in London. Lennox certainly made an effort to dissuade James from pursuing the journey. Thomas, Viscount Fenton wrote to Mar in early March 1617 reporting that the Privy Council did kneel to the king 'humbillye beshitcheing his Majestie that he wold be pleased to staye his journaye, for this yeir'.[50] But James insisted that if he did not go this year, he might never see Scotland again. When he said that, Fenton reports, 'your brother the Dewk of Lenoxe and the Erll of Arundell did kneell and excuss them selfes for moving of the matter'. Fenton adds, 'the holle pepill here [Scotland] are mutche against his Majesties cumming, but that will not prevaille'. By securing a loan of £100,000 from London's merchants, James removed a major obstacle to his plan.[51] Lennox began the journey with James; in all likelihood he did not complete the whole trip. Indeed, by the time James actually reached Scotland, not many lords remained, the exception being Buckingham.

No matter the disgruntlement among the group, which initially numbered 5,000, but dwindled to a fraction of that, James did indeed seem to be revived by being on his native soil, as he moved somewhat restlessly from city to city. Leaving in mid-March 1617, the entourage reached Berwick on 13 May and then crossed into Scotland, reaching Edinburgh on 16 May. James received a noble, if not altogether joyous, reception in the city of his birth. After touring various parts of Scotland, James began the journey back to England, arriving back at Windsor on 12 September, a nearly seven-month absence. Queen Anne did not journey with James; she had hoped to be made regent in England but James gave that honour to Bacon. Whatever the shortcomings of the trip, James saw it through royal-coloured glasses. In many ways, the journey may have been the king's last relatively peaceful time.

That Buckingham made the entire journey with James cannot be surprising. By 1617 his position as the king's 'favourite' had been well-established and he did not miss opportunities to secure that status. Somewhat ironically, Queen Anne led the way in introducing Buckingham into the court and James's attention in order to distract the king from Somerset. The Archbishop of Canterbury, George Abbot, seconded the queen's efforts. As early as 1615, Buckingham had become a Gentleman of the Bedchamber, a much-coveted position for its power and proximity to the king.[52] In 1616 the king's generosity continued to flow: Master of the Horse, Order of the Garter and the title Viscount Villiers. During the next year, the time of the Scottish journey, he became Earl of Buckingham and a member of the Privy Council.

James made a bracing statement to the Council about his love of Buckingham:

> I, James, am neither a god nor an angel, but a man like any other. Therefore, I act like a man, and confess to loving those dear to me more than other men. You may be sure that I love the Earl of Buckingham more than anyone else, and more than you who are here assembled. I wish to speak in my own behalf, and not to have it thought to be a defect, for Jesus Christ did the same, and therefore I cannot be blamed. Christ had his John and I have my George.[53]

This statement, which obliterates all kinds of boundaries, must have caused dismay, consternation, resignation and envy among members of the Council and all those who got a report of it. Buckingham's status could not be questioned; everyone, including members of James's family, had to come to terms with the situation. That also included Lennox, who had to reconcile the favour that he enjoyed with James with this new challenge, if not threat. Evidence, such as it is, suggests that Lennox responded intelligently and deftly, occasionally joining Buckingham in common purpose. Lennox, for example, participated in the ceremony on 1 January 1618 in which he and others delivered to Buckingham the 'letters patent' that created him Marquis of Buckingham. Certainly a measure of Lennox's personality and skill inheres in the recognition that Lennox served James faithfully to the end, never losing his love and respect. But Buckingham occupied some kind of superior place, enjoying an intimate love, for all that that can mean, unmatched by anyone else. After all, Jesus had his John.

In case Anne did not already recognise her status with James, Buckingham's meteoric rise made it clear. By 1617, if not sooner, Anne existed on the outskirts of James's affection. A steady decline in health, physical and psychological, followed. She had lost James to his favourites and the hunt, lost Henry to death, and lost Elizabeth to marriage and a distant home in Germany. A deep melancholy began to settle into her soul. Accumulating illnesses, such as dropsy, gout and poor circulation, compounded her difficulties, accounting in part for her absence from her various courtly functions, such as the investiture of Charles in 1616. Anne receded further into the background of court life: forgotten but not gone. Chamberlain wrote to Dudley Carleton in January 1617: 'The Quene removed yesterday to Whitehall from Somerset House where she hath lien this fortnight sicke of the gowte or somewhat els'.[54] A constant thread runs through these reports of her sickness: Anne's illnesses were as much emotional as physical. Even sending Buckingham, whom she had begun to respect, to her in March 1618 to persuade her to participate in an event did not prevail (Chamberlain, 2:152).

Her final illness began in January 1619 at Hampton Court, but James did not visit her there. Only Prince Charles and a few noblemen, likely Lennox, paid her heed. Finally, on 2 March 1619, Anne died. She had had difficulty accepting approaching death. Anne had, the Venetian ambassador Antonio Donato observed, 'released herself from the prison of perpetual death'.[55] Donato adds: 'Her Majesty died three days ago in the palace of Hampton Court . . . without seeing the king, who was at Newmarket. She breathed her last amid a few attendants in a country place. . . However, before dying, she had time to embrace the prince' (494). Ironically, as she lay in state at Denmark House, more people paid their respects than had visited her while still alive. Sadly, James could not readily arrange for adequate financing for her funeral, which kept being postponed. Finally, on 13 May, the funeral took place at Westminster Abbey, about ten weeks after her death. Chamberlain described the funeral as 'a drawling tedious sight, more remarqueable for number then for any other singularitie' (2:237). No matter, Anne finally received sufficient attention, much of which had been denied her in her last years. The procession was long and impressive, including many lords and ladies, bishops and officers of the court. The Countess of Arundel served as the 'chief mourner'; and Lennox served as her 'supporter', much as he had for Charles at Henry's funeral. Anne had had great admiration and respect for Lennox since her arrival in Scotland in 1590 and he did not waver in support of her. In the early evening of the 13th the funeral service ended at the Abbey; darkness and silence claimed Queen Anne as Lennox remained to contemplate the queen's life and his place in it.

During the period immediately following Anne's death and before her funeral, James himself experienced a serious illness, documented by Chamberlain, who wrote to Carleton on 27 March 1619 that several lords, including Lennox, went to meet the king, having learned of his illness – what Chamberlain characterises as a 'violent fit of the stone' (2:225). When the delegation met up with James between Newmarket and Royston, they found the king 'weake and faint'. The physicians ordered James to rest for at least ten days. But the situation seemed to worsen, giving, according to Chamberlain, 'a general apprehension of daunger' (227). Lennox, other lords and Prince Charles were summoned to the king's bedside. There James commended to Charles's attention several of the lords by name, starting with Lennox. This action conveys a note of seriousness on the king's part, indicating that James wanted Charles to be cognizant of the lords who might serve him admirably and faithfully. On 17 April, Chamberlain writes that Lennox and the lords, the Lord Mayor of London and members of the guilds all gathered at Paul's Cross to hear a sermon by the Bishop of London, giving God praise and thanks for James's recovery. 'The audience was the greatest that I remember to have seene there' (Chamberlain, 2:229). Clearly, many thought that the king had been in serious danger, but now they rejoice in his recovery. After the sermon, 'All the counsaille and noble-men that were present dined with the bishop who they say made a great feast' (230). A season for rejoicing and relief after a fearful interval. In early June 1619, less than a month after Anne's funeral, James made an entry into London, dressed festively in pale blue satin with silver lace and a blue and white feather – resembling more a 'wooer then a mourner' Chamberlain noted (2:242). Lennox and other lords attended James on this occasion, themselves perhaps puzzled by the king's garb. Chamberlain thought that James was more sullen than sick. In any event, the king did not waste much time in public mourning for Anne.

In 1620, Lennox made one final recorded procession into London, this one with King James on the occasion of the king's going to St Paul's to encourage repairs of the building. This event took place on 26 March 1620. James had sent word to the Lord Mayor of his intention to come into the City for this purpose. The mayor, Sir William Cockayne, responded positively and he then sent orders to the guilds to make themselves ready to stand in their livery along the processional route. The City also formed a committee to work out the details of the event. The mayor, recorder and aldermen greeted James and his party at Temple Bar. From there the large group made its way to the cathedral along streets lined with guild members. Of course, James came with numerous people in his entourage, including members of the Privy Council and Bedchamber, and Prince Charles. In the order of the procession, Lennox gets a separate entry, documenting his importance.[56] Arriving at the cathedral, James and group passed through the Great West Door and entered for a service of divine worship, but for the sermon, preached by the Bishop of London, John King, they went outside to Paul's Cross, a popular and well-used public space for sermons. The Cross had been used the previous year to give thanks for James's recovery from illness. The evening concluded with a banquet at the bishop's palace. At about six o'clock the king and his group returned to Whitehall, accompanied to Temple Bar by the mayor and aldermen. Although devoid of explicit dramatic performance, this event in late March exemplifies yet another display of royal power and prestige, embraced by the City. It certainly contained spectacle and a powerful sense of occasion, including Lennox, a royal entourage and the full panoply of City authorities and the guilds' representatives.

Chamberlain offers a slightly different account of this event in London, beginning with anticipation for it, noted in a letter to Dudley Carleton on 20 March. He writes: 'Here is great speech and expectation of the Kings coming to Paules Crosse on Sunday next, where the bishop of London should preach his court-sermon in the afternoon' (2:297). Others surmise that the king might speak on other topics: possibly 'the King will there deliver somewhat touching the matters of Bohemia, others, concerning this intended match with Spaine'. Chamberlain believes that James will focus simply on the necessity of repairing St Paul's, 'which indeed growes very ruinous'. A few days later, 1 April, Chamberlain writes again to Carleton in order to report on the event, noting the sermon by the bishop, but 'the better halfe of the time (being above two houres) he [Bishop] spent in a pathetical speech for the repairing of Powles' (2:299). At the banquet that followed, the king prevailed upon the mayor and aldermen to get busy, claiming that he would be 'content to fast with bread and water to see yt don'. Along the way to the cathedral, 'citizens stoode by companies with their banners and stremers all along the streets'. At Temple Bar the Lord Mayor and aldermen presented James with 'a purse of 1000 marks and another with 500 li to the Prince'. When James and the party entered the church, 'the Dean [John Donne] made a short speech in Latin' that was a parable about an old man who needed a physician's help in order to survive. Clearly struck by this event, Chamberlain follows up with another report of a commission, on which he has been invited to serve, that sought to get the repairs done. Chamberlain thinks himself 'very unfit for any such employment' (2:301). He cannot imagine 'how I came in unles yt be for my love to the place'. St Paul's functioned as a kind of home and place of business for Chamberlain; he thus would have been well known for his knowledge of and omnipresence in the cathedral. Alas, nothing happened quickly about repairing the cathedral, despite the kingly procession and exhortation and Chamberlain's abiding interest. The event offers a striking example of the interplay between court and city, an exchange that Lennox knew well by experience and observation.

A few days later, 3 April, Lennox made a procession from Whitehall to Westminster for an unspecified occasion, perhaps a meeting of some Parliamentary committee or other commission. A manuscript records the impressive group: 'the Companie aforesaid did proceede in manner following'.[57] It begins: 'First the knighte Marshalls men with Tipstaves' walking two by two on foot. 'Councellores at law belonging to the Marshalle' also proceeded on foot. Officers of Lennox's household followed, also two by two on foot. The document consistently refers to Lennox as Lord Steward. The 'Sheriffe of the Countie on Horsbacke' proceeded, followed by the Lord Steward's 'gentlemen on foot', also walking two by two. 'Two Typstaves bareheaded on fote' appeared. A 'Clarke' bearing the 'white Rode on foote, and bareheaded, hauing on his Lefte hand the Lo: Stewards gentlemen bareheaded and on foot', led the way with Lennox following, 'accompanied with the Lo: Chanceller on Horsebacke'. Earls and barons on horseback soon followed. And so this lengthy procession with Lennox at its centre moved towards Westminster for some unknown purpose. This impressive group seems a follow-up of the one that processed from Whitehall to St Paul's a few days earlier. In any event, Lennox as Lord Steward had no trouble putting together a large group, one that befits his status.

Having participated in Charles's investiture as Prince of Wales in 1616 and having watched with amazement and some fear the meteoric rise of Buckingham in the king's favour, Lennox in 1623 found himself involved in one last major event in the royal family: the marriage pursuit of Charles for the Infanta of Spain Maria Anna, daughter of Philip III, a process known as the 'Spanish Match'. Lennox had participated as early as 1613 in negotiations of such a marriage to a French princess, a potential marriage favoured by several, including Lennox and Queen Anne. But this process went nowhere. Therefore, attention turned to Spain. What no one had anticipated was Charles's decision, perhaps on his own, to travel to Spain to complete the marriage arrangements. Having secured a picture of the Infanta, Charles convinced himself that he was in love with her and desperately wanted to marry her. In this, Charles resembles his father and his approach to marrying Anne. Charles was almost twenty-three-years old now, clearly of marriageable age, indeed the same age as James when he pursued Anne. James and others thought that this Spanish marriage might result in the restitution of the Palatinate to Frederick and Princess Elizabeth, which had been lost to the Spanish after the couple's disastrous acceptance of the roles of King and Queen of Bohemia, contributing to the Thirty Years' War. This hope of Spanish acquiescence turned out to be a fantasy.

Charles sought Buckingham's help in persuading James to allow the slightly hare-brained idea of a trip to Spain. James opposed the idea, as did others, such as Lennox; but Buckingham insisted that if James did not allow this journey, he would not be trusted in the future. Lennox and James Hamilton had, according to a report (10 March 1623) by the Venetian ambassador, Alvise Valaresso, 'remonstrated with his Majesty' against the idea, noting the unreasonableness of the proposal, full of danger for the prince with the potential of making Charles a prisoner in Spain.[58] James faced the possibility of losing the two people whom he loved most: Charles and Buckingham, as Valaresso points out. But tearful and apprehensive, James relented, on the condition that Buckingham accompany Charles.

And so, these two, in mid-February, donned false beards, wore different clothes to disguise their identities and adopted the names Jack and Tom Smith, master and servant. (Clearly, they had been reading too many romances.) Looking slightly ludicrous, they set out on the

perilous trip by water first to France and then overland to Spain. Various
authorities throughout England and beyond almost blew their cover. In
a letter of 27 February, James addressed Charles and Buckingham as
'my sweet boys and dear venturous knights, worthy to be put in a new
romance'.[59] This charming idea, of course, flies in the face of the considerable danger lurking in this enterprise. Lennox, in a letter to his friend
Edward Herbert on 2 March, notes the amazement of 'these aduenturers
of Amade de Gaule concerning the knights errants the Prince and my
Lord of Buckingham and there journey'.[60] The Venetian ambassador had
been more precisely on target in his warnings about the danger of this
trip, which cannot be masked over by notions of romance.

On 21 February Charles and Buckingham reached Paris; by averaging
about sixty miles a day on horseback, they got to Madrid on 7 March –
to the complete surprise of the Spanish, who did not quite know what to
make of this unexpected appearance of the prince and king's favourite.
Some thought that perhaps Charles had come to convert to Catholicism,
thus potentially speeding the marriage procedures, all of which hinged on
the possibility of a papal dispensation for the Infanta. Whatever romantic notions still lingered, the intransigence of the Spanish soon dispelled.
The two would spend several more fruitless months expecting things to
be worked out to the benefit of the English and the marriage. That would
not happen. Debates, discussions and tension dominated the situation,
with no favourable result. Terms seemed to be agreed to in late August
but the English negotiators got no concessions from the Spanish about
the Palatinate; and they did not get to take the Infanta back to England,
where construction had begun on a chapel, designed by Inigo Jones, for
the Infanta.

Reports in and out of England waxed and waned about the likely
success in Spain. Lennox wrote to Edward Herbert on 2 April, saying
'I hope you haue hearde of his Highness safe arriual well in Spaine and
of his Magniifique entertainment'.[61] A few weeks later (24 April) Lennox
again writes to Herbert, reporting of 'the good success of all business
in Spain'.[62] On 13 May Lennox tells Herbert that the ships are ready to
'bring home the prince his Highnes and the Infanta, wee hope they will
bee here in July'.[63] That same May, Chamberlain reports that Lennox
and others are making their way to Southampton to begin preparations
for the Infanta's arrival (2:499). On 14 June, Chamberlain informs
Dudley Carleton that Lennox and the group have indeed made their way
to Southampton 'to take order for the reception of the Infanta when
she shall arrive, for lodging her and her traine, for mending the high
ways and for shewes and pageants, to which purpose Innigo Jones and

Allen [Edward Alleyn] the old player went along with them' (2:501). The presence of Jones and Alleyn implies a certainty about the Infanta's likely arrival; that is, even entertainments are being planned. On 21 July Charles wrote to Lennox, according to Valaresso, 'begging him to hasten on a reply to the last despatch, because he expresses his determination to leave on its arrival there'.[64] And so it went. One might be at Southampton, scanning the coastline looking for the Infanta, but she will not arrive, to the great relief of the English people.

Charles and Buckingham did, however, arrive in England at Portsmouth on 5 October, safe and sound and *sans* Infanta. The next day they entered London and soon met James at Royston. Londoners responded with wild joy; great bonfires of rejoicing lit up the skies, by the hundreds, according to various reports. A service of celebration took place at St Paul's Cathedral, including, Chamberlain noted, the 'singing of a new antheme . . . the 114th psalme, when Israell came out of Egypt and the house of Jacob from among the barbarous people' (2:516). Near the end of that October, Valaresso reported to Venice: 'For the rest I may say that they keep dead silence at Court about the marriage'.[65] Whatever enthusiasm had once existed for the Spanish marriage had almost completely vanished. Dead silence took its place. Lennox decided to keep his silence by remaining neutral on the issue in early January 1624, according to Chamberlain (2:542), doubtless understanding that for all practical purposes the marriage deal had died. Even Prince Charles had soured on it, according to a letter from Thomas, Earl of Kellie to John, Earl of Mar, 5 February 1624: 'if I be not wrong informed, the point and jump of the besines is, that the Prince wold gladlye be from the bargaine, without onye staine or imputations to lye upone the ladye'.[66] Even Parliament rose up against the whole prospect of the Spanish Match. The 'knights errant', as Lennox called them, had failed in their purported mission. Their romantic venture ended in disappointment but growth in wisdom about the wily machinations of the Spanish court. Charles would have to wait a few years for a bride.

In 1623 Lennox could verify the wisdom of the Second Lord in Shakespeare's *All's Well That Ends Well*, who observes: 'The web of our life is of a mingled yarn, good and ill together' (Act IV, scene iii, lines 70–1). For Lennox and the royal family this life together ranged from death and funeral (Henry) to wedding and rejoicing (Elizabeth). It included births and deaths of royal children (Mary and Sophia) and celebration at Prince Henry's investiture as Prince of Wales (1610) and Prince Charles's later ceremony (1616); the sombre reburial of James's mother, Mary (1612) and the joyous arrival of Prince Frederick, come to marry Elizabeth, and the delight in a visit from Christian IV, Anne's brother. Numerous dramatic performances and spectacular court masques join in the mix, along with the sad, lonely death of Queen Anne in 1619.

Through it all, Lennox remained steadfast in his devotion to King James and love and respect of the royal family, which they reciprocated. Despite the emergence of the king's 'favourites', Somerset and Buckingham, Lennox did not waver in being indispensable and trustworthy, the king's friend and confidant. The king unhesitatingly sent Lennox on diplomatic missions, trusted him to gather Prince Frederick and bring him to Westminster, placed on Lennox the care and responsibility for Princess Elizabeth as she journeyed to her new home in Germany. The status of other courtiers might wax and wane, but Lennox's position continued stable and secure, earned through dutiful service. The excitement of the royal family's arrival in England might have faded over time but Lennox's stature did not. Chosen by James to accompany him and the family to this new land, called England, Lennox became a beloved fixture in the family's activities, its sorrows and joys and everything in between.

Notes

1. *Calendar of State Papers Venetian*, 12:473.
2. From an account quoted by John Nichols, *Progresses of King James*, 2:513.
3. See previous note for the reference to the Revels Accounts. For the Chamber Accounts, see *Collections VI: Dramatic Records in the Declared Accounts of the Treasurer of the Chamber 1558–1642*, David Cook (ed.).
4. John H. Astington, *English Court Theatre 1558–1642*, offers a convenient listing of the court performances, see especially pp. 246–7 for the 1612–13 season. We have no information about the order in which the plays were performed, except for *Cupid's Revenge*.
5. Astington writes: 'we can note that comedy predominated among the Christmas performances of 1612–13; perhaps the Lord Chamberlain and the Master of the Revels deliberately chose plays which stayed clear of the sensitive matter of the death of princes' (p. 203). Given the generic diversity of the plays, one can hardly claim that comedy 'predominated'. And clearly *The Winter's Tale* confronts the matter of the death of a young prince.
6. *Letters of John Chamberlain*, 1:416.
7. For an account of the wedding festivities, see Jerzy Limon, *The Masque of Stuart Culture*, pp. 125–69.
8. *Calendar of State Papers Venetian*, 12:472.
9. John Taylor, *Heavens Blessing and Earths Joy*, sig. C4v.
10. *The Magnificent Marriage of the Two Great Princes*, sig. A2v.

11. For an account of the appearance of 'Turks' in civic pageants, see my '"Are we turned Turks?": English Pageants and the Stuart Court', *Comparative Drama* 44 (2010): pp. 255–75.

12. *Calendar of State Papers Venetian, 1610–1613*, 12:498.

13. Anthony Nixon, *Great Brittaines Generall Joyes*, sig. B3v.

14. I follow the account as found in John Nichols, *Progresses*, 2:542. Nichols reproduces *The Magnificent Marriage of the Two Great Princes*, cited above, along with other interpolated contemporary material.

15. For a twentieth-century complaint about the wedding, see David Harris Willson, *King James VI and I*. Willson writes: 'There followed a week of festivities which were elaborate, tedious, poorly managed and grossly extravagant. Why King James . . . permitted such lavish, vulgar and senseless waste is difficult to understand' (p. 286). Ask the Duke of Lennox or members of the royal family about this 'senseless waste' and one would get an incredulous response.

16. Bishop Montagu served as Dean of the Chapel Royal for many years. He also brought together the materials to form *The Workes of King James*, published in 1616, for which he wrote a most interesting prefatory essay.

17. Quotations from Campion's masque come from *A Book of Masques in Honour of Allardyce Nicoll*, T. J. B. Spencer and Stanley Wells (eds). *The Lords' Masque* is edited by I. A. Shapiro, pp. 95–123.

18. Martin Butler, *The Stuart Court Masque and Political Culture*, p. 9. Butler's excellent study focuses on the political implications of the masques.

19. These can be found in *Inigo Jones: The Theatre of the Stuart Court*, Roy Strong and Stephen Orgel (eds), 1:240–52.

20. For a critical discussion of this masque see Stuart Curran, 'James I and Fictional Authority at the Palatine Wedding Celebrations', *Renaissance Studies* 20 (2006): 51–67, David Norbrook analyses a proposed masque, 'The Masque of Truth: Court Entertainment and International Protestant Politics in the Early Stuart Period', *Seventeenth-Century* 1 (1986): 81–110. Norbrook believes that Prince Henry was involved in planning this masque that was not performed. His analysis derives from the French text by D. Jocquet, published in 1613. See also Martin Butler's discussion in *The Stuart Court Masque*, pp. 197–9.

21. For Chapman's masque, I follow the text found in *Court Masques: Jacobean and Caroline Entertainments 1605–1640*, David Lindley (ed.). For an analysis, see Martin Butler, *The Stuart Court Masque*, pp. 200–3. Butler does not pay much attention to the procession to Whitehall. I discuss the processional parts of these masques in 'Court Masques about Stuart London', *Studies in Philology* 113.4 (2016): 822–49.

22. For some of Jones's drawings see Orgel and Strong, *Inigo Jones*, 1: 253-63. This edition provides a list of expenditures for the masque, which totaled £1,182.

23. *Calendar of State Papers Venetian*, 12:532.

24. *Letters of John Chamberlain*, 1:426.
25. The text of Beaumont's masque I take from *A Book of Masques*, cited in note 19. This quotation comes from p. 132 in this edition prepared by Philip Edwards. See Martin Butler's brief discussion, pp. 199–200. Butler does observe: 'Of the performed masques, only this one envisaged the alliance as having military consequences' (200).
26. *Calendar of State Papers Venetian*, 12:525.
27. *The Correspondence of Elizabeth Stuart, Queen of Bohemia, 1605–1631*, Nadine Akkerman (ed.), 1:114.
28. *The Magnificent, Princely, and most Royal Entertainment given to the High and Mightie Prince, and Princesse*. All quotations will come from this text.
29. *The Correspondence of Elizabeth Stuart*, Nadine Akkerman (ed.), 1:123.
30. John Harrington, *Nugae Antiquae*, 2:275.
31. For a discussion of James's devotion to male favourites, see my *King James and Letters of Homoerotic Desire*. The section on Carr appears on pp. 65–97.
32. *Letters of John Chamberlain*, 1:249.
33. For a convincing analysis of this arrangement, see Neil Cuddy, 'The Revival of the Entourage: The Bedchamber of James I, 1603–1625', in *The English Court from the Wars of the Roses to the Civil War*, David Starkey (ed.), pp. 173–225.
34. *Calendar of State Papers Venetian 1613–1615*, 13:219.
35. Reported in Anne Somerset, *Unnatural Murder: Poison at the Court of James I*, p. 103. This book offers a compelling account of the whole business of Carr and Frances Howard and the murder of Overbury.
36. For a reliable account of Frances Howard and her marriages and other machinations, see David Lindley, *The Trials of Frances Howard*.
37. For a discussion of the Overbury problem, see Alastair Bellany, *The Politics of Court Scandal in Early Modern England*, pp. 25–56. See also my discussion of all of these matters in *Shakespeare's London 1613*, pp. 239–65.
38. *Earl of Mar and Kellie Manuscripts*, p. 53.
39. Gabaleone's reports can be found in John Orrell, 'The London Court Stage in the Savoy Correspondence, 1613–1675', *Theatre Research International* 4 (1979): 80; 79–94.
40. For discussion of the masque, see Jerzy Limon, *The Masque of Stuart Culture*, pp. 170–97; Kevin Curran, *Marriage, Performance and Politics at the Jacobean Court*. Curran's astute analysis of all the entertainments for this wedding appears pp. 129–60. See also the analysis of Martin Butler, *The Stuart Court Masque*, pp. 214–19. Butler writes: 'The masque confronted the marriage's problems and attempted to manage them symbolically' (p. 217). James Knowles discusses all of the entertainments for the wedding in his *Politics and Political Culture in the Court Masque*, pp. 53–92. Knowles, like Butler, focuses on the political implications of the masques.

41. All quotations come from *The Works of Thomas Campion*, Walter Davis (ed.), p. 268.
42. Orgel, *Complete Masques*, p. 200.
43. Orrell, 'The London Court Stage in the Savoy Correspondence', p. 81.
44. For discussion of this curious masque, see Martin Butler, *Stuart Court Masque*, pp. 121–3. Butler writes: 'The masque is best understood less as wanton falsification of colonial realities than as an image of what James's government thought it was achieving' (p. 122). Knowles, *Politics and Political Culture*, has an extended analysis of this masque, pp. 78–92. Knowles argues that this masque 'registers a darker political climate', prompted by the 'disquiet' over the marriage and the 'advancement of the Howards' (p. 84). He adds: 'The masque embodies and seeks to negotiate many of the strains surrounding Carr, his marriage, and the factional shifts that occurred due to the nuptials' (p. 89).
45. For a political critique of this masque, see David Lindley, 'Embarrassing Ben: The Masques for Frances Howard', *English Literary Renaissance* 16 (1986): 343–59. Lindley emphasises the smugness of the masque in its attitude toward the Irish. Lindley writes: 'The message of the masque is therefore directed *at* the benighted and comic Irish from the point of view of secure and self-satisfied English and Scottish masquers' (p. 357).
46. *The Masque of Flowers*, E. A. J. Honigmann (ed.), in *A Book of Masques*, T. J. B. Spencer and Stanley Wells (eds), p. 159. All quotations will come from this edition. Butler, *Stuart Court Masque*, observes: '*The Masque of Flowers* was the only masque to invoke a specifically British theme' (p. 216).
47. Quotations come from the exceptional compilation: Maija Jansson, *Proceedings in Parliament 1614 (House of Commons)*, p. 4. For a summary of this Parliament see David Harris Willson, *King James VI and I*, pp. 344–8 and Alan Stewart, *The Cradle King*, pp. 251–6.
48. For a helpful discussion of the whole Overbury business, see Alan Stewart's *The Cradle King*, pp. 257–82; also, my discussion in *King James and Letters*, pp. 73–80. Lennox's involvement will be discussed below in the section on 'Politics'. See Chapter Four here for Lennox's involvement in this trial.
49. Quotations come from my edition of the Middleton text found in *The Collected Works of Thomas Middleton*, Gary Taylor and John Lavagnino (eds), p. 1204. See also my introduction to this text, pp. 1202–4.
50. *Earl of Mar and Kellie Manuscripts*, p. 75.
51. For a helpful discussion of the trip to Scotland, see Alan Stewart, *The Cradle King*, pp. 283–94. For documentation of the journey, see Nichols, *Progresses*, 3:317–27.
52. For a full discussion of Buckingham and his relationship to James see my *King James and Letters of Homoerotic Desire*, pp. 98–145.
53. Quoted from *King James and Letters*, p. 104.
54. Chamberlain, *Letters*, 2:47.
55. *Calendar of State Papers Venetian*, 15:494.

56. Nichols, *Progresses*, 4:601. Nichols has rounded up several sources to document this event, 593–602.
57. Bodleian Library, Tanner MS 236, fol. 83.
58. *Calendar of State Papers Venetian*, 17:582.
59. Akrigg, *Letters of James*, p. 388.
60. National Archives, PRO 30/53/10/78, fol. 163.
61. National Archives, PRO 30/53/10/80, fol. 167.
62. National Archives, PRO 30/53/10/82, fol. 171.
63. National Archives, PRO 30/53/10/83, fol. 163.
64. *Calendar of State Papers Venetian,* 18:74.
65. *Calendar of State Papers Venetian*, 18:146.
66. *Earl of Mar and Kellie Manuscripts*, p. 190.

4

Diplomacy, Politics and the Arts

Lennox's social, cultural and political life obviously intersects that of the royal family regularly, but he also experienced a political life not wholly beholden to the king. Of course, it all begins with the king's showering him with positions, the likes of which he had held in Scotland. When James arrived in England, he determined to structure the court much as it existed in Scotland. England, of course, already had a Privy Council, and this James continued, setting out to have an equal number of Scots and English sit in this group. The king immediately appointed Lennox to the Council. James also decided to elevate the importance of the Bedchamber, which first had only Scots as members, with Lennox as its head. This group, which also included Lennox's brother Esmé, grew in political power, in many ways supplanting the Privy Council.[1] It derived part of its power from its proximity to the king's person. Perhaps this situation informs the view of the Venetian ambassador, Giovanni Carlo Scaramelli, who reports in October 1603: 'Lennox is the person deepest in the King's confidence, and some time ago has been named the nearest to the Crown'.[2]

DIPLOMACY

This personal and political position enables James to make Lennox an occasional emissary to Scotland. Indeed, Scaramelli's report includes information about the early resistance of Scottish nobles to the whole idea of a possible legal union between the two countries. The Scots see England as an 'accessory to Scotland', therefore, inferior. Several of Scotland's leading nobles endorse this idea, rendering James 'anxious about this business', the ambassador writes. Thus, the king 'had an idea of sending the Duke of Lennox to Scotland to break up the combination' (10:106).

James, however, was able to write to Alexander Seton in Scotland and persuade him to hold off any meeting of the recalcitrant Scots. But Lennox's life will continue to intersect with Scottish politics.

In the same letter of February 1611, in which Lennox laments the death of the Earl of Dunbar, he responds to increasing pressure to take a more active role in Scotland. In fact, the Laird of Kilsythe, to whom he writes, has apparently urged Lennox to become James's representative in Scotland. Lennox admits his willingness to serve James, just not in Scotland, knowing 'that I coulde do his Majestie alls good service as any'.[3] Lennox adds: 'Bot, first, I must confess that I am loathe to leave my personall attendance on his Majestie'; indeed, James has not mentioned such service in Scotland to Lennox. He wants to remain 'nearest to the Crown' literally; from this proximity, his political power derives. Thus, regarding Scotland, Lennox concludes: 'So in this I am resolved not to medle in it and so eschew it alls far as I can' (1:124). Of course, when James sends him to 'medle' in Scotland, he goes. But the relationship with his adopted country can be fraught.

Indeed, he finds himself in Scotland in June 1604, going to the Scottish Parliament as the king's representative, pursuing the elusive idea of union of the kingdoms, which Nicolò Molin characterises as the king's 'favourite scheme . . . but one which will meet with many difficulties, as he well knows, and, therefore, he does all he can to secure unanimity'.[4] Molin reports on 8 June that the English Parliament has named forty-four members for the commission on union, but the Scots, no one. They have not, Molin observes, 'on account of insults they say they have received from the English' (10:155). As a consequence, 'They refused to allow the Duke of Lennox and the Earl of Mar to sit, declaring that, though they were Scotsmen, yet having been appointed of the English Privy Council, they had no right to a share in the debates of the Scottish Parliament, for they might report to the English Privy Council with great injury to Scotland' (10:155). Eventually, the Scots relented, having first flexed their political muscles. Even with the king's blessing, Lennox would from time to time encounter Scottish intransigence, if not hostility.

He fared slightly better in 1607, when James once again sent him to the Scottish Parliament. The Venetian ambassador, Zorzi Giustinian, reported on 1 August: 'The Duke of Lennox has been sent to reside there as the King's Lieutenant', in order 'to secure for his nation a just revenge against the malicious language used in the English Parliament he has assented to the same freedom being exercised in the Scottish Parliament'.[5] At best, King James indulges in a curious logic: he will let the Scots speak offensively in order to exact revenge against the English Parliament for doing that. This logic should best be left to kings to fathom. Lennox might well have been puzzled as well. James will learn by 1610 or so that the dream of union of the kingdoms would not happen in his lifetime, making this probably his greatest foreign policy defeat.

Lennox was back in Scotland in 1616, where 'he made a posting journey to reconvoy the Marquis Huntley', Lennox's brother-in-law, who had been 'excommunicated by the kirke in Scotland'.[6] This action forms part of the ongoing battle over Huntly's religion, despite his regular protestations that he followed the teachings of the Scottish Kirk, whose leaders rightly concluded that he was Catholic. In England, however, the Archbishop of Canterbury 'absolved' him; 'and in the presence of sixe or seven bishops and many other persons of goode account receved the sacrament', Chamberlain writes. What the Scottish Kirk had done, the English church could undo. James certainly thought that the Church of England was the superior church, so better to be reinstated by it. Lennox's fingerprints rest somewhere in this episode; certainly he would want to arrange a favour for Huntly and his sister.

After the journey with Huntly, Lennox returned the next year as a participant in King James's largely nostalgic trip to Scotland in 1617, as noted earlier. Having first opposed this trip, Lennox gave in and accompanied the king on most if not all of this adventure. Apparently, this experience lingered in his memory as having been pleasant because Chamberlain takes note of the intention of several other nobles to join him and Marquis Hamilton in Scotland in late summer 1619. Chamberlain reports in a letter to Dudley Carleton on 15 July:

> divers of our great Lords as Marquis Buckingham, the Lord Chamberlain [William Herbert], the earle of Arundell and others are minded they say to take a posting journey into Scotland when the King is at Rufford to accompanie the Duke [Lennox] and Marquis Hamilton, and this *bon viage* is upon a gayetie [pleasure-seeking], and kind of promise some of them made when they were last there. (Chamberlain, 2:250–1)

Perhaps some of them had second thoughts about this trip, for Chamberlain writes in August: 'The Lord Chamberlain only is gon into Scotland with the Duke and Marquis Hamilton' (257). Lennox doubtless returned to Scotland on other occasions, whether for pleasure or political purpose. By so doing, he retained a strong attachment to this place where he had arrived as a nine-year-old boy.

Lennox's political knowledge of England took a giant step forward with his visit to London in 1601, coming there from a mission to France. His visit to England included, obviously, conversations with

Queen Elizabeth, who enjoyed his company and so wrote glowingly to
King James about the duke. But Lennox also met Cecil, chief secretary
to the queen and eventually Earl of Salisbury. Thus began an important friendship and useful working relationship, to the benefit of both,
lasting until Cecil's death in May 1612. Lennox wrote to Cecil in April
1602 about his visit and thanked him for his hospitality.[7] Establishing
this relationship clearly enhanced the skill and ease of transformation
after Elizabeth's death the following March. Lennox was able to inform
James first-hand of his impression and understanding of the working
of Cecil and the English Privy Council. When James encountered Cecil
at his estate at Theobalds in May 1603, he already knew much about
him.

Cecil had written to the Master of Gray in Scotland on 20 February
1602 about Lennox and his late-1601 visit. Cecil begins by noting some
momentary conflict between Lennox and Mar, but declaring that they
both wish 'sincerely the mutual amity of both Princes'.[8] Cecil admits
that he did not see much of Lennox after conferring with him in the
Privy Chamber, where, he professed his 'undivided duty to my Sovereign'
(14:209). He cautioned Lennox about listening to other councillors who
might mislead him and he urges Gray to 'make it appear to the Duke
that no man shall be more ready to give him his due at all times than
I shall do, nor shall be more glad of his good opinion, because I note so
many parts in him to make him worthy the service of a King' (209). Cecil
knows whereof he speaks and he has correctly understood Lennox's crucial and loving relationship with James. It will clearly be to Cecil's benefit
to curry favour with Lennox – and vice versa. In late November 1602,
just months before Elizabeth died, Cecil wrote to George Nicolson,
saying that no one in Scotland has better standing with the queen than
Lennox, 'whose carriage when he was here towards herself was very
agreeable unto her', and she has taken note 'particularly of his good
disposition to do all the best offices he can for preservation of the mutual
amity'.[9] Indeed, Cecil continues, 'if he be sent up he shall find no man
here more ready to do him all honest offices'. Cecil stands eager to serve
and assist Lennox.

In a letter of 18 April 1604 Lennox acknowledges the protocol of passing important documents through Cecil; in fact, he asks that Cecil convey
such a document about two men who wish to be named 'Registraries'
to the King 'wholly, whereby you shall have no prejudice'.[10] A few days
earlier, Lennox had written to Cecil to inform him that the king wants
Sidney Montague to become secretary to Prince Henry. In order to make
this happen, Lennox asks for Cecil's assistance: 'I desyer your Lordship

woulde give him your favoure and furtherance . . . I shall rest ready to requite your Lordship with san lyke kyndnesse that is in me'.[11] Later, in August 1604, Lennox 'protests his dutiful affection' to Cecil (Salisbury, 14:256). Two years later, on 24 August, Lennox seeks Cecil's help in dealing with 'many injuries at the hands of Anthony Besson and Richard Besson' (Salisbury, 18:246). The squabble refers to Yorkshire lands that Lennox owns and the Bessons owe him money. He has even had them arrested, but the conflict has not been resolved. He implores Cecil: 'The charges expended are quite lost, and myself without remedy unless you will by your private letter write to the Lord President of the North to take some course that I might receive remedy'.[12] No matter is too small to seek Cecil's help. This Lennox also did in 1609 in his quarrel with Christ College Cambridge, noted earlier. Lennox writes confidently in July 1609 that he has 'knowledge of your [Cecil's] worth and assurance of your love to myself' (21:113). Obviously, both Cecil and Lennox assisted each other in multiple ways, large and small. Cecil's death came as a great loss to Lennox personally and to the country.

Not only did Lennox serve regularly as an emissary to Scotland, he also undertook diplomatic missions to France on James's behalf, beginning with the one in 1601. Lennox continued to serve this purpose in England, going to France in 1605. Chamberlain reports in mid-December 1604 that Lennox makes preparations to travel to France: 'The Duke of Lennox is presently going in ambassage for Fraunce, and though yt be thought that his owne busines is his greatest imployment, yet for his coutenaunce this place is imposed upon him'.[13] The duke will receive compensation of £300. Cecil, now Viscount Cranborne, wrote to Sir Thomas Lake on 21 January 1605 about the French mission. Cecil reports: 'Immediately after the writing of this letter, here arrived this morning two dispatches, one from the Duke, and the other from the Ambassador', which James read, 'for by the one he shall see how well the Duke was received, and by the other how much his carriage deserves commendation'.[14] Cecil adds that he has learned from some good friends 'that he has done the King honour in that Court'. King James wrote to Cecil on 22 January about Lennox in France, instructing Cecil to 'send to us a letter to be directed to Sillery, as our cousin the Duke of Lennox requireth'; and he adds: 'you may cause the Duke to understand that touching the French King's complaint about our Ambassador at Venice, that we have none there nor in all Italy avowed but Wotton'.[15] Part of the discussions there involved the controversy about Lennox's relative Count d'Entragues, who was found guilty of plotting the assassination of Henri IV of France. Chamberlain and the Venetian ambassador offer rather different perspectives on the ambience of Lennox's mission. Chamberlain, on 16 February, claims that he has received word

> that he [Lennox] found but course entertainment, whether yt were by reason of his uncle Entragues disgrace, or upon complaint of the French ambassador here that he is no more respected, and therefore hath sent for his leave to be gon: or that there is some other alienation toward. (1:203)

Nicolò Molin reports to the Venetian Senate also on 16 February:

> The Duke of Lennox, who was sent as Ambassador to France, writes to say that he has not been treated as becomes the representative of so great a Sovereign. He went to audience, and found the King in a chamber with four Princes of the blood on his right and many nobles . . . on his left; after saying a few words he covered, as usual, and he complains that instantly all the others did the same. This is interpreted here as an affront to the Ambassador.[16]

Molin adds: 'This act and the late quarrel with the French Ambassador at this Court adds to the friction between the two Crowns'. Apparently, Cecil's early assessment about success was premature or incomplete. No one said that diplomacy would be easy; potential slights, imagined or real, often impede progress. Lennox was not immune to such behaviour.

After accompanying Princess Elizabeth from England to Germany in 1613 and taking leave of her, Lennox moved on to France, at the king's instructions. James wanted him to pursue the marriage negotiations for Charles to marry Princess Christine, the six-year-old second sister of Louis XIII. Lennox arrived in early July but the marriage question had been discussed for several months before then. Indeed, the whole issue has a rather macabre edge, because Thomas Edmondes, ambassador to France, had engaged the French court on the question of marriage, first for Prince Henry, whose death obviously ended that angle. King James wrote Edmondes on 14 December 1612 about the matter. First, James chides the ambassador for thinking to thus pursue the princess for Charles: 'For it had been a very blunt thing in us that you, our minister, should so soon after such an irreparable loss received by us have begun to talk of marriage, the most contrary thing that could be to death and funerals'.[17] James writes with consideration. But that is not the whole story; for he moves quickly to suggest that the French will probably bring up the matter anyway, 'therefore that you should entertain the motion and that with so much the greater hope that that great and irremediable inequality of years is now taken away', that is, Charles is closer to Christine's age than Henry was. James also urges Edmondes 'to behave yourself in harkening to this their motion as they may neither apprehend that we are becoming greedy in urging it, nor yet upon the other side to give them any sense of distaste upon apprehension of our slowness and averseness in it'. At least by the time Lennox got to France, this issue had been percolating for some time and the somewhat unseemly haste had cooled. After all, the youth of Charles and Christine assured that no marriage was imminent.

Lennox readily embraced the challenge. Zorzi Giustinian, the Venetian ambassador, located in France, on 10 July reports Lennox's arrival and purpose. Lennox should 'assure Her Majesty of his master's cordial friendship. These words he expressed in his first audience. After this he has commission to approach the queen and government upon the question, already broached of the marriage between their prince and the second princess'.[18] James has apparently instructed Lennox 'to proceed cautiously' (13:5). The ambassador thinks that 'the feeling here is favourable, as age and interests are in harmony and it is hoped that such an alliance will quiet the minds of many, especially the Huguenots'. Such an arrangement would also help balance matters with Spain. Lennox has something else also in mind while in France:

> The Duke of Lennox intends to request for himself the company of men at arms which the kings of France have in their pay by ancient conventions. The prince of England will renounce it and Lennox has good reason to hope for success as he is the principal subject of that kingdom. (13:5)

Somewhat later in July Giustinian reports that 'The duke of Lennox, at his first audience with the queen, touched upon the proposed marriage and he afterwards saw Villeroi [Seigneur de Villeroy] and did the like' (13:14). Getting a favourable response, Lennox 'sent immediately to England, and he expects to receive instructions to set the matter on foot'. But Lennox did not yet have the actual commission and his cautionary approach has raised suspicions about the seriousness of James in the marriage arrangement. The French fear that the Spanish will somehow do them in on this matter: they 'will leave no stone unturned to prevent it'. By 6 August Lennox's emissary back to England has returned; he 'brings news that the king is very gratified by the favourable reception given to the duke's proposals, and that he directs the duke to give assurances that they will find him ready to carry the matter to a successful issue' (13:18). James has no objection to the princess following her Catholic faith in England and he thinks that the dowry will not be a problem, the Venetian ambassador observes. There may, however, be opposition in England by 'the partisans of Spain', who will not offer overt opposition but will seek to divert the effort 'under divers pretexts' (13:19). The 'tender' age of the princess continues to cause some concern for James, who would prefer an older wife for Charles. 'This line of argument,' the Ambassador notes, 'favours the infanta of Savoy.' Such awareness prompts Lennox to return immediately to England in order to calm James's hesitation. Antonio Foscarini, Venetian ambassador in England, correctly concludes that Lennox is 'moved by his natural inclinations towards France and by his own interests' (13:23). Ultimately, the whole French marriage prospect collapsed despite Lennox's efforts. He did, however, succeed in getting command of the Scottish Guard, although the queen 'excuses herself for the time on account of the scarcity of money. But this matter will be easily arranged when the question of marriage is settled,' reports Giustinian (13:19).

Lennox thus travelled to France several times on missions for the king, but he also entertained ambassadors, especially the French one, with feasts in London. John Finet, one of Cecil's secretaries, assisted Sir Lewes Lewknor, the Master of Ceremonies, in dealing with ambassadors; and he offers a vivid account of their comings and goings and especially their squabbles in his *Finetti Philoxenis*. Finet would himself in 1627 become Master of Ceremonies. Other accounts, such as Chamberlain's letters, offer details of the entertainments and feasts. For example, Chamberlain writes to Dudley Carleton on 22 February 1617 about feasts for the French ambassador, De la Tour: 'The French ambassador and his companie were feasted at Whitehall on Sonday, and yesterday at Tiballs, and last night had a great supper at the Lord Mayors'.[19] Chamberlain adds: 'The Duke of Lennox feasted him before the King, and this night he is solemnly invited by the Lord Haye [James Hay] to the wardrobe to a supper and a maske', which was Ben Jonson's *Lovers Made Men*. Plays and masques at court or at aristocratic houses often include some kind of feast.

Such is the case on 20 May 1619 at Whitehall. The court gathered to enjoy a feast in honour of the French ambassador, Trémoille. Information about this occasion derives from a remarkable letter from Gerrard Herbert to Dudley Carleton, dated 24 May. This entertainment and feast occurred just a week after Queen Anne's funeral, before a rather small gathering at court. King James was probably not present, as he had been dealing with his own illness. Herbert covers several topics, but he focuses primarily on the occasion. Herbert writes: 'The Marquise Trenell [Trémoille] on thursday last tooke leaue of the Kinge: that night was feasted at white hall by the Duke of Lenox in the Queenes greate chamber: where many great Lordes weare to keepe them Company but no ladyes. the Sauoy Imbassadour was also there'.[20] Herbert enumerates the lords present 'all mixed wth the french alonge the table: the Marquise Trenell sitting alone at the tables ende'. Herbert describes the meal: 'The supper was greate & the banquett curious, serued in 24 great Chynay [chinaware] worcke platters or voyders [trays], full of glasse scales or bowles of sweete meates'. After the meal, the attendees listened to music, which included 'French singinge' and harp and lute songs. They also enjoyed a performance of Shakespeare's *Pericles* (more on that below). Chamberlain comments on this occasion in a letter of 31 May: 'The Marquis of Trinell went hence in Whitson-weeke, after he had ben feasted by the earle of Dorset, and the Duke of Lennox that made him a supper at Whitehall of 400li, which wold have cost another the double, but that he is Lord Steward' (2:240). Chamberlain counters this some-what caddy remark about Lennox a bit later in this letter when he refers to Lennox's going to the Lord Mayor, Sebastian Harvey, to 'comfort him' in his deathly illness (241).

Chamberlain reports to Carleton on 1 January 1620:

the French familiarities growes more in request: so that the French ambassa-dor [Count de Tilliers] made a feast on Thursday last at noone to the Duke of Lennox, Marquis Buckingham, Marques Hamilton and some few other courtiers, who have a meaning [intention] on Monday next to requite his curtesie with a maske. (2:279)

Things did not go quite so well the following 3 January 1621, accord-ing to an account from Finet. He reports that Lennox 'nobly enter-tained the Ambassador at Hampton Court with hawking and hunting; and on Wednesday the third, he was invited to dine with the King at Westminster'.[21] For some reason the French party encountered delays, leading to much impatience and chaos: 'They so filled the roome [in Parliament], disorderly stuffed before with an intruding multitude, as no officer was able freely to discharge his service till the King sat down to meate'. Finet adds: 'The French Noblemen of the best quality were conducted by the Duke of Lenox, and the rest by myself, to the Court of Requests'. They took their places 'promiscuously at the table, and the Duke leaving them (perhaps somewhat abruptly) before he had seen five or six of the principall set down at the upper end'. This unexpected action by Lennox prompted the French to begin 'whisperingly to mur-mure amongst themselves', believing themselves to have been neglected. Other noblemen entered and seemed also to ignore the French, who 'took their cloaks, and with shews of much discontent, departed the roome to their coaches' (633). Finet spent the next day trying to mollify the French party, who complained that they had been 'left alone by the

Duke of Lenox without any person of sort to accompany them at their sitting down to meate'. Persons of sufficient rank and stature had not joined them at their table. The ambassadorial corps in London regularly demonstrated their hair-trigger reaction to slights, real or imagined. Perhaps Lennox had simply grown tired of them; in all likelihood he had not intended purposeful disregard for the French. By the following January, calm had returned, noted by Finet: 'The French Ambassador and the Venetian supped that night with the Duke of Lennox, and entred the roome with the King. They were both seated there on his left-hand' (Nichols, 4:784). Lennox apparently stayed put this time.

During the time of the negotiations of the Spanish Match James welcomed a new Spanish ambassador to the court and provided an elaborate feast for him and his group on 20 July 1623. This took place in the new Banqueting House, which included a 'table of about eight yards long, unto which was served his Majesitie's and the Ambassador's viands, by the Pensioners, and huishered up by the Duke of Richmond [Lennox] (being Lord Steward of the King's Howse,) the Treasurer of the Howshold, and Controller' (Nichols 4:883). (The latter two possibly present to keep a bootless eye on expenses.) The ambassador and others sat in appropriate places relatively near the king, who 'dranke two healthes, the one to the King of Spaine, the other to the good successe of theise affayres [marriage negotiations]'. The Bishop of London gave thanks and Lennox and others carried the necessary implements for the meal to the king. During these festivities James entered the room, leaning on Lennox, a clear sign of his reliance on his cousin. Feasting and entertainment became hallmarks of a prosperous and welcoming court and James generally stinted no expense in order to impress the ambassadors. Such activities helped diplomatic business succeed. Lennox knew his part to play in these events.

POLITICS, POSITIONS AND TITLES

Diplomat, host, advisor, go-between, Lennox also acquired additional positions, some political and almost all with some favourable economic possibilities. James had, as noted, from their arrival in England placed Lennox on the Privy Council, made him head of the Gentlemen of the Bedchamber and bestowed on him the Order of the Garter. With letters patent issued on 16 September 1605 James granted Lennox the office of Alnager, inspector of woollen cloth. The king's proclamation states several times and in different ways: 'Now know yee that Wee of our speciall grace certaine knowledge and meere motion haue Created, ordained Constituted and appointed and by these presents for vs our Heires and Successorts, create, ordaine, constitute and appoint the said *Lodowicke* Duke of *Lenox* our Alnager'.[22] James enumerates a long list of all the imaginable manifestations of wool. The king grants this office and privilege to Lennox for twenty-one years; he will collect all the subsidies and fees due, by him or his deputies. James further asserts: 'the said *Lodowicke* Duke of Lenox, shall be reputed, named, taken and called Alnager, Sealer, Searcher and viewer of the said new Draperies, and woollen commodities and Stuffes' (p. 4).

The office of Alnager dates from the late twelfth century in an attempt to measure, regulate and standardise the woollen trade. Lennox wrote Cecil in 1605 acknowledging this new office: 'The letter of the Council to Mr. Attorney for drawing a proclamation touching the alnage of the new draperies, granted by letters patent to me, have taken no effect'.[23] Lennox asks Cecil to draw up a new document that will better enable his deputies to execute the office. Obviously, the duke will not himself be sitting around in some cluttered room measuring woollen cloth; he will delegate such functions, but he will see to it that the fees and duties are promptly collected and thereby enrich his own circumstances.

That may be one of the reasons that Lennox seems to have taken this office seriously. He often served to negotiate conflicts between the City of London and the Privy Council. The Council, for example, sent a letter to the Lord Mayor on 20 July 1612 about a complaint that 'had been made to them by John May, servant to the Duke of Lennox', who has been thwarted in his effort to establish a market in Leadenhall for 'strained cloths' and other 'stuff of the new drapery'.[24] The Council, doubtless at Lennox's urging, instructed the mayor to investigate and resolve the controversy. A different issue prompts the Lord Mayor to forward a petition in early January 1613 from the City's merchants, 'complaining of the conduct of the Deputy Alnagers, who entered their shops and demanded extraordinary duties and payments, not warranted' (*Remembrancia*, 73). The merchants lodged a similar complaint on 20 July 1614. The deputies seem to have exercised considerable, perhaps unfair, zeal in collecting fees. The petition adds that

> the City were for a long time farmers [one who collects revenues] of the alnage, view, and search of all cloth within the City and Liberties, when all things were well and peaceably carried; that the Duke of Lenox, the present farmer, would willingly pass it over to the city and prays them to contract with him accordingly. (73)

Thomas Middleton, the mayor, 'was intreated by the Court [of Aldermen] to confer and treat with the Duke of Lenox for a lease of the Alnage to be granted to the City' (74).

Lennox apparently complied to some extent, although another petition on this subject from the mayor to the duke appears on 29 April 1620. London's merchants took upon themselves in May 1621 to appeal to the House of Commons, as documented in a letter from Lennox to the mayor and aldermen. This letter notes that the merchants allege 'that a subsidy and fees for sealing of fustians had been demanded, by virtue of his Patent of the new draperies, and charging the Deputy Alnagers with divers abuses' (*Remembrancia*, 75). The duke insists that 'When he granted a lease to the City of the subsidy and alnage of the old and new draperies . . . he granted it only in as ample a manner as the King had granted it to him, and they had covenanted that the Deputy Alnagers, by them nominated to him, should execute the office lawfully' (75). Apparently the City's own appointed Deputy Alnagers have not behaved much better than the previous ones. Thus, Lennox 'prayed them forthwith to call the Petitioners and the Deputy Alnagers for London before them, and give such satisfaction to the Complainants as should appear just'. Lennox here exercises good judgement and a savvy understanding of the conflicts; he also cannot resist observing that the City's deputies have failed the merchants.

From Whitehall on 4 December 1621 Lennox again wrote to the Lord Mayor about another complaint and petition 'presented to him by the Clothiers of Suffolk, complaining of the re-search of their cloths at Leadenhall, and of seizures made contrary to law' (*Remembrancia*, 76). Lennox therefore 'requested the Lord Mayor to direct that the Order of the council for tolerated cloths might be hung up in Leadenhall, and that the City's Deputies should not intermeddle with such tolerated cloths previously searched in the country'. These documents provide superb evidence of Lennox as an officer charged with an explicit task, one that he took, perhaps surprisingly, rather seriously, often with hands-on attention. Of course, this focus on the job cannot have derived completely from his interest in woollen cloth.

Indeed, Lennox had higher ambitions beyond Alnager: he especially desired an appropriate English title to add to his collection. But he had to wait until 1613 to get one. Surely, he and King James must have had more than a few conversations about this. Of course, Lennox had to be careful not to press the king too hard on the issue. Lennox's frustration bubbles up as captured in a letter from Chamberlain to Dudley Carleton on 29 April 1613 in which Chamberlain writes: 'The Duke of Lennox is gon over with the Lady Elizabeth somewhat malcontent that he could not prevayle in a purpose he had to be made Duke of Richmond, and so an English peere of parlement' (1:444). Even Thomas Howard, Earl of Suffolk, attempted to help Lennox's cause by rounding up some nobles to support the idea. But he also encountered opposition from Arundel, the Earl of Worcester and even his son-in-law William Cecil, who observed: 'that he [Lennox] was one of the youngest of the nobilitie both in yeares and creation and therfore wold see the auncient nobilitie before him' (1:444). In other words, a question of right and precedence. The Lord Chancellor, Thomas Egerton, Lord Ellesmere, decided that the pursuit of this should be abandoned. In another letter, dated 6 May, Chamberlain makes this same point (1:449). This whole matter must have rankled in Lennox's consciousness as he went about obeying the king's orders to accompany Princess Elizabeth to Germany and then to stop in France for marriage negotiations on behalf of Prince Charles.

By the time that Lennox had returned to England the matter of his title began to percolate again. On 15 August 1613, Viscount Fenton wrote to Mar to tell him that Lennox had returned but had been in some kind of conflict with Somerset, what Fenton calls 'sume discontentment betuyx Lenoxx and Rotchester'.[25] The two were 'almost past speking kyndnes'. Fortunately, James Hay intervened and prevented further discontent. Fenton reports: 'I think my Lord of Lenoxx shall have his besines exped betuyx this and Mychellmes, quhitche is to be Erll of Ritchemond heir in England. I think that was the caws of the quarrel'. Nothing like envy on the part of competing noblemen, each seeking to maintain and enrich his status. James made his move by appointing Somerset as Lord Treasurer of Scotland and then offering Lennox the title of Earl of Richmond on 6 October 1613. Chamberlain reports that 'The Duke of Lennox hath his patent to be earle of Richmond and an English peere, at which doore (now yt is open) more are like to enter perhaps shortly' (1:481). Foscarini, the Venetian ambassador, reports on 22 November: on 'Monday the 18th he [James] created him [Carr] baron of Brancepth and earl of Somerset. To the duke of Lennox he has given the title of earl of Richmond, but with the privilege alone and without any ceremony'.[26] Somerset, as noted before, received an elaborate ceremony. In all likelihood, rather than this being a slight to Lennox, it merely recognised that he already had a ducal title. James seems intent on honouring his favourite, Somerset, but not put him ahead of Lennox, his cousin and long-time confidant. At last, Lennox could assume a seat in Parliament, the meetings of which he had attended several times but only as an honoured spectator.

In November 1616 James appointed Lennox as Lord Steward, thus in charge of the arrangements for and management of the royal household. In a letter of 21 December Chamberlain confirms this information, but not without a disparaging word. Chamberlain notes that Thomas Edmondes has just been named Comptroller of the King's Household and comments: 'God geve him joy of the honor when he hath yt for I feare there willbe no great profit to be expected, specially now there is a Lord Steward of the houshold that ingrossess [nothing withheld] all the commoditie' (2:46). Chamberlain records later, on 3 January 1618, that Edward, Lord Wotton, Treasurer of the Household wants to exchange positions with Edmondes; although the king agreed with this idea, Lennox objected. He 'interposes,' Chamberlain writes, 'as yf yt were a derogation to him that any such place shold be bestowed without his approbation, wherin he is seconded and abetted by some, whom the other tooke for his best frends' (2:125). Therein the matter rested, blocked by Lennox who, clearly, does not shy away from jealously claiming prerogatives and using his authority. Chamberlain suggested in 1619, noted above, that for the feast for the French ambassador Lennox got by with a cheap price because of his position as Steward. He could also be helpful, as in the case of two Scots who had quarrelled, leaving one dead on the field. The survivor, Robert Carr (not Somerset), a member of Prince Charles's household, sought pardon from the king, which he was reluctant to grant, as commented on by Chamberlain on 12 February 1620. But the prince intervened with 'humble and earnest intertie (assisted by the Duke of Lennox and Marquis Hamilton)', and the king remitted the offense (2:288).

Lennox gained the final and perhaps greatest prize on 17 May 1623: the title of Duke of Richmond. James had obviously been in no hurry, even though Lennox had sought this designation for some time. The Venetian ambassador, Alvise Valaresso, wrote on 2 June 1623: 'The Duke of Lennox, a duke of Scotland, to keep him the first place in England also has been made Duke of Richmond; his patent is made out to precede that of Buckingham'.[27] The ambassador refers to the dating of the patents, Lennox's being on 17 May and Buckingham's on 18 May, awarded to him while he was in Spain with Charles. James, once again, as he had done with Somerset when elevating him to Earl, made sure that Lennox had the superior position. Perhaps the desire to reward Somerset and then Buckingham prompted James to reward Lennox as well, so as not to slight him. Chamberlain suggests that Buckingham by his own consent 'wold not take place of his father, as he calls him [Lennox]' (2:497–8). He deferred to Lennox. Whatever Buckingham's motives, he shrewdly chose

Figure 4.1 Engraving of King James by Simon van de Passe, 1616, from *The Workes of King James*. Courtesy of the Department of Special Collections, Kenneth Spencer Research Library, University of Kansas.

Figure 4.2   Engraving of Ludovic Stuart, Duke of Lennox, by Simon van de Passe, 1616. Courtesy of the National Portrait Gallery.

a wise move. After forty years of unflagging service to James, Lennox became the only non-royal with a ducal title from Scotland and England. 'They call me Lennox and now Richmond'.

TRIALS

In case Lennox grew weary of inspecting woollen cloth and collecting fees, he had the opportunity to become involved in varying degrees in three trials or legal judgements, beginning in 1615. In that year Sir Ralph

Winwood got word of possible evidence that suggested that Thomas Overbury's death in the Tower in September 1613 was not the result of natural causes; rather, he had probably been poisoned. Such word spread like wildfire through the court and caused great alarm. What had been put out of mind as just bad luck on Overbury's part now had a sinister likelihood. Soon, implications began to flow in the direction of Frances Howard and Somerset. This possibility certainly caused great concern for King James: his favourite stood in danger of having committed a crime. Truth to tell, by this time the king's intense involvement with Somerset had begun to wane. To his credit, James did not decide to protect Somerset; instead, he set up a commission to investigate the story and evidence. Winwood wrote to Isaac Wake in November 1615: 'The King's love of justice led him to have the matter searched, though it might implicate some about him'.[28] James appointed Lennox, Ellesmere, Lord Zouche and Lord Chief Justice Edward Coke to serve on the commission (Coke eventually dropped out). Even by this time, things had moved rather quickly as Richard Weston, Overbury's keeper in the Tower, and Mrs Turner, the Countess's woman, had been executed for their involvement. Somerset had been sent to the Tower.

Somerset besieged James with letters, begging him to get rid of this whole process. But sometime in October 1615 the king wrote to him, beginning: 'I need not to answer your letter since Lennox hath long before this time told you my resolution in that point whereupon you have bestowed so much scribbling and railing covertly against me and avowedly against the Chancellor'.[29] James reminds Somerset that 'In a business of this nature I have nothing to look unto but first my conscience before God, and next my reputation in the eyes of the whole world'. James does try to reassure him that he has only ordered an investigation. Near the end of the letter he writes: 'To conclude then, I never had the occasion to show the uprightness and sincerity that is required in a supreme judge as I have in this. If the delation [accusation] prove false, God so deal with my soul as no man among you shall so much rejoice as it as I' (p. 344). The king will also spare no effort to track down the conspirators, if the charges prove false. James seems to be more than a little pleased with himself in all of this, following his conscience and thereby being a model king. At the same time, he holds out the remote possibility that the commission will find insufficient evidence to proceed to a trial.

In late October, James wrote to the commissioners, underscoring their task to be no less than 'the discovery of the truth' (*Letters*, p. 346). The king offers explicit instructions of how and when they should interview Weston and Mrs Turner. James writes: 'We therefore have thought it convenient to require you that, before Weston shall come to his second arraignment, you examine the Countess of Somerset, and after confront him apart . . . if you shall find it convenient, with the Earl himself'. The commissioners should for the moment hold off on examining the Lieutenant of the Tower, Sir Gervase Helwys, and Sir Thomas Monson, who had arranged for the appointment of Weston. But the commission should 'proceed against them as justice shall require, though they be our servants, as more particularly you shall understand from our cousin the Duke of Lennox, who had received his charge from our own mouth and with whom we have clearly confirmed of all these points' (p. 347). With this statement, James makes Lennox the de facto head of the commission. Their several interviews will lead to a trial.

The examinations of the Earl and Countess and others lingered into spring 1616. The questioning of Somerset encountered some delay, as Bacon, Attorney General and lead prosecutor, reported in a letter to Buckingham dated 13 April. Lennox's illness caused the delay. Bacon writes: 'we stay only upon the Duke of Lenox, who it seemeth is fallen sick and keepeth in, without whom we neither think it warranted by his Majesty's direction, nor agreeable to his intention, that we should proceed'.[30] Bacon clearly understands Lennox's importance in this whole process; thus, he asks Buckingham to confer with the king about the duke's health. Bacon also notes that they have agreed to a re-examination of the countess and that they have generally concluded they have found enough evidence to convict Somerset (5:267).

Thus, the examination of Somerset took place in the Tower on 18 April. Bacon reports: 'Yesterday my Lord Chancellor, the Duke of Lenox, and myself spent the whole afternoon at the Tower, in examination of Somerset upon the articles sent from his Majesty, and some other additionals' (5:270). They encountered a resistant Somerset: 'He is full of protestations'. But, 'my Lord Chancellor put him in mind of the state he stood in for the imprisonment; but he was little moved with it, and pretended carelessness of life, since ignominy had made him unfit for his Majesty's service' (p. 271). Somerset would maintain this defiant attitude for some time, even into the trial. Chamberlain on 20 April writes about the delays in some of the examinations, wondering if 'these delayes are to some such end' (1:623). He then notes that Coke is no longer part of the examining group and that Lennox, Bacon and Ellesmere have interviewed Somerset, 'not contenting themselves with what the Lord Cooke hath don before, who meddles no more since he delivered his papers and examination to the atturny'.

By mid-May the trial dates had been established and had begun. Chamberlain, writing to Dudley Carleton on 18 May, sets the scene: 'The stage in the midds of Westminster Hall, with numbers of scaffolds round about was finished, and Lords assembled, and all things redy' (2:1). Everything rightly suggests theatre. Spectators readily agreed to pay for seats, as Chamberlain notes:

> which at this time were growne to so extrarordinarie a rate, that fowre or five peeces (as they call them) was an ordinarie price, and I know a lawier that had agreed to geve ten pound for himself and his wife for the two dayes, and fiftie pound was geven for a corner that could hardly contained a dousen.

It would be a great show, as Bacon's extensive commentary about the trial makes clear.[31] Why would one not want to see the spectacle of the king's favourite and wife on trial for murder – too good to pass up. Chamberlain has heard that Somerset has begun to relent, and 'he desired to have the Duke of Lennox sent to him, and the Lords Commissions have ben with him once or twise since' (2:1). Presumably Somerset wants Lennox because of his impeccable standing with King James; exactly what he expected Lennox to do remains unclear.

The countess made the process easy because at her trial on 24 May she pleaded guilty to the crime of plotting Overbury's death. The next day, after hours of debate and a rambling, sometimes incoherent defence by Somerset, he was found guilty as well. William Trumbull's papers contain several items about the trial and they place Lennox in the middle of the proceedings. One document indicates that during the trial 'My Lord Steward [Ellesmere] went out of the Court to ease himself and in the meane time the Earle dranke wine and did eate a litle sucketts [sweets] sent unto him by the E. or Rutland'.[32] When the Steward returned, 'after an oyez made for silence, Sir Randall Crewe spake a great while and urged much the pardon that the E. of Somerset would have procured of the King'. Another item reports that 'the Lord Steward exhorted him [Somerset] rather to confesse and submitt himself, which he refused to do, then the Lord Steward caused pen, incke, and paper to be given unto him that he might take notes to help his remembrance' (Trumbull, 5:518). Ralph Winwood, writing to Trumbull in late May, reports that 'with the unanime consent of all the peeres hee [Somerset] was found accessorie to the murder before the fact, and accordinglie received from the mouth of the Lord Steward the sentence of death which his wief had had the day before' (Trumbull, 5:515). Lennox, who had interviewed Somerset as part of the king's commission, took an active part in this

trial, and could appreciate the irony of offering ink and paper so that
Somerset might enhance his memory.

Chamberlain writes on 8 June confirming the results of the trial, that
when he wrote last he had

> left the earle of Somerset pleading for his life; but that he saide for himself
> was so litle that he was found guilty by all his peeres: which did so litle appall
> him that when he was asked what he could say why sentence shold not be
> pronounced, he stoode still upon his innocence. (2:6)

Somerset curiously asked that instead of a judgement of death by hanging he should be beheaded. Yet, 'he stands firme in denial; though by all
circumstances and most pregnant, (yea almost infallible) probabilities he
be more faulty and fowle then any of the companie'. King James com-
muted the sentences of death; instead, he sent the couple to the Tower
where they would remain until January 1622, when the king offered a
pardon. Even though Somerset found time and money to redecorate his
quarters in the Tower, he had to endure the added punishment of occupying the space with his embittered and obviously criminal wife. Perhaps
Somerset knew and recalled the haunting and appropriate lines from
Shakespeare's Sonnet 25:

> Great princes' favourites their fair leaves spread
> But as the marigold at the sun's eye,
> And in themselves their pride lies buried,
> For at a frown they in their glory die. (lines 5–8)

The king and court have frowned and Somerset's glory has died.
Small wonder that Lennox and others were eager to move past this fasci-
nating but disturbing event and look forward to the investiture of Prince
Charles as Prince of Wales a few weeks later.

Somerset's fall marks a beginning of the fall of the House of Howard.
In 1619, his father-in-law Thomas Howard, Earl of Suffolk and Lord
Treasurer will be found guilty in a Star Chamber trial. Not murder this
time, but rather financial corruption on an impressive scale. Lennox
plays a role in the proceedings. James had made Suffolk Treasurer in
July 1614, as the king regularly proclaimed his intention of reform-
ing court finances. Practice never matched expectations. Thus, being
Treasurer under James would always be a fraught position. Further, the
Howards ran afoul of Buckingham, whom they detested, mainly because
he siphoned power away from their clan. Buckingham thus remained
eager to find ways to do them in. Finding some problem or corruption
would never be a particularly difficult matter, and he made sure that

James learned of abuses in the Treasurer's office, including the machinations of Suffolk's wife.

Chamberlain's reports track much of the procedures. As early as 14 May 1619 Chamberlain writes to his friend Dudley Carleton about Suffolk's predicament: 'The earle of Suffolkes cause and his Ladies was called upon this terme in the Star-chamber, and though to win time (as shold seeme) they pleaded that they had divers witnesses to be examined for theire clerring' (2:238). The king 'will have the matter protracted no longer'. But Chamberlain reports later in May that the trial has been delayed until Michaelmas term, in part because the earl and his countess have claimed ill health. Further complication gets noticed in Chamberlain's letter of 15 July: 'At the Kings being here on Thursday yt was expected that the Lord of Suffolkes acknowledgement and submission [confession] shold have ben accepted at the counsaile table, and so the sute in the Star Chamber to cease' (2:251). But Suffolk's verbal confession was deemed unacceptable, given his earlier insistence on innocence. So, the case will go forward. James stripped Suffolk of his position of Lord Treasurer on 19 July. When Michaelmas term began Chamberlain reported to Carleton on 30 October: 'The earle of Suffolkes cause is now handling in the Star-chamber, beeing drawne out at such length that yt hath lasted five dayes there already' (2:269). Suffolk and his wife have, Chamberlain writes, 'misemployed' the king's treasure in many ways, 'with abuse in the payments of Ireland, and finally with many extortions, concussions, and fowle corruptions in all that passed thorough theyre hands'. James had hoped that the case would have finished by now, but prosecutors, among them Francis Bacon, have found it too difficult. The trial in fact lasted eleven days and, on 13 November, the earl and his wife were found guilty on all counts. The court fined them £30,000 and sentenced them to be imprisoned.

Sir John Finet reported on 14 November the discussion and comments made by various lords during the trial. The Lord Chamberlain, William Herbert, for example, 'used few words but weighty, saying every particular point had been so well spoken by the rest of my Lords his repetition would be needless'.[33] The Marquis Hamilton agreed also with the case laid out by Lord Henry Hobart, Chief Justice of the Common Pleas, who argued against the fine supported by Edward Coke. Lennox spoke at some length, reporting

what a good servant the Earl had been in times past to his Majesty, and by comparison of those that inquiring after the heavens and astrology so long fall to consult with spirits and prove conjurors, he said my Lord might by the temptation of his place be brought from one infirmity to another, till he were at length plunged in this mischief and merit of punishment. (Salisbury, 22:112)

Lennox seems to be offering a kind of rationalisation for Suffolk's behaviour. But he finally agrees to the punishment and wishes for the king to receive even more money; thus, Lennox argues, 'his fine should be with Lord Cooke 100,000'. The court came in at a lower figure. Lennox's argument seems to be a mixture of a sympathetic understanding of how one might fall into such behaviour; nevertheless, the man is guilty and should be punished. By this moment in 1619 Lennox has had considerable experience in such legal procedures in high-level cases. James sent the couple to the Tower but only for ten days.

Bacon, who had figured prominently in the prosecution of the Somerset and Suffolk cases, found himself on the other side of the fence in 1621. Bacon had become Attorney General in 1613, thanks to the support of Somerset, and the Lord Chancellor in 1618. But in 1620 charges began to be made about the abuse of patents and monopolies, which pointed in Bacon's direction. Further, he was accused of improperly accepting gifts and taking bribes. For this Bacon stood trial in Parliament. Lennox actively participated. Bacon pleaded guilty and the court impeached him, fined him £40,000 and imprisoned him, which lasted but three days. Bacon had now ruined a distinguished career. He had to suffer further embarrassment of having to return the Great Seal in late April 1621. A commission of four lords, Lennox, the Lord Treasurer Viscount Mandeville, the Earl of Arundel and William Herbert, Lord Chamberlain, went to York House to confront him. They were sympathetic; but Bacon responded: 'No my Lords, the occasion is good. It was the King's favour that gave me this, and it is my fault'.[34] With that, Bacon handed over the Great Seal.

Other legal matters impinged on Lennox. For example, Sir Henry Yelverton, in late October 1620, appeared before the Star Chamber accused of introducing clauses not in the king's warrant in a new charter for the City of London. Yelverton chose to speak, as Chamberlain reports: 'he made a very submissive acknowledgement of his errors with teares, imploring the Kings mercie and desiring the cause might be deferred for that time' (2:323). Several opposed; but others accepted his plea, including Sir Fulke Greville, William Herbert, 'and most of all by the Duke of Lennox (who came but overnight from the King) that yt prevailed; wherby his frends hope that he hath as yt were escaped shipwracke' (2:324). Chamberlain continues: 'he is well frended in the bed-chamber, and that his fault is rather a peccadillo of indiscretion or oversight, then any great crime or malicious practice'. Lennox sits on the side of leniency. He was a little less generous in the case of Sir Francis Michell, who appeared before the King's Bench in June 1621. Here, according to Chamberlain, sat Lennox, Buckingham and Arundel 'as commissioners of the marshalls court' (2:383). The commission agreed to carry out the sentence levied by Parliament: Michell to be 'degraded from the order of knighthood'. The ceremony proceeded 'by the breaking of his sword over his head, and throwing the pieces severall ways, as likewise his spurres, and pronouncing him to be no more Sir Fraunces Michell knight, but a person infamous and a knave' (2:383). Exactly which part Lennox played in this punishment the record does not indicate. Certainly it has a dramatic flair beyond merely receiving the Great Seal.

Various other commissions required Lennox's participation, such as the one in 1623. Chamberlain writes: 'The selected commissioners for forain affaires sit much' (2:527). Presumably this group focused on the Spanish questions of that year, given the date of the letter, 21 November. Chamberlain enumerates the members of this group: the Lord Treasurer, Lionel Cranfield; William Herbert, Arundel, 'the two Dukes' (Lennox and Buckingham); Lord of Carlisle and a few others. Chamberlain concludes: 'God send them still to give a just and true verdict' (2:528). A month earlier Prince Charles and Buckingham had safely returned from Spain without the Infanta; now, the court struggled with a final decision about this proposed 'Spanish Match'. Sometimes Lennox simply had to intervene between quarrelling lords, such as in September 1622. Chamberlain reports: 'I heare of some rough and rude unkindness that passed twixt Lord Lisle [Robert Sidney] and the Lord of Doncaster [James Hay] at Sion, but the matter was presently taken up by the Duke, Lord Marquis of Buckingham, and the Lord of Northumberland, and they reconciled in shew' (2:451–2). Perhaps more personal than political, nevertheless Lennox and others served conveniently as arbiters.

Sometimes reports capture Lennox's voice in the midst of deliberations about or in Parliament. Such can be found in an account found in Francis Bacon's materials. King James had gathered the Privy Council on 24 September 1615 to determine if he could resolve matters of subsistence without a Parliament; if not, what preparations could be made for such a Parliament. After several meetings the Council agreed that a Parliament was necessary to confront financial issues. In turn, various lords spoke, including Lennox, who comes across as modest and agreeable in this case. 'The Duke's speech tended to this that he would not take upon him to interpose his own judgment in things of so great moment as these which were now in consultation; but rather rely upon the opinions of others more experienced in the affairs of this country than he'.[35] Lennox 'approved the ways of preparation which were proposed before. He concurred specially with those who had moved the disparking of some forest and chases'. But on the issue of a Parliament in Scotland, Lennox 'answered the same had been already done, and money given towards the payment of the King's debts'. Lennox might defer to the judgement of others on English matters, but on Scotland he had a special perspective and knowledge. As one who has been a member of Parliament only since late 1613, Lennox seems to be deferential to his fellow lords, considerate and shrewd, but capable of speaking his voice on pertinent issues.

Lennox also stood in the gap between aggrieved parties, seeking to bring about desired outcomes by using his political and personal influence. One such case appears in Holles, former Comptroller of Prince Henry's household, who had commiserated with Lennox after Henry's death. He found in Lennox a sympathetic respondent. Thus, when Holles got in trouble, to the point of being imprisoned, because of his support of Somerset, a patron, during the hearings, especially about Richard Weston, he turned to Lennox for help. Numerous letters followed, written from various prisons, in late 1615. The matter of Holles cuts across political and personal concerns. He had been angling for a court position for some time after the prince's death, but ran into resistance, led by Sir Edward Coke. From the Marshalsea prison Holles wrote to Lennox on 9 November, having been given the privilege of conversing with friends. He turns first to Lennox, hoping 'your Lordship will voutsafe me the accustomed place in your favour, and good opinion'.[36] Holles finds himself in the 'naturall condition of loe bottoms', and thus turns to Lennox (87). Holles hopes: 'My humble desire is your Grace divert this blow'. He cannot understand why his service to the king has not prevented his imprisonment and he honours Lennox's position. He congratulates 'the addition of honor and trust, which at the last the King hath layd upon yow; witnessing thereby to the world his acceptance of your person and meritt, wherunto I wishe all cumfort and happiness' (87). Just a few days later, and now in Fleet prison, Holles again writes to Lennox, hoping that he, 'fortified with the goodnes of my cause, and your owne knowledge of my person, will stand in the gapp betwixt me and them [his enemies] and indevor to dissipate these cloudes' (88). Holles enumerates his enemies, claiming, 'I have run over these particulars for your Graces memory, of which yow may use what yow shall fynd most proper to wourk the King to a gratious consideration of me' (88–9).

In a similar vein, Holles writes on 6 January 1616 again from the Fleet, apologising first for troubling Lennox 'with my desires, this festivall season' (100). He informs Lennox that 'I have heer enclosed my letter to his Majesty, which I beseeche your Lordship voutsafe to deliver for me' (101). Holles closes: 'with my self I lay downe before your Lordships noble consideration, and shall howsoever remain your Graces affectionate to serve yow' (101). This series of letters culminates in one of 17 July 1616, which finds Holles at long last free of prison. He apologises to Lennox for not getting to see him in Whitehall recently because Lennox had left town. Holles's mission: 'my errand was to kiss your hands at my waygate, and to bequeath to your honorable love the remembrance of my well known desires' (134). 'I am the same man to yow in devotion and service', as Holles acknowledges that words cannot fully repay his gratitude to Lennox for 'what yow have resolved'. Holles continues to write to Lennox, even while the duke was in Scotland in July 1617, again seeking his help in yet another controversy.

Indispensable, knowledgeable and even sometimes helpful may describe Lennox's relationship to politics in the Jacobean court, this man who, according to the Venetian ambassador, was 'deepest in the King's confidence'. He ranged from the Privy Council, the Bedchamber, being the king's Alnager and Lord High Steward, member of Parliament, one on whom the king leaned, metaphorically and occasionally literally. Lennox complains in a personal letter to Doncaster, James Hay, written on 3 January 1622, that he does not have complete information about Doncaster's whereabouts: 'so that a man may bee a courtier and not know perfectly the passages of all things'.[37] True, but Lennox comes as close as anyone to being the perfect courtier, knowing the passages of most crucial things and persons, standing, as he does, 'nearest to the Crown'.

ARTS: PATRON AND PERFORMER

Thinking back over the ten years since he and the king had arrived in England, Lennox could marvel at the extravagance and quantity of dramatic performances at court, such as the exceptional number beginning in the Christmas season 1612 and stretching through much of February 1613. What had brought about the court's connection to professional adult acting companies, starting in 1603? Scotland did not have well-established acting companies; indeed, Lennox had lamented the relative lack of art in Scotland. And he remembered the extraordinary action of King James on 19 May 1603, just weeks after their arrival in London, by which the king took the major adult acting companies under royal patronage. William Shakespeare's company, the Lord Chamberlain's Men, would henceforth be known as the King's Men, servants of the royal household. As such, they lined the route for James's official royal entry into London on 15 March 1604, an exceptional civic pageant, as noted earlier. They performed regularly at court and enjoyed the king's patronage. Lennox would have been among the spectators at court, revelling in the excitement and pleasure of such performances, for example, eight of Shakespeare's plays in early 1613.

On 19 May 1603, the king issued a patent to the King's Men and alerted all office-holders throughout the kingdom, announcing his action:

> Wee of our speciall grace certeine knowledge & mere motion have licensed and authorized and by theise presentes doe license and aucthorize these our Servauntes [here follows a list of the actors, including Shakespeare] . . . and the rest of their Associates freely to use and exercise the Arte and faculty of playinge Comedies Tragedies histories Enterludes morralls pastorals Stageplaies, and Suche others like as theie have already studied or hereafter shall use or studie aswell for the recreation of our lovinge Subjectes, as for our Solace and pleasure when wee shall thincke good to see them duringe our pleasure.[38]

This singular and unexpected action provided the actors unusual protection and patronage and assured their preferred position for court performances. Nothing in James's background quite anticipates this action, although Scotland enjoyed some dramatic performances, including visiting English players.[39] Certainly the king might have seen this move as an expression of royal power, whatever else motivated him. Beyond self-interest, the king solidified the status of the King's Men and protected them against attack. These actors could move about the country secure in the king's support, 'authorised' by him and the royal patent; they provide 'recreation' for the country's citizens. But they also noticeably offer something quite different: what James refers to as 'Solace and pleasure'. Clearly solace must have been one of the primary effects, for example, of the dramas presented at court in 1612–13.

Although King James brought London's adult acting companies under royal patronage in 1603, other companies, nevertheless, continued to exist under the patronage of noblemen, including Lennox. About his troupe relatively little information survives. No records exist of performances by them in London; instead, they seem to have been a travelling company of actors. An early record of the Duke of Lennox's Men can be found in the Dulwich Manuscripts that relate to Henslowe's *Diary*, an entry dating from 13 October 1604. In this warrant, Lennox addresses mayors, justices of the peace and others 'on behalf of his company of players, who had apparently been forbidden to act'.[40] Another item in this collection 'is a bond from Francis Henslowe to Philip Henslowe in £60 to observe certain articles of agreement between Francis, John Garland and Abraham Saverie, "his ffelowes, servantes to the most noble Prince the duke of Lennox", dated 16 March 1605' (Henslowe, 298). From this at least some of the actors' names appear. As Chambers notes, both Garland and Henslowe had been Queen Elizabeth's men and 'it is possible that when these men were left stranded by her death in 1603, they found a new patron in Lennox'.[41]

The *Records of Early English Drama* reveal some of the places where the Duke of Lennox's Men performed: Canterbury (two weeks in April 1604), earning 13s 4d; Norwich Common Hall (8 April 1604); Barnstaple, Devon, Guildhall (September 1604–September 1605); St Mary's Guildhall, Coventry (November 1604–October 1605); St Mary's, Coventry again (November 1607–October 1608); Bath, Somerset, Guildhall (May 1609–September 1609). A final entry appears for a performance in Folkestone, Kent, Town Hall (September 1617–September 1618), earning 1s.[42] (Lennox also had a company of trumpeters, who may have on occasion accompanied the players.) These entries tantalise because so much remains unrecorded and therefore unknown. The last one in Folkestone is puzzling because it comes so late and with payment of a measly one shilling. Unfortunately, these fragmentary records say nothing about what this company may have performed – the kinds of plays, let alone titles. For at least ten years and possibly longer, however, these players owed their protection and support to Lennox.

Lennox also provided protection to dramatists, as in the case of George Chapman. The duke had intervened to help prevent Chapman's arrest for his play *The Conspiracy and Tragedy of Byron*, performed in 1608. The play had stirred the antipathy and anger of the French ambassador who convinced Cecil to issue a warrant for Chapman's arrest. A letter survives from Chapman in which he thanks Lennox for the 'Shelter' he has been accorded during the 'Austeritie of the offended time'.[43] Chapman may literally mean 'Shelter', such as Esmé Stuart provided Ben Jonson for an extended period of time. In the following year (1609) Chapman offered praise for Lennox in a dedicatory sonnet (in Shakespearean form) to his translation of *The Iliad*. A series of such sonnets follows Book 12, but one directed to Lennox occupies the first place. The heading is: 'To the right Gracious and worthy, the Duke of LENNOX, &c'.[44] Chapman begins: 'Amongst th' Heroes of the Worlds prime yeers, / Stand here,

great Duke, and see them shine about you'. The poet concludes: 'To
this soule, then, your gracious count'nance give; / That gave, to such as
you, such meanes to live'. Like the heroes of the past, Lennox will 'live
ever'. Chapman's case provides explicit evidence of how patronage of
dramatists worked sometimes and it underscores Lennox's interest in the
theatrical world.[45]

Not only did Lennox serve as sponsor of an acting company and offer
protection to dramatists, he also participated actively in dramatic performances at court, especially court masques, a rarefied form of drama,
consisting of dance, music, elaborate costumes, speeches and action.
Samuel Daniel, writing a lengthy epistle dedicatory (longer than the text
of the masque itself) to the Countess of Bedford in his 1604 masque,
The Vision of the Twelve Goddesses, claims that such entertainments
serve as 'necessary complements requisite for state and greatness'.[46]
The same claim might be made for all courtly entertainments, or those
presented in honour of the royal family.

The first show that Lennox experienced in England was the entertainment at the estate of Sir Robert Spencer at Althorp on 25 June 1603,
as the duke accompanied Anne and Prince Henry on the final stages of
their journey to London. Ben Jonson, the author, had already become a
leading figure among dramatists; a few months later, he would be a principal writer for the royal entry pageant on 15 March 1604, as the royal
family and Lennox processed from the Tower towards Westminster. At
Althorp Jonson created a world of romance, populated with satyrs and
fairies. The satyr greets the royal party, looking at the queen, prince and
duke, and concludes that surely 'they are of heavenly race'.[47] Following
his speech, the fairy queen also welcomes the group. Queen Mab arrives
with fairies who dance and Mab speaks words of welcome to Anne.
But the satyr, who is hiding in a bush, warns the queen about this fairy:
'Trust her not'. So, the contest continues between these two. The character Nobody explicitly refers to the 'Queen, Prince, duke' (409). A song
follows in praise of Anne and the fairies present her with a jewel. In such
an entertainment Anne, the prince and Lennox have been welcomed to
England.

While in Scotland Lennox had helped plan and then participate in
the royal entry pageant that officially welcomed the king and the new
queen to Edinburgh in May 1590. Similarly, in late August 1594, Lennox
functioned actively in all the festivities that surrounded the baptism of
Prince Henry at Stirling Castle. That he showed similar interests once he
came to England cannot be surprising. Indeed, he helped plan the first
Jacobean masque, performed at Hampton Court on New Year's 1604.

Evidence for this derives from Dudley Carleton's letter of 15 January to Chamberlain. Unfortunately, no text of the masque exists, which some have named the *Masque of the Orient Knights*.[48] Carleton refers to Lennox as the '*rector chori*' for the masque. Carleton writes of the various festivities at court, including the observation that on that night the court first saw a 'play of Robin Goodfellow and a mask brought in by a magician of China'.[49] Robin brought in 'certain Indian and China Knights to see the magnificency of this court'. Lennox led the all-male corps of eight masquers, who danced and 'called out' a comparable group of women, beginning with Anne and those of her inner circle. Esmé and the Herbert brothers, William and Philip, also participated. The men wore 'loose robes of crimson satin embroidered with gold and bordered with broad silver laces'. Carleton complains that 'their attire was rich but somewhat too heavy and cumbersome for dancers' (54). Nevertheless, Lennox has invigorated the new court by imagining and creating the first Jacobean court masque, understanding this form as a complement to state. Others, notably Queen Anne, will build on this step. Lennox has shown the way.

A week later, on 8 January, Lennox also danced in the masque arranged by Queen Anne and written by Daniel, *The Vision of the Twelve Goddesses*. These masques, performed in quick succession, confirm Carleton's observation: 'We shall have a merry Christmas at Hampton Court, for both male and female maskers are all ready bespoken: whereof the Duke [of Lennox] is *rector chori* of th' one side and the La: Bedford on the other'.[50] Daniel's masque focuses on the women, the twelve goddesses, performed by Anne, Arbella Stuart and others. Carleton in his letter to Chamberlain describes their costumes: 'loose mantles and petticoats, but of different colors, the stuffs embroidered satins and cloth of gold and silver' (Carleton, 55). After the goddesses appear and speak, Sibylla, '*having placed their several presents on the altar*', also speaks with the hope that the gifts will 'Make glorious both the sovereign and his state' (36). '*After this the Masquers danced their own measures, which being ended and they ready to take out the Lords, the three Graces sang*' (Daniel, 36). The lords included Lennox, Pembroke, Suffolk and several others. Carleton notes that the dancers unmasked about midnight, and 'from thence they went with the king and the ambassadors to a banquet provided in the presence, which was dispatched with the accustomed confusion' (56). This entertainment and banquet indeed helped make this a 'merry Christmas'. The two January masques have complemented and completed each other, making glorious the sovereign and the state. Lennox again has led the way.

His interest in court masques and related activities continued on a regular basis. In some he performed; in others, he participated by hosting feasts for ambassadors and distinguished guests. For example, Lennox performed in Jonson's *Hymenaei* on 5 (masque) and 6 (barriers) January 1606, in honour of the marriage of Essex and Frances Howard (unfortunate marriage as it turned out). Lennox appeared in the indoor tilt or barriers where he led the sixteen knights who represented champions for Truth, who fought vigorously and successfully against Opinion's supporters with what Jonson calls '*alacrity and vigour as if Mars himself had been to triumph before Venus, and invented a new music*'.[51] But suddenly '*a striking light seemed to fill all the hall, and out of it an ANGEL or messenger of glory appearing*' (697). After the Angel speaks, Truth offers her triumphant speech. The lords all exit together in harmony.

Similarly, on 9 February 1608, Lennox along with his brother, the earls of Arundel, Pembroke, Montgomery and others danced in Jonson's *The Haddington Masque*, in honour of the marriage of John Ramsey to Elizabeth Radcliffe. Jonson describes the lords' costumes, of carnation and silver colours with feathers and jewels on their heads, as '*most graceful and noble, partaking of the best both ancient and later figure*'.[52] The playwright characterises the masquers' performance as '*so magnificent and illustrious that nothing can add to the seal of it but the subscription of their names*'. Thus, such a list follows, beginning with 'The Duke of Lennox'.

Prince Henry's first formal chivalric appearance came in *Prince Henry's Barriers*, as noted above, the event that began the memorable year of celebration in 1610, including his investiture as Prince of Wales that summer. On the night of 6 January, the court gathered at the Banqueting House in Whitehall. Lennox participated, much as he had in the Barriers that formed part of the *Hymenaei* masque earlier. The subject matter, apparent in the speeches written by Ben Jonson for the occasion, derives from Arthurian legend, with appearances of the Lady of the Lake, Arthur and Merlin. Henry assumes the name of 'Meliades'. According to an account by Sir Charles Cornwallis, Meliades wanted to test the valour 'of his young years in foreign countries', and knights have returned from their long travels, bringing joy to young Meliades. This became the pretext for the presentation of 'the first fruits of his [Henry's] chivalry at His Majesty's feet'.[53] In speaking of Meliades, Merlin likens him to Henry V, 'to whom in face you are / So like . . . and so in worth' (534). After the Barriers, Merlin closes with a speech of praise for Henry and his bright future (538–9).

Howes sets the stage for the event:

The sixt of January, at the pallace of white-hall in the presence of the Kinge and Queene, and the Ambassadours of Spayne, and Venice, and of al the peeres & great Ladies of the land with a multitude of others: in the great banqueting-house all these were assembled, at the upper end wherof was the kinges Chaire of State.[54]

From a sumptuous pavilion, Henry and his assistants descended into the middle of the room and 'there the Prince performed his first feats of armes'. According to Howes, 'These feates of armes with their triumphal shewes began before ten a clocke at night, and continewed there untill the next morning'. Before the formal fighting began, Lennox and the prince participated and enjoyed the scenes and speeches devised by Jonson and Inigo Jones. Surviving drawings show Jones's sketch for the House of Chivalry and St George's Portico, as well as the costume for Merlin.[55] Jonson established an Arthurian setting as the entertainment began with the speech of the Lady of the Lake, situated near Merlin's tomb. She praises the kingdom's renewal under King James, who has laid claim to Arthur's seat. Arthur, celebrating the union of this isle, appears '*as a star above*' (525). The Lady of the Lake summons Merlin, who arises out of his tomb and calls forth 'fair Meliadus'; at which point '*Meliadus and his six assistants here discovered*' (528), residing in St George's Portico. Merlin redefines romance so that it does not confine itself to antique knights who rescue ladies and slay giants. Rather, Henry must accept the task of governing and giving laws. After reviewing the history of many of Henry's predecessors, Merlin closes by commenting on the uniting of the kingdoms. Immediately before the Barriers, Chivalry appears, claiming that Henry has revived his spirit and orders that the 'rusty doors' be thrown open. After the jousting, Merlin again speaks, prophesying Henry's bright fortune, 'Which shall rise brighter every hour with time' (538). The long night had ended on a triumphant note.

The Barriers were fought across a barrier in the middle of the hall, with Henry leading the way. He had six challengers (supporters), including Lennox, Arundel, Southampton, Sir Thomas Somerset, Lord Hay and Richard Preston. These fought against numerous defendants, ranging from forty to fifty-six, depending on the account cited. The performance took place in the presence of James, Anne and the ambassadors of Spain and Venice, with many noble spectators. Howes in Stow's *Annales* (1615) writes that 'Against these Gallant challengers came six and fiftie braue defendants . . . who in the lower end of the room had erected a very delicat and pleasant place . . . Euery Challenger fought with eight seuerall defendants two seueral combats at two seueral weapons'.[56] The account adds that Henry 'performed this challenge with wonderous, skill, and courage, to the great ioy and admiration of all the beholders'. Henry and Lennox's costumes of crimson velvet and gold lace dazzled the spectators. Not surprisingly, apparently no one was eager to leave.

The wedding of Somerset and Frances Howard on 26 December 1613 provoked ten days of festivities in which Lennox participated fully (as discussed earlier in Chapter Three). These performances included, on the evening of the wedding, Thomas Campion's masque, generally known as *The Somerset Masque* or *Masque of Squires*. The knights in the masque eventually gain release and they come forward to dance, including among them Lennox, the earls of Pembroke and Montgomery and three of Frances' brothers. The next evening offered Ben Jonson's *A Challenge at Tilt, At a Marriage*, the first part of which took place on 27 December, followed by the tilt on 1 January. Chamberlain cannot recall the names of all the challengers; but he does remember Lennox and the earls of Pembroke, Montgomery, Dorset and Rutland. After the masque and the tilt, Lennox had not yet finished his performance in these events.

Just as Campion's masque shifted its scene to London, so does the entertainment for Frances Howard and Somerset. King James on 31 December requested that the Lord Mayor of London, Thomas Middleton, entertain the newly married couple. When the mayor objected that he could not accommodate such a gathering, the king urged him to think again. As Chamberlain puts the issue succinctly: 'he making an excuse that his house was too litle to receve them, yt was not accepted' (1:499). Therefore, the mayor arranged for the city to present entertainment at the Merchant Taylors' Hall, apparently chosen for its size, beauty and previous theatrical performances, and perhaps also because the king had officially visited this guild in 1607. With only four days' warning, the city had to come up with something and thus hired Thomas Middleton, the playwright, to write a masque, which was performed on 4 January 1614. Middleton had, of course, already written the pageant for the opening of the New River on 29 September and the following month on 29 October, the splendid Lord Mayor's Show; therefore, he would have been well known to the city authorities. City records reveal a payment to Middleton for his masque, generally known as the *Masque of Cupids*, of which no text survives.

The court thus went to the city. Roger Coke explains: 'But *White-hall* was too narrow to contain the Triumphs for this Marriage, they must be extended into the City'.[57] London becomes the outlet for court entertainment. Chamberlain reports the spectacular procession: 'they went yesternight about sixe a clocke, thorough Cheapside all by torchlight, accompanied by the father and mother of the bride, and all the Lords and Ladies about the court. The men were well mounted and richly arrayed making a goodly shew, the women all in coaches' (1:499). With Lennox leading the way, the procession created quite a stir, moving smartly through Cheapside to the Merchant Taylors' Hall as citizens marvelled.[58] Out of the dark and chill of this January night, the elegant procession, its lights puncturing the darkness and creating a joyful glow, became part of the entertainment. The dazzling lights recall the ones that moved along the Thames for Beaumont's February wedding masque as it moved from Southwark along the river to Whitehall. The Italian envoy Gabaleone confirms many of the details of this event: 'The wedded couple left their lodging at five in the afternoon accompanied by a hundred knights, all lords, earls and barons, dressed most superbly, on horseback, ranked two by two . . . Every knight had a single groom with a torch in his hand walking at his side'.[59] This procession moved through 'the whole length of the city. There the people had gathered, making a wonderful sight because of the great quantity of lights they had with them at windows and in the streets' (82). Chamberlain concludes his report: 'I understand that after supper they had a play and a maske after that a banket' (1:499). Another report indicates that the 'Aldermen of London, in their scarlet robes, entertained them with hearty welcome, and feasted them with all magnificence'.[60] The noble guests did not return to Whitehall until three o'clock the next morning. Lennox had thus vigorously participated in these entertainments, underscoring his interest in such and willingness to perform.

Not only did Lennox perform, he also sometimes offered feasts attached to the occasions, provided needed mediation between quarrelling ambassadors, who struggled to get the proper invitation to the masque performance, and soothed ruffled feathers of the ambassadorial corps – a fractious lot. A particularly egregious example occurs in the correspondence of the French ambassador, Antoine Le Fevre de la Boderie, to the King of France, first on 22 December 1607 and then on 5 January 1608, in anticipation of a performance of Jonson's *Masque of Beauty* on Twelfth Night. The ambassador resents not having been invited, whereas the Spanish ambassador had been. Lennox becomes the intermediary between several interested and aggrieved parties.

The ambassador begins the first letter: 'I will tell you that M. the Duke of Lennox did me the favour of coming to dinner here, to tell me that yesterday the Queen of England had spoken to her husband the King'.[61] Lennox revealed that Anne told James that she had invited the Spanish ambassador to the masque, 'which Lennox thought good to warn me, because of the respect that he had for the French King, and because of his friendship towards me'. As an alternative, James will invite M. de la Boderie to a dinner. The ambassador responds in outrage at this slight. Lennox tries to mollify him by saying that the matter was not completely resolved and that 'he would see the lords of Salisbury and Dunbar today to try to defuse this trap'. The ambassador senses a conspiracy: 'Without doubt it is a ploy conceived by the Queen', who clearly prefers the Spanish over the French and here exercises her control over James. Things get only worse, according to the French ambassador in his next letter: 'I informed him [Lennox] how much this could offend the King [of France]'. James has apparently said, according to Lennox, that no remedy exists. This does not satisfy the ambassador, who imagines the Spaniard enjoying the masque and then a supper with the king and 'would be seen by ten thousand people'.[62] 'Therefore,' the ambassador writes, 'I begged him [Lennox's messenger] to ask the Duke on my behalf to break off this dinner because I was totally resolved to refuse it.' Everywhere the ambassador looks he sees slights: 'with my own eyes I had seen the Lord Chamberlain's coach enter the Spanish Ambassador's house when the last tournament took place, and my servants had seen him getting out at the house of the Lord Chamberlain's son-in-law'. Imagined insults abound.

Even the Privy Council got involved and debated at length this whole matter, 'where most were inclined to uninvite the Spanish Ambassador'. Queen Anne refused. The Council 'begged the Duke of Lennox to find me himself and encourage me once again to accept the offer of a feast'. To this De la Boderie will not consent, given the magnitude of his grievance. So, the ambassador writes in pain: the Spanish ambassador 'will dance and we will not eat'. He blames Queen Anne completely, adding, 'The Queen has now turned against the Duke of Lennox for the refusal I made to go to their feast, and swore yesterday two good oaths that she would make him [Lennox] feel sorry for it'. Fantasy begins to take over. If Anne felt annoyed with Lennox, it did not last. But these rich letters underscore how seriously the ambassadors took the matter of precedence and how petty they could be, leaving Lennox often in an untenable position. He seems, however, to have weathered these temper tantrums well. Masques can be a tricky business, apparently.

De la Boderie gets cranked up again in conjunction with the performance of Jonson's *Masque of Queens* (1609); he has not lost the edge in feeling aggrieved. Lennox gets in the middle of this uproar also. The ambassador writes again to King Henri IV of France, 29 December 1608, beginning with noting that Cecil summoned him to his house, 'where I would find him and the Duke of Lennox'.[63] Cecil has been offended by something that the ambassador has said and he wants Lennox present to witness the ambassador's response because Cecil had detected 'so much bitterness and passion in this language'. The whole thing boils down, again, to being irked that the Spanish and Flanders ambassadors have been invited to a feast and De la Boderie finds it 'very strange' that they were invited before him. The ambassador adds: 'I begged His Majesty not to do me wrong. If it pleased him to compensate [me] with another favour for the feast . . . I asked that it be to be invited to the Queen's ballet [masque]'. James has instructed Lennox to tell the ambassador that 'he would excuse what I proposed to him'. The rest of the discussion seems to have satisfied the ambassador: 'although they were not more explicit, they have given me to understand that they would have me dance [go to the masque]'. If they don't follow through on this, 'I will spot it and make them aware of it'. It seems that the ambassador does not care so much about the masque itself as he does the annoyance that some other ambassador might be invited and not he.

Jockeying for position continues unabated. Thus, for the *Masque of Augurs*, to be presented on Twelfth Night 1622, John Finet provides in his notebooks a lively account of the attempt of the Venetian ambassador and others to be invited. Finet reports that he went to Girolenio Landi with the message that although he had been told a few days ago that no ambassador would be included at the masque, apparently the wily Spanish ambassador (Gondomar) had managed to get an invitation, causing much chagrin among the diplomats. Therefore, if the Venetian ambassador receives an invitation he should refuse it on some grounds. Understandably, the ambassador is not keen on this proposal and eventually he prevailed 'with the like respect as was the Spanish Ambassador'.[64] At the masque itself Gondomar makes his presence felt, seated near the right hand of King James with 'other strangers promiscuously on a Scaffold behind the King'. The visiting Prince Landsgrave of Hesse 'was brought in by me the back way through the Garden, and supping with the Duke of Lenox . . . was seated amongst the great Ladies'. The French ambassador did not attend, insisting that 'his stomach would not (he said) agree with cold meat, and desired therefore his absence might be pardoned' and also pointing out the presence of the Spanish ambassador 'in the first place'. Some scores seem never to be settled. At least this time, Finet seems to be the intermediary, leaving Lennox simply to provide a feast. Such controversy continues into the next year at the time of Jonson's masque *Time Vindicated*, performed on 19 January 1623, although originally intended for Twelfth Night. Finet again reports on the negotiations, each ambassador wanting to be invited and preferring to sit near the king. The potential presence of the Spanish ambassador continues to annoy others. But finally, 'The French Ambassador that night [of the masque], and the Venetian supped with the Duke of Lenox, and entered the Roome with the King, both seated there on his left hand'.[65] Lennox has smoothed the way by offering a feast to these ambassadors.

He did something remarkably different at the performance of Jonson's *The Golden Age Restored* (1616), as recorded in a dispatch sent from Francesco Quaratesi back to Florence. The emissary reports that 'On Saturday night a wonderful masque was performed. The ambassadors of France, Venice, and Savoy were present'.[66] (The seeming harmonious gathering of ambassadors may have been possible because the Spanish ambassador was not present.) The report indicates that King James attended: 'His Majesty came to see the masque. He was helped by the Duke of Lennox and the Earl of Worcester who held him up', the king apparently suffering from gout. Lennox thus had a wide array of experiences with the court masques: dancer, performer, tilter, spectator, intermediary, negotiator and, on at least one occasion, propper-up of kings.

Lennox had a different kind of experience nearly twenty years after Jonson's entertainment at Althorp, the first entertainment that greeted Anne, Henry and Lennox in 1603: *The Gypsies Metamorphosed* (1621), performed three times at Burley-on-the Hill, then Belvoir, and finally at Windsor in the presence of King James all three times in August and September of that year. Textually complicated, the masque had first focused on Buckingham and his father-in-law, the Earl of Rutland. But the final performance at Windsor put its emphasis on the royal courtiers, especially appropriate for this royal castle. This masque may have been James's favourite. Lennox gets special notice at Windsor. The Prologue greets James: 'But you, sir, that twice / Have graced us already, encourage to thrice; / Wherein if our boldness your patience invade, / Forgive us the fault that your favor hath made'.[67] The gypsies at Windsor get underway with their fortune-telling, dancing and singing. Jackman and the gypsies tell the fortunes of the Lord Chamberlain (William Herbert), Lord Keeper of the Great Seal (Bishop John Williams), Lord Treasurer (Baron Montague), Lord Privy Seal (Edward Somerset), the Earl Marshal (Thomas Howard, Earl of Arundel), and then the Lord Steward, the Duke of Lennox.

The Fourth Gypsy turns to Lennox, while holding his hand, and says:

I find by this hand
You have the command
Of the very best man's house i' the land.
Our captain and we
Ere long will see
If you keep a good table;
Your master's able,
And here be bountiful lines that say
You'll keep no part of his bounty away.
There's written frank
On your Venus' bank,
To prove a false steward you'll find much ado,
Being a true one by blood and by office too. (pp. 341–2)

Wittily, the gypsy refers to Lennox's control of the household management and purse of the king, in referring to 'bounty', 'bountiful' and 'good table'. Lennox would have been in charge of the expenditures here at Windsor. Therefore, he controls 'the very best man's house'. Lennox can be understood as being a 'true steward' by his blood relationship as a Stuart ('steward') to the king and by his careful management of the office. All these observations can be seen in Lennox's hand, so says the gypsy. Jonson has thus offered, through the playful yet serious speech, the most explicit reference to Lennox that occurs in any of these entertainments. No such show could have ignored this crucially important courtier, confidant of the king and patron of the arts.

In addition to being a part of these indoor court entertainments, Lennox also regularly participated in outdoor, chivalric and martial jousts or tournaments. In conjunction with Princess Elizabeth's wedding February 1613, for example, Lennox joined others in a rigorous running at the ring in the Whitehall Palace tiltyard, located just below Lennox's windows in the Holbein Gatehouse. The royal family, noblemen and spectators gathered in the tiltyard on 15 February to see the king, Prince Charles, Frederick, Lennox and other nobles of the realm engage in running at the ring. The tiltyard, elaborately decorated, included many Heralds at Arms, the Yeoman of the Guard and the King's Trumpeters, all in rich embroidered coats. Queen Anne, with Elizabeth, watched from gallery windows, accompanied by many noble ladies. First, King James 'mounted upon a steed of much swiftnes', began the activity; he took 'the ring upon his speare three severall times together, whereat the trumpets still sounded to the great joy of the beholders'.[68] Prince Frederick, 'upon a horse of . . . brave courage', took his turn, 'so lightly and so nimbly, that the whole assembly gave him high commendations' (Nichols, 2:550). Then Charles followed on a Spanish jennet; he took the ring four times in five attempts. Lennox and Arundel, with a few other lords, 'in honour of the magnificent Marriage, performed very worthy races, and many times tooke the ring'. Spectators of all kinds delighted in this chivalric activity, which added another layer of colour, spectacle and celebration to the wedding, only slightly less idealistic than the masques.

Each 24 March the court celebrated Accession Day in honour of the day that James became King of England. These occasions usually included a tournament with Lennox among the participants. The Accession Day tilt in 1605 took place at Greenwich because the court had gathered there awaiting Anne's delivery of their first English child. Samuel Calvert writes to Ralph Winwood about the event: 'The tilting on Sunday last (Coronation-day) was not performed with the accustomed solemnity; the Lords the Dukes of Holst and Lenox were the chiefest runners, though our English outran them in every respect' (Nichols, 1:500). Although providing no details, Calvert adds: 'The shows were costly and somewhat extraordinary'. Lennox competed the following year, but one account complains of lacklustre performance and the lack of stunning costumes.[69] Another account agrees, calling the tilt 'poor and penurious' with the exception of Pembroke and Montgomery who were 'rich and dainty' (Nichols, 2:43). The report adds: 'There was more expected for devise and cost (at least) at the hands of the Duke of Lenox, and the young Earle of Arundell for the maidenhead of their running'. The writer thinks that perhaps Montgomery ran the best.

Penurious would not be the word to describe the Accession Day Tilt of 1610. The tilters included Lennox and the other usual participants, such as Pembroke, Montgomery and Arundel. This joust at Whitehall contained triumphal chariots that conveyed allegorical characters delivering speeches of compliment to the king. Richard Preston appeared in a pageant, 'which was an Elephant with a castle on the back', which moved very slowly, 'creeping about the Tilt-yard'.[70] This contemporary account describes Lennox's costume: 'The Duke of Lennox exceeded all in feathers'. (One longs for an illustration of Lennox bedecked in feathers!) The writer describes only Lennox's costume, which obviously made quite the impression.

Information about the tournament in 1612 comes from the Venetian ambassador, Antonio Foscarini, who had the great honour of being invited to attend. He reports: 'The Prince ran a match with marvelous grace'.[71] The ambassador adds proudly: 'the Duke of Lennox, Lord Hay and other gentlemen of the Court . . . informed me that his Highness would be glad if I could be present. I accepted, and was received by the Princess, and at the close of the joust I was welcomed by the Prince'. Foscarini even dined with the king: 'Thus I have received a favour not common to any other Ambassador'. The familiar issue of the struggle among ambassadors for invitations to such court events appears even here. Foscarini seems not particularly concerned with what took place in the tiltyard.

On 24 March 1613, the annual Accession Day Tilt took place at Whitehall with Lennox as one of the principal participants. In Chamberlain's view, 'Yesterday was the great tilting at court, where there was more gallantrie both for number and braverie then hath ben since the King came in'.[72] Lennox, and the earls of Arundel, Rutland, Pembroke, Dorset and Montgomery, and six lords were among the tilters. Chamberlain says that 'they all performed theyre parts very well specially Sir Harry Rich with Sir Sigismond Alexander'. But rain hindered the spectacle 'to the disgrace of many fine plumes'.[73] Nevertheless, Sir Henry Rich and his brother Sir Robert Rich offered a speech to the king, one written by Ben Jonson. The poem offers the brothers' 'lives, their loves, their hearts' to the king.[74] Jonson's verse also interprets the emblems that the brothers presented; for example, Robert 'Presents a royal altar of fair peace; / As an everlasting sacrifice'. Henry offered a 'prospective' glass, which when looked at correctly enables the knight to appear as a new creation to the king's eyes. The other tilters presented their *imprese*, 'whereof some were so dark, that their meaning is not yet understood, unless perchance that were their meaning, not to be understood', Wotton suggests (2:17). (*Imprese* were allegorical or symbolic visual designs, typically accompanied with mottoes of some kind, such as can be found in the tournament in Shakespeare's *Pericles*.) Wotton further says that the

> two best, to my fancy, were those of the two Earls brothers [Pembroke and Montgomery]: the first a small exceeding white pearl, and the words, *Solo candore valco*. The other a sun casting a glance on the side of a pillar, and the beams reflecting, with this motto, *Splendente refulget*.

This Accession Day tournament joined the earlier one on 15 February as part of the nearly three-month-long courtly entertainments, all prompted by Princess Elizabeth's wedding.

Perhaps unexpectedly, Shakespeare intersects this tournament explicitly. He designed the *impresa* for Francis Manners, the socially ambitious Earl of Rutland, obviously at the earl's request. For this artistic endeavour Shakespeare received a payment of 44 shillings. The earl's steward's records also include a payment of 44 shillings to the actor Richard Burbage, who painted the *impresa*.[75] Thus, two of the King's Men earned income from the Accession Day tilt and thereby participated in it, just as Burbage had performed in the many dramatic performances at court over the past several weeks.

Chamberlain offers a full report of the tournament of 1620 in which he gives Lennox only glancing notice. He observes that Charles 'who runs very faire . . . came in goode fashion accompanied by his owne people, six trumpetts, fowre pages, six groomes and six footmen, all very well and richly appareled in his colours' (2:298). The prince even had 'a fayre tent of those coloured damasks to repose himself'. Many lords performed, presumably including Lennox, although not named. Chamberlain complains about Arundel who was 'every way so poorely accoutered that he did himself nor the place litle honor'. The report also notes the presence of the Spanish ambassador (Gondomar) who had a place near the prince's tent. But the French ambassador did not attend, refusing because he would not have a sufficient place from which to observe the tilt. Chamberlain suggests 'in truth in some mens opinion he shold have ben placed to his disadvantage in a corner of the Duke of Lennox lodging' (298–9). This refers to the Holbein Gatehouse, Lennox's palace residence. King James did not accede to the ambassador's complaints.

Into the squabble about the French ambassador Lennox enters with two letters to his friend Edward Herbert, now serving as English ambassador to France. The first letter, dated 24 March, occurs on the day of the tournament itself, suggesting Lennox's determination to record his version of things. Lennox begins by noting 'some discontent the French Ambassador hath taken about his place at the tilting day'; but he had little reason to complain, Lennox suggests, 'considering the conditions were offered him . . . and [he] had the aduantage of the place to all men's judgment'.[76] Given his preference for France, Lennox says that he should have been sympathetic to the ambassador, but not even the Ambassador of Savoy's efforts 'could persuade him to accept of the place was offered him'. A few weeks later, on 11 April, Lennox again wrote to Herbert, having received his letter of 3 April. Lennox writes: 'for the occasion the french Ambassador tooke to absent him selfe from seeing the running at tilt I trust it will breed no harm for I assure your L. that the french

King could haue receaued no prejudice if hee had accepted of that place was offered him'.[77] Fortunately, Lennox observes, the ambassador 'is a well disposed gentleman and was Lothe to doe any thing that might bring any imputation vpon him and that made him somewhat more scrupulous then was needful'. Obviously, Lennox and Herbert have been communicating about this episode, eager to diffuse any lingering effect. These tournaments, most of which involved Lennox, became arenas of royal display, beautiful costumes, speeches, chivalric exploits, physical accomplishment and sites of ambassadorial dispute. Small wonder that the duke should have been present in multiple ways.

During the exceptional season of late 1612 and early 1613 at court, Lennox attended the almost nightly performances by the King's Men and other acting troupes, enjoying the plays and pondering their significance. He also travelled with Prince Charles and Prince Frederick in March 1613 first to Oxford and then Cambridge. At Cambridge they saw two different plays performed, one of them lasting between seven and eight hours, according to Chamberlain. They also heard theological and philosophical disputes. Hacket captures the scene at Trinity College:

> His [Dr Nevile's] Table was Graced with the Company of Prince *Charles*, Prince Elector *Frederick* the Bridegroom, Count *Henry* of *Nassau*, *Lodwick* Duke of *Lenox*, with a most comely Concourse of Nobles and Gentlemen . . . In two distinct Nights a Comick and a Pastoral Fable, both in *Latin*, were Acted before their Highnesses, and the Spectators, by the Students of the same College.[78]

Chamberlain adds, however: 'The King is very angrie and out of love with our Cambridge men for theyre questions at the Palsgraves beeing there specially whether *electio* or *successio* were to be preferred in kingdoms, and is out of patience that yt shold be so much as argued in schooles' (1:440). James clearly preferred that he alone be allowed to ruminate on kingship and succession. Records attest to Lennox's presence at other dramatic performances, such as the one at Whitehall in May 1619.

The primary source for knowing about and understanding the dramatic event in May 1619 comes from a letter, dated 24 May (noted above), written by Gerrard Herbert, who, rather like Chamberlain, moved in court circles and reported on many activities there. Herbert's identity and family connections, however, remain uncertain. But he did write numerous letters. In letters to Dudley Carleton, Herbert wrote regularly about court events, including performances, especially of masques.[79] He, for example, notes the performance at court of *For the Honour of Wales*, performed before the queen in February 1618, and Jonson's revision of his *Pleasure Reconciled to Virtue*, first performed on 6 January of that year. Accounts of the build-up to what Herbert refers to as the 'Prince's masque' occur in several letters, especially that of 6 December 1617, in which Herbert writes: 'A greate Maske is appointed to be for the Christmas, wherin the Prince himselfe wil be one'.[80] Then, on 12 January 1618, Gerrard reports to Carleton: 'the maskeres beynge suted wth siluer lace for the most parte & the Prince, (& the rest also performing very well the daunces, the Queene not beynge well to be present at it, and beynge the Prince his first maske . . . the maske therefore is to be on shroffsunday', which the queen did attend.[81] The February performance Herbert documents in a letter of 22 February 1618.[82] On 20 January 1619, Gerrard reports to Carleton the burning of Banqueting House (more of which below). All of these reports on dramatic events serve as preparation for writing about the performance of Shakespeare's *Pericles* on 20 May 1619.

Another letter from this period confirms the event at Whitehall, this one from William Herbert, Lord Chamberlain, who wrote on 20 May to James Hay, Viscount Doncaster. In this letter William Herbert refers to the feast and also to the recent death of Richard Burbage, the great tragic actor, who had died on 13 March, just a few days after Queen Anne's death. His death prompted much grief in the theatrical world, some suggesting that his got more attention than the queen. Chamberlain also reported Burbage's death. William Herbert provides the first record of the play performance at court and he calls attention to Lennox. He writes: 'Lenox made a great supper to the French Embassador, this night here. Even now all the company are at the play', which Herbert 'could not endure to see so soone after the loss of my old acquaintance Burbadg'.[83] This touching response to Burbage's death underscores this actor's power, such that Herbert could not bear to watch the play, which he does not name. In part, then, this feast and performance at Whitehall occur in the context of the recent death and funeral of the queen and of Burbage. These events may account for the rather small crowd gathered at the palace.

Gerrard Herbert's letter about *Pericles* contains valuable content, beyond the account of the play, serving multiple purposes. The letter begins with a comment about the queen's funeral and comes full circle at the end by discussing the breakup of her royal household. Herbert starts by stating his intention to have sent some news of the funeral; 'but that the bearer by whom I meant to sende deceaued my expectacions, & partinge to the contrye till wth in thies fewe dayes althoe[84] it wold now be to late to speake thereof'.[85] This statement comes across as rather amusing, placing blame on the letter-bearer who unexpectedly went out into the country. Herbert next moves to various items of information about the court, establishing clearly that he has close connections to it and serves as an eyewitness. He, for example, remarks on the king's going to the chapel, 'looking very well (God be thancked)' (an obvious response to the king's recent serious illness). Later that day, James announced his intention to elevate a number of noblemen, including Lennox's brother, Esmé, Lord D'Aubigny, who will become an earl. The Feast of St George had been postponed, presumably because of Anne's death, until some time the following week. The account of the feast and play performance then follows (more on that below). The last section of the letter focuses on the dispersal of the queen's household. Herbert writes: 'On Wednesday last, after Whittson hollidayes ended, the Queenes Court broke vpp' (fol. 101). The Lord Chamberlain and other lords gave 'very hopefull wordes & promises from the Kinge to all the servantes'. Clearly the letter holds great interest for anyone concerned with the Jacobean court, especially in the aftermath of the queen's death and funeral.

The letter notes a much smaller, more private performance than typically occurred with court masques, certainly compared to the 1618 Jonson one which had an audience of more than six hundred. Herbert focuses on the various noblemen present for the feast and play at Whitehall. The portion of the letter devoted to the festivities in fact begins with a listing of these noblemen who were present for this occasion in honour of the departing French ambassador, Marquis Trémoille. Lennox arranged for the feast, held in the queen's great chamber. Confirmation of this comes from a letter that Chamberlain wrote to Carleton, dated 31 May, cited earlier. Herbert enumerates the noblemen, including the Marquis of Buckingham, by this point clearly James's 'favourite', who sat intermixed with French counts. But no ladies were present. The absence of women at the *Pericles* performance underscores the limited, private nature of this entertainment. Herbert describes some features of the feast, then the movement into the queen's privy chamber for a presentation of French music by the late queen's musicians. In the queen's bedchamber the guests heard more music in this 'moveable feast' before proceeding into the king's great chamber for the performance of *Pericles*, 'wch lasted till 2 aclocke' (fol. 100b).[86] The production paused after 'two actes' for refreshments; then the players began again. The rest of the pertinent account focuses on the French ambassador, his departure and gifts received from King James.

Herbert's original letter resides in the National Archives. A transcription of the feast and performance of *Pericles* follows below:

[100b] The Marquise Trenell [Trémoille] on thursday last tooke leaue of the Kinge: that night was feasted at white hall by the Duke of Lenox in the Queenes greate chamber: where many great Lordes weare to keepe them Company but no ladyes. the Sauoy Imbassadour was also there: The english Lordes, was the Marquise Buckingham my lord Pryuy Seale, my lord of lenox, my lord of Oxford, my lord Chamberlayne, my L: Hamelton, my lord Arundell, my Lord of Leycester: my lord Cary, my lord Diggby, mr Treasurer, mr Secretary Callvart: my lord Beaucham, & my Lord Generall, the rest English Gallantes, & all mixed wth the french alonge the table: the Marquise Trenell sittinge alone at the tables ende: at the right hande, the Sauoy Imbassador, by him the Marquise Buckingham, then a french Counte, &c. mixed: on his left hand my lord Priuy Seale, the earle of Oxford, a french Marquise, my lord Chamberlayne & so forth mixed wth french & English. The supper was greate & the banquett curious, serued in 24 greate Chynay [chinaware] worcke platters or voyders [trays], full of glasse scales or bowles of sweete meates: in the middst of each voyder a greene tree of eyther, Lemon, orenge, Cypers, or other resemblinge. After supper they weare carried to the Queenes pryuy chamber, where french singinge was by the Queenes Musitians: after in the Queenes bedd Chamber, they hearde the Irish harpp, a violl, & mr Lanyer, excellently singinge & playinge on the lute. In the kinges greate Chamber they went to see the play of Pirrocles, prince of Tyre, wch lasted till 2 aclocke. after 2 actes, the players ceased till the french all refreshed them wth sweetmeates brought on Chinay voiders, & wyne & ale in bottells. after the players, begann a newe.[87]

This long evening of entertainment underscores yet again Lennox's involvement in such events. Certainly he arranged for the feast. Who arranged for the play performance remains unclear. But the celebration marks a kind of respite after Anne's funeral, reminiscent of the power of drama to assuage grief after Prince Henry's death in 1612. Gerrard Herbert's letter places Lennox at the centre of the festivities and documents explicitly his attendance at a performance of a Shakespeare play.

A few months before the court performance of *Pericles* a great theatrical and political disaster occurred: the burning of the Banqueting House in Whitehall on 12 January 1619. Letters by Gerrard Herbert and Chamberlain report the event. Herbert wrote on 20 January to Dudley Carleton, saying, in part: 'the fyre hapned at white hall, on Tuesday 10 dayes paste, beginninge at 10 a clocke in the morninge & lastinge till 2 the afternone w[ch] burnt downe all the banquettinge house: & was generally feared the burninge of the whole house of Whitehall'.[88] Herbert reports that two fellows carried candles into the upper part of the structure; and, 'one of the oyle clothes or hanginges took fyre from one off these candles' and so suddenly burst into flame 'as the two fellowes dayne they no way cold quenche it'. But the fellows seeing the fire, 'fearing to haue it knowne', simply 'shut the doore, & went away'. Herbert credits the provident presence of the Lord Chamberlain for preventing an even worse disaster.

Chamberlain, also writing to Carleton on 16 January, offers an equally compelling, if at points at odds with the Herbert report.[89] He begins: 'we have had here a great mischance by fire at Whitehall, which beginning in the banketting house hath quite consumed yt, and put the rest in great daunger' (2:201). Fortunately, help appeared; 'and so goode order taken by the presence of the Lord Chamberlain, the Duke [Lennox], and the earle of Arundell, that all passed with as much quiet as was possible in such a confusion' (201–2). Chamberlain points to the political loss: 'One of the greatest losses spoken of, is the burning of all of most of the writings and papers belonging to the offices of the signet, privie-seale and counsaile-chamber'. The fire occurred at midday, thus avoiding the increased danger of a night-time fire. Chamberlain has a theory of how it all happened: 'a mean fellow searching in the masking or tiring house with a candle for certain things he had hid there, fired some oyled painted clothes and pastboords . . . and seeing he could not quench yt alone, went out and lockt the doore after him' (202). Whatever the cause, this was a great disaster. Fortunately, the presence of the Lord Chamberlain, Lennox and Arundel created some sense of order and prevented total destruction. The 'two fellowes', Herbert reports, 'are putt in prison'.

Shortly after the fire James appointed a commission to rebuild the Banqueting House; this commission included Lennox, doubtless because of his status but also because of his manifest interest in the arts. Arundel, renowned for his art collection, partly inherited and then augmented by a trip to Italy with Inigo Jones in 1613, also served, as did William Herbert, Lord Chamberlain, who had many connections to the theatre companies.[90] This body wisely selected Inigo Jones to design the new building. Jones, England's most outstanding architect in the early seventeenth century and designer of many court masques, eagerly accepted the task and by April had drawn up the first design, a building, influenced by Jones's travels in and knowledge of Italy, unlike any before it in England. The building was ready for use by 1622. Jones's magnificent Palladian achievement still stands in Whitehall.

Another manifestation of Lennox's interest and participation in the arts can be found in his patronage of writers. How involved Lennox

became cannot be determined, but the dedication of books to him constitutes a measure of patronage or at least participation in the opera-
tive patronage system.[91] John Ford offers an example connected to the
entertainment in 1606 for King Christian IV of Denmark. Although the
proposed tilt for King Christian lacked the romantic lustre that Lennox
had intended, a version of it survives in John Ford's *Honor Triumphant*
(1606), which includes the challenges that four knights would have given.
Indeed, Ford dedicates the first section to 'To the Right Noble Lord, the
Duke of Lennox his Grace'.[92] Lennox represents the chivalric argument
that 'Knights in Ladies service have no free-will'. Thus, a knight 'ought
not to be their owne, nor subject to their owne pleasure, unlesse to please
themselves in the recreation which tendeth to their ladies honor' (B3v).
This dedication calls attention to the just over twenty texts that various writers dedicated to Lennox, only two before his arrival in England.
Burel's volume of poetry (1596) in Scotland, cited earlier, was the first.
Although Henry Peacham dedicates his emblem book *Minerva Britanna*
to Prince Henry, he includes a specific emblem in honour of Lennox, 'To
the thrice Noble, and excellent Prince: Ludowick Duke of *Lennox*'.[93]
Peacham begins the accompanying verse: 'Nor may my Muse, greate
Duke, with prouder stile, / Ore-passe your name, your birth, and best
deserts'. The writer claims that Lennox is 'yet belou'd in forrein partes'.
Peacham closes: 'Our Muse, that shall her loftiest numbers frame, / To
eternize your STEWARTS Roiall name'. The emblem itself depicts a
strong arm holding a shield with the fleur-de-lis of France.

These epistles dedicatory seek patronage of some sort or they simply
acknowledge Lennox's prominence. Walter Quin, responding to the
Gowrie Plot of 1600, addressed Lennox: 'thou him [James] hardst complaining in the snare, / Thy grief did then thy faithfull love declare: / Thy
running eke with speed to make him free; / Wherein thow didst no paines,
nor peril spare'.[94] Similarly, John Davies celebrates the close relationship
of king and duke: 'Thou like the Moone, among heav'ns lamps dost
shine, / While Sol thy Sov'raigne goest to the Globe about'.[95] Gervase
Markham dedicates part of his *Cavalarice* to Lennox and praises his skill
as a horseman, citing also 'the noble favours which you extend to your
admirers'.[96] In 1605 James, as previously noted, appointed Lennox as the
king's alnager (inspector of woollen cloth); in recognition of that office,
John May dedicates his book on clothing to him, insisting that no cause
can obscure May's 'love and duty' to Lennox.[97] Late in his life Lennox
even became the recipient of a dedication in a book in Spanish about
learning this language.[98] Through these dedications Lennox emerges as
a noble and heroic figure, a close companion to the king. In a sense they

only acknowledge, albeit in glowing, idealised terms, what most people recognised: Lennox as paragon, in the tiltyard, on diplomatic missions, in political negotiations and in books.

Lennox's vital interest in and participation in the arts offers a worthwhile and important insight into his character. Not only an astute politician and reliable confidant of the king, Lennox ranged widely in his interests. He served as patron to an adult acting company and patron to several writers, a protector of dramatists, a mediator between ambassadors for position at performances, a performer himself in court masques and tournaments, spectator at masques and plays, host of feasts associated with dramatic events and defender of the burning Banqueting House and commissioner for its rebuilding. Few in the Jacobean era could surpass him in his commitment to the arts.

Notes

1. For a full discussion of this development, see Neil Cuddy, 'The Revival of the Entourage: The Bedchamber of James I, 1603–1625', in *The English Court from the Wars of the Roses to the Civil War*, David Starkey (ed.), pp. 173–225.
2. *Calendar of State Papers Venetian*, 10:106.
3. The letter occurs in the *Report on the Laing Manuscripts*, 1:124.
4. *Calendar of State Papers Venetian*, 10:142.
5. *Calendar of State Papers Venetian*, 11:20. Lennox could not have been disappointed in some features of this trip to Scotland. The 'Household Accounts of Ludovick Duke of Lennox, when Commissioner to the Parliament of Scotland', in *Miscellany of the Maitland Club*, 1:161–91, overflow with the expenditures for food and other items during Lennox's 1607 visit. No restraint is apparent.
6. *The Letters of John Chamberlain*, 2:19–20. The article about Lennox in the *Oxford DNB* incorrectly states that Lennox was excommunicated by the Scottish church. Clearly, as Chamberlain's report makes clear, it was Huntly who had a long and vexatious relationship with the Church of Scotland.
7. *Calendar of Scottish Papers*, 13:974.
8. *Calendar of the Manuscripts of the Marquess of Salisbury*, 14:208.
9. *Calendar of Salisbury Manuscripts*, 14:285–6.
10. *Calendar of Salisbury Manuscripts*, 16:56.
11. *Calendar of Salisbury Manuscripts*, 23:153.
12. *Salisbury Manuscripts*, 18: 246–7.
13. *Letters*, 1:198.
14. *Salisbury Manuscripts*, 17:27.
15. *Salisbury Manuscripts*, 17:30.
16. *Calendar of State Papers Venetian*, 10:22.

17. G. P. V. Akrigg (ed.), *Letters of King James VI & I*, p. 329.
18. *Calendar of Venetian State Papers*, 13:5.
19. *Letters of John Chamberlain*, 2:55.
20. This is my transcription of the original letter, which is found in the National Archives, London as item SP 14/109, folio100b; 100–101. I discuss this letter in my article, '*Pericles*: A Performance, a Letter (1619)', in *Performances at Court in the Age of Shakespeare*, Sophie Chiari and John Mucciolo (eds), pp. 107–19.
21. Reported in Nichols, *Progresses of James*, 4:632.
22. *By the King James by the grace of God, king of England, Scotland, France and Ireland*, p. 3.
23. *Salisbury Manuscripts*, 17:610.
24. *Analytical Index to the Records Known as the Remembrancia*, p. 72. All such reports will come from this collection of records.
25. *Earl of Mar & Kellie Manuscripts*, p. 53.
26. *Calendar of State Papers Venetian*, 13:68.
27. *Calendar of State Papers Venetian*, 18:28.
28. *Calendar of State Papers Domestic*, 9:329.
29. Akrigg, *Letters*, p. 343.
30. *The Life and Letters of Francis Bacon*, James Spedding (ed.), 5:266.
31. *Life and Letters*, 5:275–338.
32. *Report on the Manuscripts of the Most Honourable the Marquess of Downshire*, 5:509. The volumes contain the 'Papers of William Trumbull the elder'.
33. *Salisbury Manuscripts*, 22:112.
34. Quoted in Nichols, *Progresses*, 4:664. For full details of Bacon's experience, see volume 7 of *The Life and Letters of Francis Bacon*.
35. *Life and Letters of Francis Bacon*, 5:204.
36. *Letters of John Holles 1587–1637*, P. R. Seddon (ed.), 1:86. All quotations from Holles will come from this edition. Holles is a kind of textbook example of those would-be courtiers who sought patrons or at least 'brokers' who might help them achieve a court position. For a helpful discussion of Holles and his search, see Linda Levy Peck, *Court Patronage and Corruption in Early Stuart England*, pp. 20–9.
37. British Library, Egerton MS 2595, fol. 28.
38. Quoted from Andrew Gurr, *The Shakespeare Company, 1594–1642*, p. 254. Tom Cain in his edition of Jonson's *Sejanus* in *The Cambridge Edition of the Works of Ben Jonson* claims that 'The Stuart brothers are, indeed, the most likely courtiers to have pushed James . . . to move so quickly to issue the patent to the King's Men' (2:200). This tantalising idea is hard to substantiate.
39. Jane Rickard has countered the usual idea that Scotland provided few theatrical experiences. In *Writing the Monarch in Jacobean England*, Rickard writes: 'It would seem, then, that for James there were important

continuities between the activities of English players at his Scottish court and his patronage of the King's Men in England' (p. 50). Taking all the adult acting companies under royal patronage within weeks of arriving in London still seems unexpected. The King's Men obviously attained special status through the king's patronage. The importance of the court for Shakespeare's career has been skilfully delineated by Richard Dutton in *Shakespeare, Court Dramatist.*

40. *Henslowe's Diary*, second edition, R. A. Foakes (ed.), p. 298.
41. Chambers, *Elizabethan Stage*, 2:241. Chambers derives much of his information from John Tucker Murray, *English Dramatic Companies 1558–1642*, 1:228–9.
42. This information comes from a distillation of *REED* materials found on their 'Patrons and Performances Web Site'. For more information consult *Coventry*, R. W. Ingram (ed.); *Norwich 1540–1642*, David Galloway (ed.); *Devon*, John M. Wasson (ed.).
43. Cited by Richard Dutton, *Mastering the Revels: The Regulation and Censorship of English Renaissance Drama*, p. 185.
44. Chapman, *Homer, Prince of Poets*, following p. 118. The editors and printer of the Shakespeare Folio adopt this same practice of an '&c' following the nobleman's name.
45. For further discussion of patronage and drama, see *Patronage in the Renaissance*, Guy Fitch Lytle and Stephen Orgel (eds); *Shakespeare and Theatrical Patronage in Early Modern England*, Paul Whitfield White and Suzanne R. Westfall (eds); and my *Textual Patronage in English Drama, 1570–1640.*
46. I quote from the edition of this masque, edited by Joan Rees, in *A Book of Masques*, p. 25.
47. Quotations are from *The Entertainment at Althorp*, James Knowles (ed.) in *The Cambridge Edition of the Works of Ben Jonson*, David Bevington, Martin Butler and Ian Donaldson (eds), 2:401.
48. The suggestion comes from Leeds Barroll in his *Anna of Denmark, Queen of England: A Cultural Biography*, p.83.
49. *Dudley Carleton to John Chamberlain 1603–1624: Jacobean Letters*, Maurice Lee, Jr. (ed.), p. 53. All quotations come from this collection.
50. Cited in E. K. Chambers, *The Elizabethan Stage*, 3:279.
51. *Hymenaei*, David Lindley (ed.), in the *Cambridge Edition*, 2:696.
52. *Haddington Masque*, David Lindley (ed.), in the *Cambridge Edition*, 3:270.
53. From Cornwallis *Life and Death of Prince Henry*, quoted in David Lindley's edition of *The Speeches at Prince Henry's Barriers* in *The Cambridge Edition*, 3:519. Quotations come from this edition.
54. John Stow, *The Annales or Generall Chronicle of England*, p. 897.
55. For a reproduction of these drawings and discussion, see *Inigo Jones: The Theatre of the Stuart Court*, Stephen Orgel and Roy Strong (eds), 1:158–67.

56. Quoted in *The Masque Archive* in the online edition of *The Cambridge Edition*, item 10.
57. Roger Coke, *A Detection of the Court and State of England*, 2:69.
58. Edmund Howes reports that the bride and groom moved through London 'being accompanied with the Duke of Lennox'. Cited in Nichols, *Progresses*, 2:731.
59. John Orrell, 'The London Court Stage', pp. 81–2.
60. Quoted in *The Collected Works of Thomas Middleton*, Gary Taylor and John Lavagnino (eds), p. 1030. See there the discussion of this lost masque, pp. 1027–33. The editors attribute two songs about Cupid that presumably were used in the masque. One wonders if Middleton has cast his eye back on Jonson's *Challenge at Tilt*.
61. Quoted in the *Masque Archive* in the online edition of *The Cambridge Edition* in a translation by Karen Britland and Line Cottegnies, Item No. 12.
62. *Masque Archive*, item No. 13 for *Masque of Beauty*.
63. *Masque Archive,* item No. 16 for *Masque of Queens*, translated by Karen Britland and Line Cottegnies.
64. *Masque Archive*, item No. 1 for the *Masque of Augurs*.
65. *Masque Archive*, item No. 1 for *Time Vindicated*.
66. Found in the *Masque Archive*, item No. 10, for *Golden Age*.
67. Quoted from *The Complete Masques*, Orgel (ed.), p. 318.
68. Nichols, *Progresses*, 2:549.
69. See Alan Young, *Tudor and Jacobean Tournaments*, p. 41. Young includes a helpful Appendix that lists all the tournaments in the late Tudor and early Stuart periods.
70. Nichols, *Progresses*, 2:287.
71. *Calendar of State Papers Venetian*, 12:328.
72. *Letters*, 1:440.
73. Henry Wotton's letter to Sir Edmund Bacon, found in *The Life and Letters of Sir Henry Wotton*, Logan Pearsall Smith (ed.), 2:17.
74. Ian Donaldson, *Ben Jonson: A Life*, p. 448.
75. Reported in *The Letters of Henry Wotton*, 2:17.
76. National Archives, PRO 30/53/10/34, fol. 64.
77. National Archives, PRO 30/53/10/38, fol. 71.
78. John Hacket, *Scrinia Reserata*, p. 24. Hacket also reports the theological disputations that took place.
79. See my 'Gerrard Herbert's Reports about Drama Performances (1617–1619)', *Studies in Philology*.
80. National Archives, SP 14/94, fol. 78r.
81. National Archives, SP 14/95, fol. 24a.
82. National Archives, SP 14/96, fol.51r.
83. William Herbert to Doncaster, 20 May 1619, British Library, Egerton MS 2592.

84. This nearly indecipherable word appears to be 'althoe'. Herbert seems to have tried to correct it in some way. Herbert's letter appears in the National Archives, London, SP 14/109, folios 100–1. J. O. Halliwell prepared a transcription in the nineteenth century: *A Copy of a Letter of News Written to Sir Dudley Carleton* (London: privately printed, 1865). Halliwell in his transcription simply omits the word altogether, either because he thought that Herbert was trying to cancel it or because Halliwell could not figure it out. This is a sobering reminder about relying on transcriptions that have not been checked against the original. Halliwell does not indicate that any problem exists here. I discuss these matters fully in my '*Pericles*: A Performance, a Letter (1619)', in *Performances at Court in the Age of Shakespeare*, Sophie Chiari and John Mucciolo (eds), cited above.
85. National Archives, SP 14/109, fol. 100.
86. The Great Chamber was sometimes used for dramatic performances, plays and masques. It was, according to John Astington, *English Court Theatre*, pp. 44–51, about half the size of the hall, making it the appropriate venue for this intimate gathering. Jonson's masque the previous year was performed in the Banqueting House.
87. The transcription is my own.
88. National Archives, SP 14/105, fol. 75v.
89. *The Letters of John Chamberlain*, 2:201–2.
90. G. P. V. Akrigg, *Jacobean Pageant: The Court of King James I*, p. 284.
91. For a discussion of patronage through dedications see my *Textual Patronage in English Drama, 1570–1640*. Helen Willcox in the *Oxford Dictionary of National Biography* in the entry on George Herbert suggests that Lennox was a 'likely patron' of the poet in his search for court appointment. Given Lennox's close relationship with George Herbert's brother Edward Herbert, this idea is plausible; but I know of no confirming evidence.
92. John Ford, *Honor Triumphant*, sig. B1.
93. Henry Peacham, *Minerva Britanna*, p. 102.
94. Walter Quin, *Sertum Poeticum*, sig. F2.
95. John Davies, *Microcosmos. The Discovery of the Little World*. I quote from the 1607 edition, p. 255.
96. Gervase Markham, *Cavalarice, or, The English Horseman*, sig. Xx2.
97. John May, *A Declaration of the Estate of Clothing Now Used within this Realme of England*, sig. A3.
98. Juan de Luna, *Arte Breve*.

5

Last Years: Good and Ill Together

MARRIAGE

On the subject of marriage, Lennox might well recall King James's somewhat wistful words in the *Basilicon Doron*: 'First of all consider that Mariage is the greatest earthly felicitie or miserie that can come to a man'.[1] Lennox's experience could readily offer documentation of the king's judgement, which the king based on his only marriage and doubtless observation of other marriages. Indeed, Lennox's previous two marriages can be characterised thus: the first one, too short, lasting only one year because of the wife's death; the second one, too long, although it lasted only twelve unpleasant years. (In fact, it had in effect ended long before her death in 1610.) Not until 1621 did Lennox venture to marry again, obviously feeling no sense of urgency on this matter. One source claims that Lennox had 'shared his pleasure with many Ladis' before launching another wedding.[2] Lennox, handsome, accomplished, wealthy and the only duke in England, would have been a highly desirable target for many. Finally, in June 1621, Lennox married Frances Howard (not the criminal of the same name married to Somerset), who had herself been married before. Her two previous marriages can be characterised thus: first, the one to Henry Prannell, too short; the second, to Edward Seymour, Earl of Hertford, far too long. Quite likely, Lennox and this Frances Howard had been intimately involved while she was still married to Seymour. In any event, both potential partners shared a similarity in having no surviving children. Perhaps a third marriage would be the charm. Having experienced considerable misery, maybe now felicity would be their lot.

Frances was born in 1578, four years after Lennox, the daughter of Thomas Howard, Viscount Howard of Bindon, who died when she was three years old. At the age of thirteen Frances married Prannell, a wealthy vintner of London and Hertford.[3] Unfortunately, he died in December 1599, making her a widow at age twenty-one, but a wealthy one. Frances developed a bootless infatuation with Henry Wriothesley, Earl of Southampton, which led only to anguish for her. She regularly consulted the notorious Simon Forman for prophecies about her fortunes in love. Being bright and beautiful, not to mention wealthy, Frances had many suitors, but not Southampton. One unfortunate suitor was Sir George Rodney, who, failing in his love quest, wrote her a letter in his own blood and then took his life. Arthur Wilson, not always reliable but interesting, reports on Rodney's suicide, noting that Rodney 'wrot a large paper of well-composed *Verses* in his own blood (strange kind of *Composedness*) wherein he bewailes and laments his own unhappiness'.[4] Wilson thinks that Rodney offers a 'desperate and sad Spectacle of *Fraility*'.

Frances finally settled on Seymour, a sixty-one-year-old wealthy widower (his first wife bore the name, of course, of Frances Howard). They married in 1601. Despite Forman's forecast, Hertford lived for another twenty years, until 1621, forcing Frances to endure an unpleasant marriage to a jealous husband. Chamberlain, one of the gossips responsible for information about her, writes of Hertford's death in a letter of 18 April 1621: 'The earle of Hertford hath left his Lady in goode state, better then 4000li [pounds] joynter, besides his house in Channon-row to her and her heires, and a faire house with a parke . . . to her and the heires of her body lawfully begotten, wherof there is no great daunger'.[5] Thus, the wealthy Frances accumulated even more wealth and had rid herself of an undesirable husband.

Socially ambitious and well placed in court circles, having been many years earlier a good friend of Cecil, Frances offered most attractive prospects. A few weeks after Hertford's death in April, Lennox and Frances wed secretly on 16 June. (All of Lennox's weddings took place in some kind of secrecy.) Such unseemly haste seems to confirm the probability of their having had an affair long before Hertford's death. Indeed, Wilson offers a kind of proof, insisting that during her unhappy marriage, 'She was often courted by the Duke of *Lenox*, who presented many a fair offring to her, as an humble *Suppliant*' (*History*, p. 258). Wilson says that Lennox courted her 'sometimes in a blew Coat with a Basket-hilt sword, making his addresses in such odd disguises; yet she carried a fair fame during the *Earl's* time'. Exactly why would Lennox need 'odd disguises'? Clearly this information points to an illicit affair, which may have been common knowledge since she apparently maintained a respectable reputation. Wilson accuses Frances of being 'greedy of *Fame*, and loved to keep great *State* with little Cost' (259). A marriage with Lennox would certainly enhance her fame; and he gained a compatible wife, his knowledge of her already well seasoned.

Chamberlain writes rather harshly of the duchess, underscoring her delight in her new title and status. Clearly, she took seriously her newfound position, wife of one of the Jacobean court's most important noblemen and, furthermore, cousin of the king. She guarded the status jealously. She may have on occasion used it to her advantage. Chamberlain writes in May 1622 of a dinner with the king. According to the report, the Spanish ambassador Don Gondomar 'invited himself to dine with the Duke of Lennox and his Duchesse this day at Whitehall' (2:436). Further, 'Yt is whispered (I know not how trulie) that the Duches hath gotten of the King 10000li to pay her husbands debts, upon pretence she was promised yt before she wold yeeld to the marriage'. This seems very strange and may well not be true, as Chamberlain suggests. That James might award that amount of money, which he probably did not have, to Lennox is not unthinkable. But was it in fact necessary? A year later, just before James made Lennox Duke of Richmond, Chamberlain reports in a letter to Dudley Carleton on 5 April that the king had planned to elevate several noblemen to ducal status. This possibility chagrined the duchess: 'to the great disgust of the duchesse of Lennox who is saide to labour all she can to raigne still alone and not become retrograde' (2:488). The duchess wants no competition. In fact, James, for whatever reason, did not follow through with this plan, elevating only Buckingham to ducal status and granting Lennox a new, additional title: Duke of Richmond, which surely pleased the duchess. After Lennox's death in early 1624 the duchess continued to comport herself in a regal, if not imperious, style. Chamberlain reports on 8 January 1625 of a visit by the Duke of Brunswick to her. She 'admitted him with a proviso that he must not offer to kisse her, but what was wanting in herself was supplied in her attendants and followers who were all kist over twise' (2:594). Chamberlain continues to document her style: 'We have much talke of this Diana of the Ephesians, and her magnificence in going to her chappell at Ely House . . . where she had her closet or traverse, her fowre principall officers steward, chamberlain, treasurer, controller, marching before her in velvet gownes with white staves'. Others joined the procession. Assuming the accuracy of Chamberlain's account, the duchess seems to have created her own court, full of display and opulence. Perhaps she continued to harbour the illusion that James might marry her.

Post wedding, the duke and duchess sought more property in the form of houses, beginning with York House in London, the current residence of the disgraced Francis Bacon. Lennox wrote to Bacon in January 1622 asking for the house. The letter begins: 'I am now a married man, I have more reason than before to think of providing me some house in London, whereof I am yet destitute; and for that purpose I have resolved to intreat your Lordship that I may deal with you for York-house'.[6] As part of the proposed deal, Lennox offers the use of 'the house at Channon-row, late the Earl of Hertford's, being a very commodious and capable house, wherein I and my wife have absolute power' (7:327) – not exactly 'destitute' of a residence in London. This house had come as part of Frances's legacy. Lennox adds: 'though I have not been without thoughts of this house before your Lordship had it, yet I was willing to give way to your Lordship's more pressing use thereof then . . . I do not doubt that your Lordship [will] endeavour to gratify me in this' (7:327). Bacon's current vulnerable position makes Lennox's appeal compelling. Or, so he thought.

Bacon's response came immediately. He begins: 'I am sorry to deny your Grace anything; but in this you will pardon me. York-house is the house where my father died, and where I first breathed, and there will I yield my last breath' (Bacon, 7:327). Bacon admits his straitened circumstances but insists: 'At least no money nor value shall make me part with it'. Another suitor enters the picture: George Villiers, Marquis of Buckingham. Bacon writes: 'as I never denied it to my Lord Marquis, so yet the difficulty I made was so like a denial, as I owe unto my great love and respect to his Lordship a denial to all my other friends'. Bacon hastens to add his devotion to Lennox as well, and closes: 'So, not doubting that you will continue me in your former love and good affection, I rest'. In March 1622 Sir Edward Sackville wrote a long letter to Bacon, informing him of Buckingham's dismay at also being refused York House, what Sackville refers to as 'the old distaste concerning York-house' (7:343). But Buckingham's annoyance has been somewhat mitigated by the recognition that Lennox has also been denied. Sackville explains: 'I can assure you the tender hath much won upon him and mellowed his heart towards you, and your genius directed you aright when you writ that letter of denial unto the Duke'. Even King James apparently approved of the strategy. Buckingham continued with several clever moves to pursue this property, even though he had recently acquired Wallingford House in London and scarcely needed Bacon's home. In the long run, he prevailed; and Bacon surrendered York House, deciding that he might live out his life somewhere else rather than deny two powerful lords who were in a position to help him.

If not York House, perhaps Ely House in Holborn; thus began the pursuit of this London property as early as August 1621. Chamberlain writes somewhat optimistically on 18 August: 'The Duke of Lennox is in possession and hath taken a lease of Hatton House, but upon what termes or for how long I cannot learn' (2:397). Things did not happen that quickly. Chamberlain reports the terms on 13 July 1622: 'The Lady Hatton hath bargained with the Duke of Lennox for her house in Holbourne, rating yt at 12000li [pounds] present monie, or 2000li in hand and 1500li a yeare during her life, which later condition is accepted by the Duke and Duchesse' (2:446). Even in December 1622 negotiations continue with the additional terms: 'besides that she [Lady Hatton] reserves to herself the lodgings over the gate and a doore into the new gallerie' (466). Not until 17 May 1623 can Chamberlain report: 'The duke and Duchesse of Richmond have gotten the graunt of Ely House in lieu wherof the bishop is to have that which was the earle of Hertfords house in Chanon-row' (2:498). The house has currently been occupied by the Spanish ambassador, Chamberlain adds. The duchess 'layes in hard to have all the furniture of Ely House'.

In June 1622 the Lennox couple had also been negotiating for additional property outside of London. Chamberlain reports King James's visit to Lady Kildare at Cobham where he sought the approval of the lady to 'be brought to part with yt [Cobham] to the Duke and Duchesse upon reasonable conditions' (2:441). But by the next year, the duke and duchess engaged in a swap of this property for another. Lady Finch, widow of Sir Moyle Finch, paid £12,000 to the Duke and Duchess of Richmond, Chamberlain reports on 28 June, 'or the value thereof in exchaunge of Cobham in Kent for her faire house of Copt-hall and other landes in Essex' (505). Could it be that Lennox wanted property in Essex to compete with Buckingham, who had recently established New-Hall there? Whatever the motive, the couple knew that part of one's status could be measured in property.

LETTERS

Lennox initiated his discussion with Bacon about the desire to acquire York House by writing a letter. Lennox had many occasions to write letters, especially in his last five years, often in line with official duties, such as from the Privy Council, but also personal ones, which help expand an understanding of his character. Unlike his garrulous cousin, King James, Lennox mainly exhibited a certain restraint or reserve in personal letters. With a limited number of letters available, it can be difficult to reach conclusions about what they reveal about personality. As an exceptionally important courtier, Lennox may simply have felt that he should be prudent in letters. But he did not hesitate to express his heart-felt grief about the death of the Earl of Dunbar, in a letter cited earlier. Not reticent about friendship, for example, but not effusive, as in the manner of the king. Lennox may seem chaste by comparison, especially by contrast to the king's letters to Somerset, and particularly the letters to Buckingham in the 1620s, whose content has managed to scandalise some across the centuries.[7]

Lennox shares a perspective on the function of letters in friendship as defined by John Donne, who wrote regularly to his friend Henry Goodere, a member of the Privy Council and thus known to the duke. Donne wrote to Goodere on 15 August 1607, offering a rich metaphor: in friendship, 'a Letter, which is of a mixed nature, and hath something of both [words and deeds], is a mixed Parenthesis'.[8] The writer explains: 'It may be left out, yet it contributes . . . to the verdure, and freshnesse thereof [of friendship]'. Parenthesis suggests a kind of embrace of friends, but the letter can only be partial: some things will be left out, by choice or by necessity. Certainly Lennox's letters to friends expanded and enriched their relationships.

The duke exchanged letters earlier in the period with, among others, Robert Cecil and John Holles, as already noted. He wrote to friends who typically were out of the country, underscoring how letters often derive from the absent other. In these letters Lennox regularly seeks help of some kind, usually for his mother and sister, Gabrielle, in France. Clearly, he has not forgotten familial obligations. He wrote with frequency to his friend Edward Herbert, who served as ambassador to France, beginning in 1619. Lennox's letters show him to have an affable and pleasant relationship with others. He certainly demonstrates generous consideration in his ongoing search for help for his mother and sister, and he honours requests from his friends. A few of the letters comment on political issues, as when he muses about the Spanish Match. His letters serve multiple purposes and further document his character, offering the opportunity to hear his voice.

On 3 December 1621 Lennox wrote to James Hay, Viscount Doncaster, one of his fellow transplanted Scots who had followed James to England and remained. At the moment Doncaster was in France on a special diplomatic mission from King James. Lennox responds to Doncaster's illness and begins: 'My Lord I am glade to heare that in end yow haue ouercome that Long and tedious sicknes which afrighted all those that are your frenids: wherof I wanted not my parte ase one that pretends [feigns] a great deal of interest in any thing that concernes your L[ordship]'.[9] The letter continues: 'There are hearr a great many that rejoyce at your conualesence and wold bee hartyle content to see yow at home: which we all hope shall bee shortly'. Lennox then makes an important transition: 'but before yow come away I must entreat this fauour from yow'. Lennox seeks Hay's help and assistance for his mother and sister, 'concerning her pensione, or an Abbey for my Sister'. He signs the letter: 'your L. most Louing frenid'. But Lennox also offers an intriguing postscript: 'My wyffe comends her to your L. and nothwithstanding all old quarrells She wisheth your happy returne'. Sent from Whitehall, this letter offers a reliable pattern for Lennox's letters, although others will not carry a message from his wife of a few months. What 'old quarrels' exist with the duchess remains unclear. Thus, a straightforward and genuine concern for a friend's health takes a few deliberate turns, underscoring the various purposes of friendly letters. Lennox's voice comes through clearly.

Lennox writes Doncaster again a month later, on 3 January 1622, anticipating his imminent return, complaining first that he had not been sure of his whereabouts and makes the witty observation: 'so that a man may bee a courtier and not know perfectly the passages of all things'.[10] Lennox continues: 'I ame so muche the glader, that wee shall see your L. the sooner heare'. He concludes by offering help: 'if I can any way bee vsefull to yow, yow may vndoubtedly bee assured of the best offeces'. Lennox also notes that the bearer of the letter 'can informe yow particularly of all occurrences in these partes'. This observation calls attention not only to the letter but also to its delivery and deliverer, who may convey all kinds of additional messages, sometimes ones that should not be written down.

As early as 24 June 1610 Lennox wrote to Thomas Edmondes, ambassador to France, assuring him of friendship and then asking for a favour: namely, a letter to Lennox's mother 'and other of my private friends'.[11] The precise content of these communications remains unspecified. On 3 October 1614 Lennox again wrote to Edmondes, transacting business and assuring the ambassador that he will remind King James of his services, although the king is currently at Royston. Lennox states that he will also soon be in Royston: 'so soune as I shalbe at royston I will take occation to remember His Ma^te [Majesty] of your selfe and that your absence in His seruice make yow not to be forgott'.[12] Further, Lennox writes: 'I assure your lo: that I shall aduertise you of His Ma^tes [Majesties] answer and shall not also feall to remember yow still to my lo. [treasurer] who still assures me of his loue toward yow' (fol. 75). Lennox concludes somewhat cryptically: 'concerning the matter of mariage I can only pray for it: for of it the king saye nothing to me'. He presumably refers to negotiations in France for a possible marriage between Princess Christine and Prince Charles, a subject that Lennox had himself broached in his time in France in late summer 1613. Nothing came of this eventually. Edmondes had first negotiated on behalf of Prince Henry, a process cut abruptly short by the prince's death in late 1612.

Not surprisingly, Lennox also wrote to Dudley Carleton, as did many other people, most notably Chamberlain, who wrote regularly, if not excessively, to Carleton. During the time that Lennox writes, Carleton serves as ambassador to The Hague, to which Princess Elizabeth and Prince Frederick had moved after their ignominious expulsion from Prague and Bohemia; and in The Hague they remained. On 20 July 1621 Lennox seeks a favour for a nephew, Alexander, the son of his sister, married to Mar. Lennox begins: 'My Lord, when any occasion presents that concerneth my selfe or my freinds I make bold to bee troublesome to yow without ceremonye; I haue a sisters sone of myne . . . who hath a great inclination to follow the warrs'.[13] Lennox does not wish to interfere or insert this nephew ahead of some other: 'hee wold bee content to haue the comand of a horse company wherefore if any more Levies bee made I wold entreat yo[r] L. to deale with the Estates and the prince of Orange to procure this fauor for him'. Lennox would write the prince himself, 'but I will deffer till I heare from yow againe'. Deal with this as you can, Lennox assures Carleton, 'and doe mee the fauour to wryt to mee againe so soone ase conuientently may bee'.

A month later, on 31 August, Lennox writes Carleton, this time on behalf of someone else, Mr Lundy, 'a gentleman whome I respect', who also needs assistance in a military pursuit.[14] Lennox, thinking about such matters, approaches the familiar topic of his nephew: 'I must also entreat yo[r] L. to remember the busines I wrote to yow concerning my Nephew . . . for which courtesies I shall bee much beholden to yow'. Having reinforced concern for his nephew, Lennox moves to ask for help for Sir Peter Regementes, in a letter of 16 September 1622, who 'desired that I wold wryt to your L. in his behalfe'.[15] Lennox, recognising this person as 'being a gentleman who I respect', urges Carleton: 'I must entreat your L. to grant him your assistance for the furthering of his busines there, and to befrend him in any his Lawfull affaires'. Lennox signs the letter as 'yo[r] L. most Louing freinde'. Not only does Lennox not hesitate to ask for help for relatives, he also reaches out on behalf of others. Clearly, Lennox's stature commands attention and assurance of assistance: a recurring subject in his letters.

Beginning in 1619, when Edward Herbert went to France to be the English ambassador there, Lennox wrote to him regularly. Two topics recur: request for assistance for his mother and sister and commentary about the 'Spanish Match', the proposed marriage of Prince Charles to the Infanta of Spain. Occasionally, some other political topics appear. Surely Lennox's ongoing concern for his mother and sister reflects well on him; and he uses the opportunities, such as with Doncaster as well, to seek help. In the letter of 22 May 1619, Lennox begins with 'remembering' his love and respect for Herbert. He also reminds him of 'this gentleman whome I did recommend to your L. before yow went from here I wold entreate yow to take notice of him if he haue occasione to vse your fauor, for hee is doubly my cousin: and I loue him'.[16] In addition to this unnamed cousin, Lennox asks Herbert to assist 'my Lady My Mother, or my Sister'.

He continues this request on 1 March 1620: 'I must entreat yow to remember that busines of the Abbey for my Sister [Gabrielle] whereof there haue bene many promises made' – but apparently not yet fulfilled.[17] Lennox informs Herbert of a political problem, namely, that an 'Ambassador from the King of Bohemia' remains in London. He adds in a postscript that the Spanish ambassador Gondomar will be arriving in 'four or fyue dayes, and then I hope we shall resolue what to doe in this busines of Bohemia'. Alas, vain hope, for the problems only got worse after the Spanish had invaded Prince Frederick's Palatinate and cut him off from his own principality. And part of the problem rests with James's hesitation and well-founded uncertainty about what to do. Lennox writes: 'and yet his Ma^te our Master is Backward to expresse himself what he will doe'. In November 1620, at the Battle of White Mountain, Frederick and the Bohemians suffered a stunning defeat and Frederick and Elizabeth fled Prague, never to return. James feared, of course, possibly antagonising the Spanish.

Lennox returns to the subject of his mother and sister in a letter to Herbert just a few weeks later, on 30 March. Lennox begins with thanks: 'My Lord, I haue vnderstood by My Lady my Mother of the great fauor yow did her in solliciting her busines about her pension'.[18] Lennox adds: 'I must still rest beholden to yow for all your courtesies till occasions present of requitall'. The duke acknowledges that he has also written to a cardinal and others: 'I haue also entreated them furthermore concerning the Abbey for my Sister'. But he cannot give up: 'I must make bold to entreat the continuance of your fauorable respect towards these busines'. On 6 May 1620 Lennox again records his indebtedness to Herbert, writing somewhat wittily: 'although I should forget to giue your L. thanks for the obligations I owe yow my selfe yet my Lady my Mother will not giue me leaue to bee vnmyndfull of your courtesie to her for the

paines you took in her busines'.[19] Indeed, 'in euery letter shee writs to
mee, I ame put in mynd to giue yow thanks which I doe very hartily'.
Obviously, the son and mother carry on a conversation about her needs.
Lennox closes the letter by mentioning that Lord Digby will be going to
Spain shortly 'for the busines of Bohemia, the king is to send one ouer
to mediat a peace but wee know not yet who shall goe'. No such desired
peace took place.

A letter to Herbert of 7 November 1620 begins with Lennox expressing his 'Loue and respect vnto your L. and to giue yow many thanks
for all yo\[r\] fauors bothe to my selff and conferred vpon many others for
my sake'.[20] This statement would obviously include the favours done
on behalf of Lennox's mother and sister. Lennox mentions an upcoming Parliament and adds: 'there are no newes Lately from Bohemia may
when any thing occurreth worthy yo\[r\] knowledge I will acquaint yow with
it'. Lennox adds a telling statement of hope: 'I pray god all things may
succed well'. A common refrain continues in the letter of 19 July 1621, in
which he begins by observing that Doncaster, to whom he has also written, is now in France. Lennox asks Herbert that he 'wold furnishe him
[Doncaster] with yo\[r\] aduis and best fartherances in the pursuite of My
Mother and Sisters busines'.[21] I know, Lennox adds, that 'hee will leaue
nothing vndone that Lyeth in his abilitie to procure them content but hee
will haue need of Instructions how to proceed'. Perhaps with the com-
bined efforts of Herbert and Doncaster Lennox can get some satisfaction
on behalf of his mother and sister. Lennox's admirable persistence of five
years may yet pay off. Certainly he functions as a dutiful son and helpful
brother through these letters seeking help.

Other letters to Edward Herbert reveal Lennox's ruminations on the
'Spanish Match', discussed earlier. Lennox had clearly preferred some
kind of match with France rather than with Spain. But he tried occasionally to reflect some optimism about the Spanish marriage arrangement
for Prince Charles. Thus, he writes to Herbert on 3 January 1623: 'wee
hope to see the Infanta heere this Spring'.[22] In early March, Lennox refers
to Charles and Buckingham as 'knights errant', which attempts to see
them as romance figures on a quest.[23] The reality, of course, was not so
glamorous. A cheerful tone appears also in Lennox's letter to Herbert
on 2 April, when he writes: 'I hope yow haue harde of his Highnes safe
arriual well in Spaine and of his Magnifique entertainment'.[24] And on
24 April Lennox hopes that Herbert has heard of the good success in
Spain. On 13 May Lennox anticipates the arrival of Charles and the
Infanta: 'the Ships are ready to goe away to bring home the prince his
Highnes and the Infanta, wee hope they will bee heere in July'.[25] But

on 3 October 1623 Lennox writes to Herbert with a different kind of expectation: 'wee doe bothe curse and pray the Windes for wee expect with great impatience the prince his returne which now dependeth only vpon the Wind'.[26] Indeed, in a few days, Charles and Buckingham landed safely on English soil, but without the by now hated Infanta. And yet, on 9 November, after reporting that James has been ill with the gout, Lennox comments that 'the prince is in good health . . . wee expect that the Infanta shall bee heere in the Spring'.[27] Lennox adds that 'the king hath not yet seene the Spanish Ambassador that came with the prince'. The elusive Infanta never appeared in England. Indeed, by January 1624, the court and Parliament had largely given up the idea of a Spanish match. Certainly Lennox had.

Lennox's letters manifest restraint rather than passion. Often he simply conducts business. But that 'business' often included asking for favours, especially for his mother and sister. His ongoing concern for their welfare redounds to his credit. He also vows to reciprocate such help, as he promises these friends. Political thoughts about Bohemia and Spain appear, as Lennox attempts to convey his thoughts to ambassadors abroad. Perhaps his occasional expressions of hope about the Infanta's arrival may even be tinged with a touch of irony – admittedly difficult to know for certain. But as one not keen on the Spanish match in the first place, Lennox might well have begun to hope that the 'Spring' of her anticipated arrival would never occur. The letters reflect a serious friendship that Lennox enjoys with several people for whom he expresses his love and respect.

DEATH

'To every thing there is a season. A time to be born, and a time to die. A time to weep . . . a time to mourn' (Ecclesiastes 3: 1–4). No less true for Lennox, who died in his sleep at Ely House in Holborn on 16 February 1624, in his fiftieth year. His death shocked and saddened all.

Because no one actually witnessed his death the various accounts need to be regarded for what they represent: imagined narrative versions of the event. None is far-fetched and they rely on an oral tradition that developed about Lennox's death. They, along with reports of reactions to his death, constitute a 'scripture' of his ending. Reactions certainly form a kind of gospel – good news, embellished and often idealised.

John Hacket, eventually Bishop of Coventry and Lichfield, created a biography of John Williams, Lord Keeper and Bishop of Lincoln, whom

Hacket served as household chaplain in 1621 before becoming a chaplain to King James. Hacket resided in the Holborn area while serving St Andrews parish, and Williams obviously knew Lennox well. Hacket claims also to know the duchess and her orderly housekeeping. These connections give certain credence to Hacket's report. He writes: 'He [Lennox] had Supp'd chearfully the Night before, complain'd of nothing when he went to Bed, slept soundly'.[28] His servant went to wake Lennox the next morning so that he could get ready for the opening of Parliament, which he would attend: 'but found that he had breathed out his Spirit'. Thus, no effort could rouse Lennox. This simple narrative presents the basic facts without any embellishment.

Alvise Valaresso, the Venetian ambassador, reports on 1 March: 'The good gentleman [Lennox] expired shortly before his time to rise from bed, without any one being aware of the fact. When he first awoke he complained of some pain in his head, and accordingly some say that he died of apoplexy'.[29] This curious statement implies that Lennox had died and then complained of pain. The ambassador claims that 'The day before his death, I was with him and his wife for a good while, when the prince [Charles] also came up'. This ambassador and Charles may have been the last people, not of Lennox's household, to have seen him alive. Valaresso adds his reaction: 'He was fifty years old, the king's cousin, beloved by everyone . . . This loss is deeply felt by the king, but even more by the prince' (18:226). This succinct statement of loss captures the sentiment of most people.

Even the title page of Abraham Darcie's *A Monumental Pyramide* asserts the time of the duke's death: Lennox 'departed this transitory life . . . on Monday, being the sixteenth day of February 1624. Betwixt sixe and seauen of the clocke in the morning, to the great griefe of many thousand people of sundry Nations'.[30] How Darcie could know this remains a mystery. The suggestion of Lennox's apparent momentary awareness before dying gets further treatment in James Cleland's *A Monument of Mortalitie*. Not only has Darcie pinned down the time of death but Cleland elaborates on the event, making Lennox a kind of saint. Cleland writes: Lennox died 'meekely, patiently, like a Lambe; and so soone as hee felt his *paine of the head* increase, and more then heretofore, he turned his eyes towards heauen, and carried his thoughts whether his extreme griefe did conduct him'.[31] Cleland is not finished: 'Hee prayed vnto God in his *Bed*, beleeuing assuredly, hee who is in all places where hee is called on' will hear his prayer, as God had with others, and send 'his Angels thither to assist this soule

and bring it vnto him'. Cleland seems to have been in the room of
Lennox's death:

> when the *Doctor of Physike*, and the *Groome* of his Bed-chamber, drew the
> Courtaine, and found him cold Dead, without breath or motion, hauing one
> hand lifted towards heauen . . . so this *Comely Lord*, desiring to Die decently
> in his *Bed* (as he carried himselfe in all his actions of his life) hee pulled vp
> the vpper sheet close about his necke, and so quietly gaue vp the Ghost, not
> so much as giuing one groane. (p. 29)

This narrative achieves mythic status, moving a long way from Hacket's
simple account. How can Cleland possibly know the particulars of
Lennox's death? He cannot, but that did not stop the creation of an
idealised version of Lennox's saintly death. Myth triumphs over factual
evidence.

That Cleland served as a chaplain to Lennox would probably explain
why his text in many ways resembles a sermon, pointing repeatedly to
how Christians need to face death, for example. And this may explain
his desire to create a kind of hagiography of Lennox. He also reports
on the immediate action after discovering Lennox's death; this he may
have actually witnessed. Cleland writes that the duchess 'went to his
[Lennox's] Bed-side, *Closed his eyes, shut vp his mouth, kissed him*, and
I may say (in some sense) *washed him* . . . with her teares' (*Monument*,
45). Further, she ordered him to be bowelled, embalmed, 'and then
Wrapped vp in the best and *finest* white linen cloth'. These acts Cleland
describes as 'Christian-like' and pious. The next night, around ten o'clock,
Cleland reports that Lennox's body 'was carried by his owne Serruants,
and accompanied with a great number of Knights and Gentlemen vnto
the Abbey Church of Westminster, and there in King *Henry* the Seuenths
Chappell . . . *Honourably buried*'. There Bishop John Williams read the
burial of the dead service. Next intense preparations began for the actual
funeral, appointed for 19 April.

Chamberlain reports on some of the preparations and the time leading up to the funeral. He writes to Dudley Carleton on 10 April: 'There
hath ben a herse, with his statue [effigy] on a bed of state above these
six weekes at Hatton House, where there hath ben great concourse of
all sorts, and all things are like to be performed with more solemnitie and
ado then needed'.[32] Chamberlain credits the wife with a determination
for planning the funeral and being sure that it would be magnificent: 'yt
so pleaseth her Grace to honor the memorie of so deare a husband, whose
losse she takes so impatiently and with so much shew of passion that
many odd and ydle tales are daylie reported or invented of her'(2:551).

Chamberlain takes a dim view of the duchess's reaction, thinking that it might all be just distress about a loss of position at court. Cleland adds details about the vigil at Ely House where six rooms were hung with 'Blackes, and the *Effigie* of *My Lord his Grace*, to be made, and set vp in the best chamber of the House, apparelled with his Parliament Robes, lying in a blacke *Veluet Bed*' (*Monument*, p. 46). The creation of an effigy – a life-like figure – was common for royal funerals, giving credence to Lennox's important status and the forthcoming splendour of his funeral. Cleland concludes that such an effigy demonstrates that 'this life of ours is but an *Image*'. Scores of people came to the house to pay homage to Lennox and to observe this effigy.

Chamberlain, a couple of weeks after the funeral, reports to Carleton:

> The Duke of Richmonds funeralles were performed with great charge the 19th of this month, for there were about a thousand mourners one and other, besides sixe or eight horses covered all with velvet, and his picture or figure [effigy] drawne in a coach by sixe horses clad in like manner. (2:554)

Chamberlain adds his comparative judgement: 'his herse at Westminster (that stands yet) equall in all points (or rather more elevated) then Quene Annes'. (As noted earlier, Chamberlain did not much care for Anne's funeral.) He finds Lennox's funeral more impressive than Anne's, confirming this judgement by adding: 'I have not heard of such a titularie prince and a subject, so magnificently enterred'. Given that Lennox was not an immediate member of the royal family, his funeral may have struck others as unusually grand. Chamberlain concludes by noting that Bishop Williams preached the funeral sermon and 'gave him [Lennox] his full commendation for mildnes and many other vertues'.

Two other accounts, those of Cleland and Darcie, add to the knowledge of the funeral. Cleland writes in *A Monument of Mortalitie*: 'That great extent of persons & honors, which proceeded, from the gate of *Richmond House*, to that of *Abbey Church*, may as well bee comprehended by imagination, as by discourse, if we will figure to our selues one thousand men in *Mourning*', plus all the other features of the procession itself (p. 47). In Cleland's view, the procession beggars reckoning. He may be right, if judged by the pamphlet, attributed to Abraham Darcie, *Frances Duchesse Dowager of Richmond . . . her Funerall Teares*, which requires fifteen published pages of double columns just to list the participants in the procession, including nineteen trumpeters, scattered throughout; this list appears in the section called 'The Proceeding to the Funerall'.[33] Cleland enumerates the other features, such as those cited by Chamberlain.

Darcie's list includes a who's who among courtiers and clergy, notably, the various earls, such as Pembroke (William Herbert), Montgomery (his brother, Philip), Arundel (Thomas Howard); the Scottish lords, Gordon and Arran; Darcie himself, and Cleland; Lennox's nephews: James Stuart, son of Esmé, and Alexander and Henry Erskine, sons of Mar and Marie, Lennox's sister. Lennox had written to Carleton on Alexander's behalf, as noted above. And somewhat surprising, the great architect Inigo Jones, who presumably worked with Lennox on the rebuilding of the Banqueting House, appeared in the procession. The list also notes: 'The Banner of Steward alone borne by Sir Iohn Steward Knight a close mourner' (*Duchesse*, sig. A4). This may refer to John Stewart, the illegitimate son of Lennox, who would certainly be appropriately designated a 'close mourner'. The only meaning of 'close mourner' given in the *Oxford English Dictionary* is 'a close relative of the deceased'.[34] Such an understanding would fit John Stewart perfectly. If so, the duke's role as Lord High Steward would be recognised by this son, whose presence and importance in the commemoration of his father thus becomes acknowledged. John Taylor, in a one-page broadsheet of elegy about Lennox, includes in a column in the middle of the sheet 'The manner of the Funerall'. This item, similar to Darcie's, enumerates the participants in the procession. Taylor lists, among many others, 'The banner of *Steward*, borne by Sir *Iohn Steward*, accompanied with an Officer of Armes'.[35] Taylor names only one or two other people in his long list, thereby calling attention to the likely importance of this John Stewart.

Darcie notes that the chariot carrying the effigy included at the head John Houston, the duke's Master of the Wardrobe, and at the foot William Wood, chief gentleman of the duke's bedchamber. Alexander and Henry Erskine surrounded the chariot, as did the Lords Gordon and Arran. Cleland and Darcie both cite as chief mourner Lennox's brother, Esmé, now his brother's successor as Duke of Lennox. George Villiers, Duke of Buckingham, served as chief supporter to Esmé. It would be hard to improve on this arrangement of chief mourner and supporter, given King James's esteem and love for Buckingham.

The Archbishop of Canterbury, George Abbot, moved in the procession and participated in the service at Westminster, along with other bishops. As Cleland rightly observes: 'it was maruellous to behold; the whole streets being full of common people, the Windowes, Leads, and Tyles full on both sides of the better sort' (*Monument*, p. 48). Bishop Williams' sermon took as its text an obscure one from the Old Testament, found in 1 Kings 4: 5: 'Zabud the son of Nathan was principal officer, and the king's friend'. This the bishop found to be an accurate assessment of Lennox. Cleland agrees and comments: 'And why should hee not haue praised him, who was so Praise-worthy; seeing it is commended, if not commanded in the Bible' (48–9). Cleland adds that the scripture 'Paralleling our *Prince Lodouick* in euery particular' (p. 51), expressed 'abundantly, his [the bishop's] Learning and Loue, towards *My Lord Duke*, in declaring his Christian Life, and Heroick Deeds'. Darcie calls the bishop's sermon 'excellent and most learned' (*Duchesse*, A8v). Darcie adds Williams 'caused (contrary to custom) [the sermon] to be deliuered and giuen to the poore the next day after'.

After the sermon, 'all *My Lord's Armes, Armor, Standers, Banners, Shield,* and *Ensignes* were offered by Noblemen . . . vnto *My Lord Duke of Lenox* now is, who was his onely *Brother*' (Cleland, 51). Then, all of Lennox's officers 'brake their *Staues* ouer the *Effigie*, after all the *Offerings* were ended' (53). The service concluded, grief acknowledged and possibly assuaged, and Lennox's life celebrated in word, music and images. From his religious perspective, Cleland concludes that Lennox 'is ascended vp into Heauen before *God*, on a *Chariot of Triumph*, there to receiue . . . a *Crowne of Immortall Glorie*' (54). Whatever Lennox's eternal fate, Westminster Abbey had witnessed a remarkable event, rich in its outpouring of love for the deceased. The abbey's candles burned out, the mourners left, silence prevailed; but, Lennox's effigy and body remained, silent testimony to his exceptional life. As Chamberlain had written, Lennox was 'magnificently enterred'.

Published reactions to the death followed, glorifying Lennox, his character and accomplishments. The accounts, not surprisingly, idealise him; but, that seems to be the purpose of such elegies. Cleland does not disappoint on this score in his *A Monument of Mortalitie*. Early in the text, Cleland resorts to a familiar theatre metaphor. He writes: 'There is not an *intreat* [entrance] without an *exit* in this life's *Tragedie*; a very *Tragedie* (I say) for the most part, because wee are all borne crying, wee crie dying' (p. 9) – Cleland's echo of King Lear's reflection: 'We came crying hither' (Act IV, scene vi, line 178). Cleland says that a person enters life with a moan and exits with a groan. Death, he writes, 'in the end is the end of the *Play*'. Both good and bad actors die. The 'good are *Actors* of a *Comedie*; and howsoeuer they beginne, they end merrily: but the bad, are *Actors* of a *Tragedie*, and howsoeuer they beginne . . . yet their end miserable, their *Catastrophe* lamentable' (10). This theatre metaphor sets the stage for Cleland's assessment of Lennox's life, which he finds noble and fulfilling: an actor in a comedy. Or, as he writes a few pages later: 'our *Great* and *Gracious Prince, Lodouick*, who hath crowned all the actions of his Life with immortall *Crownes* of glorie and reputation' (16).

Cleland also records the reactions of others. He describes, for example, the duchess's apparent extreme response: 'she cast herselfe vpon the ground, teared her faire haire from her head, beating her breast, blubbering or disfiguring her face, and renting her clothes from her backe' (*Monument*, 30). King James 'was amazed at the first dolefull newes, *My Lord Duke is Dead*, and euer since hath missed him'. This restrained account continues: 'Nor yet can I tell you how the *Prince his Highnesse* [Charles] and the whole *Court* tooke these sorrowfull newes of my *Lord* his *Death*; otherwise then by silence, and by all mens teares'. Sometimes, Cleland says, 'Teares are better vnderstood then words' (31). His report expands:

> To tell now what the lamentation of *London* was, it is impossible and incredible; the people sighed and lamented one to another so; nor can I tell you how the poore people of the Countrie, euen such as neuer saw him, were sorie for his Death, because they heard of his goodnesse. (32)

Cleland acknowledges his lack of precise information, but he surmises the likely reaction of London and the country. But he sums up his own reaction: 'For my part, I cannot but grieue and lament so long as I liue, in remembering his loue, fauour, and liberalitie towards mee himselfe' (34).

Abraham Darcie in his *Framces Duchesse Dowager* devotes 116 pages to lamenting Lennox's death. He opens with a whole section of poetry, 'Funerall Teares', told from the perspective of the duchess, who begins: 'In Sea of Sighes and Teares I doe not know / Vnto what place of quiet I should row'.[36] In the first of several sections called 'Funerall Complaints' Darcie addresses the reader: 'Reader, admire, dissemble not in moane, / A Maruell hes extinct beneath this stone' (sig. A2). Darcie informs the reader: 'His [Lennox's] Soule and Corps were perfect, Honors hie, / Iustly he was admir'd on earth, in skie. / That he was admirable, his deeds do proue'. The writer adds: 'His death would not obserue the common way, / The Court was fil'd with cries and matchlesse mone, / Because its obiect maruellous was gone' (A4). Such outbursts counter Cleland's view of silence. Indeed, before the account of the funeral procession, Darcie imagines that the senses have been adversely affected by Lennox's death; for example, 'The World was dy'd in Blacke when Richmond dyde / No pleasing obiect can be now espiede'. The 'dull eare' can no longer hear music; smell has been affected; even taste is 'poudred with my Teares'; and feeling has been dulled: 'I can feele nothing since this lucklesse crosse, / But this, a feeling of Great Britaines losse' (Darcie, *Duchesse*).

In the second section of 'Funerall Complaints' Darcie constructs a momentary dialogue between France and Great Britain, as each acknowledges loss; they are 'mute', the writer says. France urges Britain: 'Put on blacke weeds for your vnhappie fate: / Ordaine a solemne fast' (C4v). And this country responds to France: 'True I haue cause to grieue, and so haue you'. France blames Britain for allowing Lennox to slip away; and Britain responds: 'Oh, do not blame me, twas not want of loue, / Which did him from my haplesse soyle remoue'. France rightly concludes: 'Then let vs ioyne our cries, and wailing keepe'. Darcie follows this with an imagined response of servants: 'He was a Maister like to God aboue, / If we did any fault or crime commit, / He didst freely forgiue and forget' (C5). Unlike other elegies about this death, Darcie thinks of the impact on the arts. He writes: 'The arts and Academies Complaints had ioynd, / As quite vndone but that you [Duchess] staid behind' (C8). Without her presence, all poets 'Would to the pit of darkesome despaire fall'. Their 'patron's' death has affected them deeply – an unexpected acknowledgement by Darcie of Lennox's exceptional contribution as patron of the arts and performer also.

In this same section of 'Funerall Complaints' Darcie comments on the reaction of the royal family. The text sets off these references with distinctive typographical features, as if to highlight them. First, Darcie reports about the king: 'first our mightie King doth act his part: / Whose part is passion, and whose actions teares, / From whom these words do seeme to pierce my cares' (B8). Later in this section Darcie imagines a more telling response from James than had Cleland: 'Oh Royall King, your eyes in teares may swim, / Cause You a subiect haue forsooke in him. / A Cousen and a friend whose loyall loue, / Did alwaies true and trustie to you proue' (C7). Of Prince Charles, Darcie writes: 'His fathers teares do no whit his impaire. / For he in sorrow seemeth more then heire. / Who wailes his losse' (C2). News of Lennox's death has flown to The Hague, where Princess Elizabeth and Frederick now live. They learn that Lennox lies 'asleepe in graues darke loathsome bed' (C2v). Even Elizabeth's children note her grief: 'With little ioy their mothers griefe espie: / And with their speech and gesture seeme to woe' (C3). Of course, while the royal family weeps, the duchess' 'mournfull heart doth bleed, / All knowes her griefe doth farre all theirs exceed' (C6v). In Darcie's view Lennox's death has prompted far-flung grief, from the king to the lowest servant.

Samuel Tailboys pays homage in his *A New Lachrymentall and Funerall Elegy*, which opens with an image of a skeleton and the inscription '*sic transit Gloria mundi*'. Tailboys addresses readers and observes that Lennox was 'so beloued . . . and had so many deserued titles of Honour, and was so gracious and good a member, for the good of all *Brittaine*'.[37] In the poem that follows, Tailboys appropriates the theatre metaphor: 'In worldly Stage, where all our liues are Plaies, / Whose Sceane hath end, in better Ioyes to rest'. (B2v). The poet claims that Lennox enjoyed respect for his merits in both Scotland and England. In fact, 'Our *Steward* high whose life and loue was iust, / That high and low did faithfully him trust' (B2). Tailboys calls him 'Graue, wise, iust, true, a mirrour of mankinde' (B1v). The poet enumerates his various titles and offices, such as Privy Council, Scotland's Admiral and Chamberlain, Steward and Member of Parliament. Great and small sought him out in Parliament. Now, Tailboys asserts, Lennox sits in a 'Parliament in Heauen where is no lacke / Of Honour, Beautie, Riches, and true Fame' (B4). His earthly role has ended.

Three broadsheets join the elegiac outpouring for Lennox. John Taylor's 'True louing sorrow', cited above, includes his assessment of the duke, in addition to providing another account of the funeral procession. Taylor writes of Lennox: 'True to his King, as did his seruice proue: / Discreet in Counsell, Noble in his minde'. The poet also characterises him as 'Affable, so hopefull vnto all'; and he asks, 'Who of this Duke a bad report can giue'. Taylor imagines seeing numerous woeful mourners as they visit Lennox's monument. George Marcelline, who had written earlier about Lennox as the one always at the king's right hand, continues in a vein similar to Taylor in his 'A Funerall Elegie', a broadsheet with a black border that suggests some kind of architectural structure. Death, in Marcelline's view, has tried to 'pull downe vertues great mansion place', one occupied by Lennox.[38] This cruel death has 'made our *King* / The dolefull tune of *Lachyrma* to sing'; it has likewise adversely affected Prince Charles, the country's nobles and the commoners. Lennox was, Marcelline writes, 'a Steward after Gods owne minde' and a '*Solomon* for true intelligence'. This poet also highlights the duke's steadfastness in religion, a pillar of the church. But he emphasises what others, other than Darcie, have not paid much attention to: Lennox's work as patron of the arts. Marcelline writes: 'Me thinkes I heare *Art* in the streets complaine, / She hath lost him who did her state maintaine. / *Vertue* in sable weeds mournes all alone, / Because her patterne and her Patron's gone'. Later, the poet adds: 'Let all the Muses to him honour giue, / He gaue them house roome whiles he here did liue'. Lennox's death leaves a vacancy, including for artists, perhaps Marcelline himself.

Patrick Mackguear produced the last of these broadsheets (Fig. 5.1). It has the notable distinction of including an impressive black border

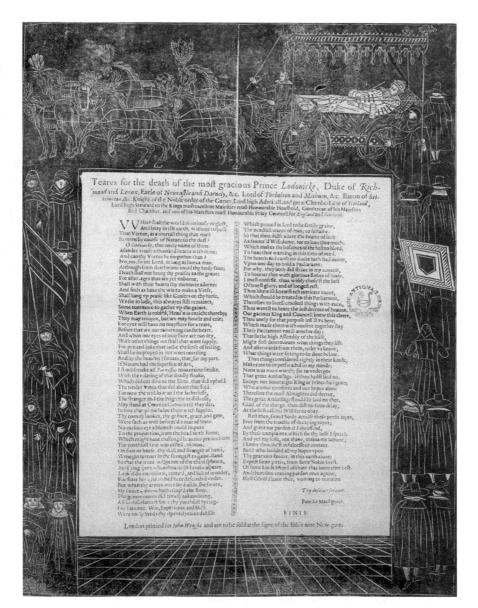

Figure 5.1 Drawing of the Duke of Lennox's funeral procession from Patrick Mackguear's broadside, 'Teares for the death of the most gracious Duke of Loduicke', 1624. Courtesy of the Society of Antiquaries of London.

that depicts a funeral procession, presumably Lennox's. Starting at the
bottom right-hand corner, the eye moves up the page with shrouded
mourners. The top of the border shows a funeral carriage, drawn by
horses, with a recumbent figure, again, presumably Lennox, or his effigy.
Moving down from that on the left side is a group of more mourners.
Printed by John Wright, this broadsheet offers the only visual depiction
of Lennox's funeral procession. The author asserts that 'Death shall not
bring thy praises to the graue'.[39] Unlike the writers of the other broadsheet elegies, Mackguear focuses on Lennox's body: 'Thy comely looks,
thy gesture, grace, and gate, / Were such as well beseem'd a man of State. /
No curious eye a blemish could impute / To thy proportion, from the
head to th' foote'. Indeed, Lennox's body might have prompted 'beauties
praises'. Mackguear likens Lennox to both Mars and Adonis. The writer
also notes the delay of Parliament because of the duke's death. Lennox
himself has now gone to a higher Parliament, the 'high Assembly of the
blist'. Mackguear closes on a personal note: 'I who builded all my hopes
vpon / Thy gracious fauour, in this earth alone; / Expect some pittie, from
some Noble brest'. Expectations of patronage thwarted seems to be the
writer's view, underscored by his closing before his name: '*Thy desolate
seruant*'. These three single-sheet elegiac documents flesh out additional
qualities of Lennox's person, presence and patronage.

Not an elegy but a letter: one from Esmé Stuart, Lennox's brother, to
Sir David Carnegie, who became Earl of Southesk, dated 20 February
1624. Esmé wrote:

> The occasion of the sorrowfull newes of my Lord, my late brother's deathe,
> hath given mee to just subject to require the assistance of my frendes. I need
> not to relate vnto yow how willing hee was to deserue the good opinion of
> those hee respected, and how desirous to requite it. As I ame neerest to him
> in blood, so shall I striue to come as near to him in that as my abilitie will
> giue mee leaue.[40]

The letter closes with a plea for Carnegie to continue the support and
assistance that he had given Lennox. The brother's love comes through
this succinct message, as he confirms Lennox's good opinion among
many and the desire to emulate him. Lennox and his brother had enjoyed
a long, cordial relationship, participating together in meetings of the
Privy Council or performing in court masques. Lennox revelled in the
delight of Esmé's children. Esmé feels the weight of trying to live up to
his brother's accomplishments and reputation.

Another letter enters the conversation of response to Lennox's death:
the letter from Princess Elizabeth in The Hague to Thomas Roe in

Constantinople, written on 11 March 1624. James's daughter begins by thanking Roe for his many letters; then, she moves to respond to the failure of the 'Spanish Match', which, upon Charles's return from Spain in October 1623, 'all is changed from being Spanish'.[41] Elizabeth hopes that the issue will be settled by the upcoming Parliament. She writes: 'the parlia[ment shoulde haue bene vppon the] 16 of the last month but by reason of the good Duke of Richemondes death who was found dead that morning [in his bed] you know how well I loued him and therefore may [easilie guesse that I am not a little sorie for his losse]' (445). Elizabeth's simple words of love convey all that need be said about the loss of Lennox, which she feels keenly.

John Spottiswood wrote of Lennox's death, which came 'to the great regret of all that knew him; a Nobleman of excellent parts, whose very aspect and countenance did promise much good'.[42] Hacket describes Lennox as 'Affable, Humble, Inoffensive, contented with so much Favour as was never Repin'd [complained about]: One that never Wrestled with the King's Privados [favorites], and was never near a fall; One whose Wit and Honesty kept him great, and much belov'd of all'.[43] Hacket lists not only Lennox's active virtues but also his ability not to do certain things, such as antagonise James's favourites. That surely must be part of political and personal wisdom. His attributes kept him from 'falling'. Sorrowful news, cited by Esmé, meets its counter in the outpouring of elegies and statements of love and esteem.

Shakespeare, whom Lennox would have known either personally or certainly through performances of his plays enjoyed by Lennox at court, writes compellingly about the flux of life and the ultimate victory of time, for example, in Sonnet 60:

> Like as the waves make towards the pebbled shore,
> So do our minutes hasten to their end,
> Each changing place with that which goes before,
> In sequent toil all forwards do contend . . .
> And Time that gave doth now his gift confound. (1–4, 8)

Lennox's 'sequent toil' has ended, as his minutes hastened to their end, the inevitable movement of time.

The story of Lennox does not end here, however. The Merchant Taylors hired the playwright John Webster, a guild member, to prepare the mayoral pageant for 29 October 1624 in honour of John Gore's inauguration; and the guild spent more than £1,000 for the show. In this Lord Mayor's Show, named *Monuments of Honour*, Webster circles back to Thomas Dekker's 1612 show, *Troia-Nova Triumphans*, which also honoured a Merchant Taylor and which Lennox had seen. Webster's last device, called the *Monument of Gratitude*, includes a representation of Prince Henry, fulfilling twelve years later that 'perticular roome' that Dekker had created in the House of Fame. Dekker and now Webster respond to the prince's motto: *'fax gloria nuntis honestae'* (fame incites honest minds), a motto suggested by Ben Jonson.[44] The Monument of Gratitude Webster places on an artificial rock, decorated with many signs appropriate to Henry. Webster writes: 'the Rocke expresses the riches of the Kingdome Prince *Henry* was borne Heire to, the Piramids, which are Monuments for the Dead, that hee is deceased'.[45] Webster adds: 'upon a pedestall of gold stands the figure of Prince *Henry* with his Coronet, George and Garter; in his left hand hee holds a Circklet of Crimson Velvet, charged with foure Holy Lambes, such as our Company choose Masters with'. Numerous symbolic figures surround Henry, highlighting his virtues, such as *'Peace* sleeping vpon a Canon, alluding to the eternall Peace he now possesses' (C2).

Why should Webster commemorate Prince Henry twelve years after his death? Webster had, of course, written a moving elegiac poem, *A Monumental Column*, at the time of the prince's death in 1612; thus, he clearly had an affinity for the prince. In all likelihood, Lennox's death earlier in 1624 and the advent of another Merchant Taylor mayor prompted Webster to create a pageant full of monuments of honour. In the text of the pageant, the dramatist enumerates former kings and noblemen who have been free of the guild, echoing what Dekker had done. But Webster singles out Lennox: 'with Prince *Henry* in the yeare 1607. the Duke of *Linox*' (sig. B3v). Thus, Webster perceives an obvious link between the prince and Lennox. Both had, of course, become members of the Merchant Taylors during their visit to the guild in 1607. The pageant's closing speech, delivered by 'Amade le Graunde' (Amadeus the Great of Savoy), celebrates Henry, 'fames best president, / Cald to a higher Court of Parliament' (C2). One part of this speech may refer to Lennox as well. The speaker says: 'Such was this Prince, such are the noble hearts; / Who when they dye, yet dye not in all parts: / But from the *Integrety* of a Brave mind, / Leave a most Cleere and Eminent Fame behind' (C2v). Such a characterisation fits Lennox well, whose memory now lives on in a London civic entertainment, befitting one who frequented such entertainments and participated in them, leaving behind an indelible impression. His 'representation' may have passed through the streets in April but his legacy lives on, now enshrined in Webster's text. He has not, in the words of the speaker, died 'in all parts'; he has left behind a 'Cleere and Eminent Fame', an embodiment of Prince Henry's personal motto.

Fame certainly continues for Lennox in the funeral monument, commissioned by his wife and erected in Henry VII's Lady Chapel in Westminster Abbey. A large monument of black marble and bronze, by the sculptor Hubert Le Suer, dominates the small chapel (Fig. 5.2). Bronze reclining effigies of the duke and his duchess, holding hands and appropriately dressed, rest underneath a bronze canopy. A brilliant figure of Fame sits atop the canopy, complete with wings and a trumpet. Large bronze figures of Hope, Truth, Charity and Faith anchor each respective corner and support the canopy, reminiscent of the four Cardinal Virtues that accompany the effigy of Robert Cecil in his monument at Hatfield House. The Latin inscription enumerates Lennox's various offices and distinctions; and it cites the scriptural text, slightly abbreviated, which comes from 2 Samuel 3: 38: 'And the king said unto his servants, Know ye not that there is a prince and a great man fallen this day in Israel?' Courtiers and citizens alike in England and Scotland would readily concur. Or, they might think of Lennox as Zabud the son of Nathan, described as the 'principal officer, and the king's friend', in another passage from the Old Testament and the sermon text for Bishop Williams at Lennox's funeral. Or they might appropriate the theatre metaphor used by James Cleland in his elegy and see Lennox as an actor in a comedy. How fitting that works of art, the Lord Mayor's pageant and the magnificent monument should capture and perpetuate Lennox's reputation and legacy, providing a compelling and lasting memorial of this man respected and beloved by many. 'You know how well I loued him', Princess Elizabeth wrote, upon learning of his death.

Another art image captures something of Lennox's character: the painting (c. 1621) by the Flemish artist Paul van Somer, who had taken up residence in London where he created portraits of several court figures, including King James. This portrait (Fig. 5.3), housed in the National Portrait Gallery, London, shows a standing Lennox, handsomely clad in red and silver garments, with a flowing, full-length cape. His left hand holds a white staff, symbolic of court office. He wears on his left leg a garter, indicative of the Order of the Garter; his left side bears a silver sword. Lennox holds a headpiece in his right hand. His shoes are stunning. (Interestingly, Daniel Mytens, Van Somer's neighbour in London, painted a well-known portrait of King James [c. 1621], which includes several of the features of Van Somer's picture of Lennox, such as the colour of the garments and the garter, with the person facing leftward.) Lennox, with a full, reddish-coloured beard, looks strong and resolute, with possibly a hint of an emerging smile. Everything about this portrait suggests a successful person, possibly at the height of his powers

Figure 5.2   Funeral monument of Duke of Lennox and wife in Henry VII's Lady Chapel, Westminster Abbey. Courtesy of the Dean and Chapter of Westminster Abbey.

and accomplishments. He looks, for all the world, like the quintessential courtier that he was, full of confidence and authority. Van Somer's portrait offers an excellent snapshot of the mature Lennox and it reinforces the multitude of reports and judgrments about the courtier. This portrait confirms the earlier representations of Lennox, such as the one in the early part of the century, Isaac Oliver's miniature (Fig. 2.1). Oliver portrays Lennox with red hair and full beard, blue eyes looking expectantly left, and a firm, rather long nose. These qualities continue in Simon de Passe's 1616 engraving (Fig. 4.2), which depicts Lennox in full regalia but with brow somewhat furrowed and a high forehead. The wording refers to Lennox as 'Prince', a term sometimes used with him, although he held no princely title. But, of course, all portraits can only be incomplete, partial, because they cannot encompass the preceding nearly forty years of service to King James, from an uncertain nine-year-old boy from France to this moment of maturity and clarity of purpose.

In 1584, as discussed earlier, King James published his poem *Phoenix*, which commemorates his intimate, if brief, relationship with Esmé Stuart, Lennox's father. This thinly veiled allegory of this beautiful, mythical bird provided an artistic means that enabled the king to confront Esmé's death. The poem ends on an expectant, hopeful note, especially in its closing lines. That hope rests clearly on the son, Ludovic, who will take the place of the dead phoenix by himself becoming a new phoenix, surrounded by the glory of Apollo. James hints at this in these lines that refer to 'one of her race, / Ane worme bred of her ashe'.[46] The remains of the burnt phoenix 'lacks but plumes and breath / To be lyke her, new gendred by her death'. The death of the father leads to the invitation to the nine-year-old son to come to Scotland, creating a new phoenix: 'so heir [here] / Let them be now, to make ane *Phoenix* new / Euen of this worme of *Phoenix* ashe which grew' (p. 229). If this can happen, the poet continues, 'This if thow dois, as sure I hope thou shall, / My tragedie a comike end will haue'. New generation out of death defines comedy; thus, Lennox becomes a metaphorical actor (as well as a real one) in his service to James. He fulfills the expectations of the poem in ways that could not have been imagined in 1583. He transcends what his father could accomplish and overcomes James's sense of loss and tragedy. Phoenix supplants phoenix.

The transformation of the young French boy to the mature courtier of the Jacobean court came about in large measure because of Lennox's trustworthiness. All across the spectrum of forty years Lennox dutifully served James without failing. He did not always please the king, as in the case of his first marriage, but he remained steadfast in service. In

Figure 5.3   Portrait of Ludovic Stuart, Duke of Lennox, by Paul van Somer, c. 1620. Courtesy of the National Portrait Gallery.

that sense, Lennox fulfilled the scripture description of being the king's 'principal officer'. Being trustworthy seems to have come to Lennox naturally, perhaps a lesson learned from his father. Thus, James could send him on numerous diplomatic missions to France, for example, asking him to proceed with marriage negotiations for Charles in 1613. Lennox returned to Scotland several times at the king's request to wrangle with the Scottish Parliament. He garnered the trust of Robert Cecil and thus smoothed the potential accession of James to the English crown. Queen Elizabeth in her meeting with him in 1601 readily sensed his importance for James and his devotion to the king. He alone was trusted to head back to Scotland after the journey in 1603 to the new kingdom and intercede with Queen Anne, mollifying her intransigence about securing the person of Prince Henry for herself. James entrusted the care of Princess Elizabeth to him in her post-wedding journey to Germany in 1613. Lennox regularly served as the representative of the Privy Council in negotiations with the City of London. James sent him to greet King Christian IV of Denmark, when he landed in England in 1606, and bring him to London. Similarly, the king commissioned him to retrieve Prince Frederick, Elector Palatine, future husband of Princess Elizabeth, and escort him to London. Tellingly, James, possibly against all expectations, chose the fifteen-year-old Lennox to head the commission in charge of governing Scotland in 1589–90, during the king's trip to Denmark to marry Anne. How quickly and firmly Lennox had earned the king's trust, a trust warranted by Lennox's behaviour.

His trustworthiness manifested itself throughout the relationships with the royal family. Anne welcomed Lennox as a friend and counsellor. James initially thought of Lennox as his 'child', but this grew into a mature, loving, although not excessively intimate, mutually shared, understanding with him. The more intense male relationships James reserved for his 'favourites', which Lennox shrewdly never interfered with. He clearly understood the sentiment in these lines from Shakespeare's Sonnet 25: 'Great princes' favorites their fair leaves spread, / But as the marigold at the sun's eye, / And in themselves their pride lies burièd, / For at a frown they in their glory die'. Thus, James appointed Lennox to a commission to investigate and interrogate Somerset, after the disclosure of his involvement in the murder of Thomas Overbury in the Tower in 1613. Lennox served as godparent for several of the royal children. The royal family included Lennox in the procession and pageant that moved through London on 15 March 1604, in celebration of James's accession to the English throne. Lennox developed a close relationship with Prince Henry, even being able on at least one occasion to chastise the prince's behaviour. He felt deeply the unexpected death of Henry. A measure of Lennox's esteem with the royal family can be seen in his selection as chief supporter to Prince Charles in the funeral procession for Henry. Lennox went along with Charles's ill-conceived secret trip to Spain in an attempt to woo and win the Infanta for his bride, although the duke had first wisely opposed the bizarre plan. Princess Elizabeth could refer in 1613, after her safe arrival in Germany, to the 'unutterable pleasure' of having Lennox accompany her. One image may capture the reciprocal love, trust and devotion that King James felt with Lennox: in 1594, James journeyed from Edinburgh to Stirling 'with Lennox alone', the report says. Lennox would accompany James in many real and figurative journeys in the years to come, always supportive and helpful, a view shared by the other members of the royal family. Princess Elizabeth's words, written to a friend in response to news of Lennox's death, succinctly capture their love: 'you know how well I loued him'. Small wonder that George Marcelline, writing in 1610, could characterise Lennox's position thus:

> You wise and prudent *Lodwicke* . . . that haue left *France* (your Natiue country) to be alwayies by and at the right hand of *Our King*, as not able to loose the sight of him; neither be further off from his Maiesty, then the Sun from the Eccliptick line.[47]

Such value enabled Lennox to carry out other 'political duties', for example, on the Bedchamber in both Scotland and England. This body, with Lennox as its head, became increasingly important in the English period, sometimes superior to the Privy Council itself, on which Lennox also served. In 1611 Lennox did not pursue the possibility of being the king's representative to Scotland, noting, shrewdly, that he was loathe to leave his personal attendance on the king. This choice suggests informed political judgement. Nothing can supplant his position of the king's trust, being, as some described him, 'nearest to the crown'. His talent assisted him in forming and nurturing a mutually beneficial relationship with Cecil. Lennox understood Cecil's importance and carefully avoided impinging on Cecil's prerogatives. Many foreign ambassadors sought out Lennox's help in gaining audiences with the king and with negotiating tricky situations. He regularly entertained ambassadors, thereby gaining their trust and admiration. In 1605, James appointed Lennox as the king's Alnager. This position, if not strictly political, nevertheless required his skill, including trying to satisfy City merchants and their dealings with the Privy Council. Not incidentally, this position enhanced Lennox's economic status. In 1613, James made Lennox Earl of Richmond, thereby gaining for him a seat in the English Parliament where he took, on occasion, an active role, learning to move skillfully among competing agendas. The appointment as Lord High Steward in 1616 solidified his political stature. During this time, James also selected Lennox to serve in various ways on the commissions that dealt with the trials of Somerset, Suffolk and Bacon. These responsibilities Lennox discharged determinedly and faithfully. The final reward came with the title of Duke of Richmond in 1623. At that moment, Lennox became the only person with both a Scottish and English ducal title. Clearly,

Lennox's fingerprints can be found on many important political matters that affected the crown. His activities of this sort grew out of the basic trustworthiness seen in him by King James and others.

Lennox also supported his own extended family by initially encouraging his French siblings to leave their home there and join him in Scotland, which they did. Two of the sisters, Henrietta and Marie, married, respectively, George Gordon, Earl of Huntly and John Erskine, Earl of Mar, arguably two of the most important noblemen in Scotland. The third sister, Gabrielle, decided to return to France to enter a convent but not return to the family home. The brother Esmé eventually joined the clan in Scotland in time to make the transition to England. Surely Lennox was crucial in their decisions to relocate to Scotland. He developed close relationships with his brothers-in-law, although sometimes the connections were fraught. Lennox certainly had his difficulties with Huntly, at one point succeeding in forcing his temporary exile. And doubtless he intervened on Huntly's behalf on the numerous occasions of Huntly's conflicts with King James. Lennox's fondness for Huntly enabled him to mitigate the king's anger and to bring Huntly back in favour, which was never very difficult because of James's own attraction to Huntly. Occasionally, Lennox had a minor squabble with his sisters, such as when he tried to convince Henrietta to abandon her Catholic faith. His letters show unmistakable regard and concern for the welfare of his mother and sister, as he tried repeatedly to gain a pension for his mother in France and to win access to an Abbey for Gabrielle. The letters also demonstrate Lennox's attempts to find a position for his nephew Alexander Erskine. Lennox's visits to France were infrequent but he did occasionally spend some time with his mother there. Esmé enjoyed a close relationship with Lennox, especially when they moved to England. The brothers became mainstays of the Jacobean court and participated together regularly in masque performances, and they both served as significant patrons of the arts. Although difficult to document, in all likelihood the family members benefitted economically from their connection to Lennox. Their initial status they clearly owed to Lennox.

Ambition and impulsiveness complicate Lennox's portrait. He was not reticent about seeking certain advantages. In Scotland he doggedly sought to gain control of Edinburgh Castle and Dumbarton Castle; he did not give up until he had succeeded, to the humiliation of the overseers of these castles. This pursuit looks like naked ambition. With similar fervour, he sought property in London after his third marriage. He knew that he had power and he determined to use it, and he jealously guarded all his advantages and appointments. Not surprisingly, he maximised the benefits, personal and economic, of being the king's Alnager. He created a far-flung array of 'deputies' to carry out the duties of the office. Lennox also obviously sought the titles of Earl of Richmond and the more important one, Duke of Richmond. He made no secret about desiring these titles. Impulsively, in 1591, he forcefully took Sophia Ruthven out of the lodging where James had placed her and together they eloped and married, much against the king's wishes. This impetuous act could have been disastrous for Lennox, but fortunately for him James forgave him. He had a few physical fights as well during the Scotland period when angered or provoked. And he, perplexingly, got involved in helping Bothwell gain admission to the king's chambers in Scotland – another potential disaster from which Lennox escaped unscathed. Some of these encounters and actions may simply underscore that, despite his many virtues and esteem, he was thoroughly human and not immune to less admirable qualities.

As this discussion of Lennox's character began with art works, so it ends that way. Lennox's interest in and support of the arts has received few comments, and yet this aspect of his character and personality is of great importance. As noted earlier, Lennox served as a significant patron of the arts, especially drama. He did this by performing regularly in the early years in England in court masques as a dancer and character in the spectacle. In fact, he was responsible for the first Jacobean court masque in January 1604, for which, unfortunately, no text survives. During that same month he also performed in Daniel's *The Vision of the Twelve Goddesses*. He danced or participated in the barriers associated with several of Ben Jonson's masques. Lennox actively involved himself in trying to settle disputes among ambassadors about their seats at these events, the ongoing problem of 'precedence'. The athletic activities of the barriers, along with running at the ring and other tournament events, required considerable skill on Lennox's part. He regularly performed in the Accession Day Tilts, held on the tournament grounds at Whitehall; he received notice for the wearing of excessive feathers in the 1610 tilt. He helped arrange the civic pageant for Queen Anne's official entry into Edinburgh in 1590, he rode in the procession of James's royal entry in London in 1604, and he appeared in the pageant for King Christian IV in 1606. He led the procession from Whitehall to the Merchant Taylors' Hall in 1614 as part of the wedding celebrations for Frances Howard and Somerset. Obviously, Lennox attended many performances of regular plays at court, especially during the exceptional season of 1612–13 and its presentation of several of Shakespeare's plays.

Lennox's connection to theatre runs deep. For several years he served as patron of an adult acting company, the Duke of Lennox's Men. The records reveal very little about this company, but apparently they performed away from London. Nothing shows up about which plays they performed, but the records do indicate payments to the company in various towns. Lennox also had a company of trumpeters that may have accompanied the actors' troupe. He also intervened in the attempt to arrest the playwright George Chapman because one of his plays offended the French ambassador. Chapman thanked him for 'shelter', which he may have meant literally. Given that Lennox's brother provided lodging for the playwright Ben Jonson over the course of several years, that the duke might have done similarly would not be surprising. A number of authors dedicated their books to Lennox, another sign of his patronage of the arts. In 1619 after the burning of the Banqueting House, James appointed Lennox to a three-person commission for the rebuilding; they wisely chose Inigo Jones to design the new hall. Thus, in addition to supporting the king and the royal family loyally and exercising his own ambitions and political skills, Lennox found time to move in a distinctly different realm: the arts. All of these activities underscore and confirm Lennox as the quintessential Jacobean courtier.

Lennox, always at the right hand of the king, according to George Marcelline, occupied an enviable and unsurpassed place in James's life and court. As early as 1593 in Scotland, an anonymous Spanish source refers to Lennox as 'the most powerful person' at court, whom the 'King loves dearly'.[48] A person of great accomplishment but also, according to John Hacket, affable, humble, witty and honest, he created a valuable legacy, as noted in the elegies that followed his death. In 1609 a visiting Italian poet, Antimo Galli, watching the performance of Jonson's *Masque of Beauty* and seeing Lennox there captured the essence of him: 'grave in countenance and of courteous appearance. He is a greatly esteemed knight, and, believe me, is gifted with great prudence and intelligence'.[49] Lennox embodied the portrait of a beloved person as captured in Shakespeare's Sonnet 55: "Gainst death and all oblivious enmity, / Shall you pace forth; your praise shall still find room, / Ev'n in the eyes of all posterity / That wear this world out to the ending doom'. Phoenix and paragon, Lennox left behind a clear and eminent fame.

Notes

1. *Basilicon Doron*, James Craigie (ed.), 1:121.

2. Quoted in G. P. V. Akrigg, *Jacobean Pageant*, p. 391. Akrigg speculates that Lennox had conducted some affairs along the way.

3. Much of this information comes from Donald Foster's entry on her in the *Oxford Dictionary of National Biography*.

4. Arthur Wilson, *The History of Great Britain . . . King James*, p. 258.

5. *Letters of John Chamberlain*, 2:364.

6. *The Letters and Life of Francis Bacon*, James Spedding (ed.), 7: 326. Spedding dates the letter as 29 January 1621 but, of course, at that point Lennox would not yet have married Frances Howard.

7. For a discussion of James's letters, see my *King James and Letters of Homoerotic Desire*.

8. Ibid., p. 18.

9. British Library, Egerton MS 2594, f. 181. I have here and in the other letters slightly modernised the text.

10. British Library, Egerton MS 2595, fol. 28.

11. British Library, Stowe MS 171, Edmondes, vol. 6, fol. 262.

12. British Library, Stowe MS 175, Edmondes, vol. 10, fol. 74–75.

13. National Archives, London, SP 84/101/106, fol. 299.

14. NA, SP 84/102/39, fol. 134.

15. NA, SP 84/109/34 fol. 66.

16. NA, PRO 30/53/10/7.

17. NA, PRO 30/53/10/32, fol. 61.

18. NA, PRO 30/53/10/36, fol. 67.

19. NA, PRO 30/53/10/39, fol. 73.

20. NA, PRO 30/53/10/57, fol. 103.

21. NA, PRO 30/53/10/66, fol. 134.

22. NA, PRO 30/53/10/74, fol. 159.

23. NA PRO 30/53/10/78, fol. 163.

24. NA PRO 30/53/10/80, fol. 167.

25. NA PRO 30/53/10/83, fol. 173.

26. British Library, RP 4931 (facsimile). This letter Lennox signs with his additional title: Richmond.

27. NA PRO 30/53/10/87, fol. 180.

28. John Hacket, *Scrinia Reserata*, p. 173.

29. *Calendar of State Papers Venetian*, 18:226.

30. Abraham Darcie, *A Monumentall Pyramide to all Posterities*, title page, which has considerable content. All quotations will come from this original edition.

31. James Cleland, *A Monument of Mortalitie*, p. 26. All quotations come from this text.

32. *Letters*, 2:551.

33. Abraham Darcie, *Frances Duchesse Dowager of Richmond . . . her Funerall Teares*, beginning on sig. A1.

34. The *OED* attests the first example from the late seventeenth century, but that seems to be the meaning that Darcie has in mind here. Admittedly, five other people in the long procession also have the designation of 'close mourner'. Their relationship to Lennox remains unclear. Precisely what Darcie has in mind is thus muddled.

35. John Taylor, 'True louing sorrow, attired in a robe of vnfeigned griefe'.

36. Darcie, *Frances Duchesse*, the page or signature is not indicated in the text, which is a problem that recurs throughout this text, making references difficult.

37. Samuel Tailboys, *A New Lachrymentall and Funerall Elegy*, sig. A4v. Darcie in his *A Monumentall Pyramide* makes a few of the same points in his brief elegy.

38. George Marcelline, 'A Funerall Elegie vpon the death of . . . Lodovick *Duke of Lennox*'.

39. Patrick Mackguear, 'Teares for the death of the most gracious Prince Lodouicke . . .'

40. *Seventh Report of the Royal Commission on Historical Manuscripts*, Appendix, p. 723.

41. *The Correspondence of Elizabeth Stuart, Queen of Bohemia*, Nadine Akkerman (ed.), 1:445.

42. *The History of the Church of Scotland*, p. 546.

43. *Scrinia Reserata*, p. 173.

44. See Ian Donaldson, *Ben Jonson: A Life*, p. 303.

45. Quotations come from John Webster, *Monuments of Honor*, sig. C1v. A modern critical edition can be found in *The Works of John Webster*, David Gunby, David Carnegie, and MacDonald P. Jackson (eds), 3:223–94. David Carnegie edited the text and provides a helpful Introduction and Commentary. He makes much of the political context of 1624, but does not mention Lennox as a possible influence on this entertainment. I have explored the matter of the pageant's connection to Lennox in my 'The Duke of Lennox and Civic Entertainments', in *Civic Performance: Pageantry and Entertainments in Early Modern London*, J. Caitlin Finlayson and Amrita Sen (eds), pp. 157–75.

46. Quoted from the edition of the poem in my *King James and Letters of Homoerotic Desire*, p. 228.

47. George Marcelline, *The Triumphs of King James*, p. 75.

48. *Calendar of Letters and State Papers . . . in the Archives of Simancas*, 4:604.

49. Antimo Galli, *Rime di Antimo Galli*, English translation by Maria Dougu in the *Masque Archive* for the *Masque of Beauty* in online version of the *Cambridge Edition of the Works of Ben Jonson*.

Bibliography

MANUSCRIPTS AND ARCHIVES

Bodleian Library
Tanner MS 236

British Library
Egerton MS 2592, 2594, 2595
Harley MS 6986, 7007
Stowe MS 171, 175
RP 4931

Corporation of London Records
Journal 37

National Archives (London)
PRO 30/52/10; 30/53/10, 30/53/10/36, 30/53/10/38, 30/53/10/39, 30/53/10/57, 30/53/10/66, 30/53/10/74, 30/53/10/78, 30/53/10/80, 30/53/10/83, 30/53/10/87

SP 14/94, 14/95, 14/96, 14/105; SP 52/47; SP 84/82/49; SP 84/101/106, 84/102/39, 84/109/34

National Records of Scotland
GD 220/6/2003 (7)
GD 220/6/2006/1

PRIMARY PRINTED SOURCES

Analytical Index to the Records Known as the Remembrancia, London: 1878.

Bacon, Francis, *The Works of Francis Bacon*, James Spedding, Robert Ellis and Douglas Heath (eds), 14 vols, London: 1868–90.

_____, *The Letters and Life of Francis Bacon*, James Spedding (ed.), 7 vols, London: 1861–74.

A Book of Masques in Honor of Allardyce Nicoll, T. J. B. Spencer and Stanley Wells (eds.), Cambridge: Cambridge University Press, 1967.

Bowes, Robert, *The Correspondence of Robert Bowes*, Joseph Stevenson (ed.), London: 1842.

Burrel, John, *[Poems]*, Edinburgh: 1596.

Calderwood, David, *The History of the Kirk of Scotland*, Thomas Thomson (ed.), 8 vols, Edinburgh: 1842–1926.

Calendar of Letters and State Papers Relating to English Affairs . . . Archives of Simancas (Spain), Martin A. S. Hume (ed.), vol. 4, London: 1899.

Calendar of State Papers Relating to Scotland, Markham John Thorpe (ed.), 2 vols, London: 1858.

Calendar of State Papers Relating to Scotland and Mary, Queen of Scots, 1547–1603, 13 vols, Edinburgh: H M Register House, 1898–1969.

Calendar of State Papers Venetian, 1603–1625, vols 10–18, London: HMSO, 1900–12.

Campion, Thomas, *The Works of Thomas Campion*, Walter Davis (ed.), New York: Doubleday, 1967.

Coventry, R. W. Ingram (ed.), Toronto: University of Toronto Press, 1981.

Dudley Carleton to John Chamberlain 1603–1624: Jacobean Letters, Maurice Lee, Jr (ed.), New Brunswick, NJ: Rutgers University Press, 1972.

The Letters of John Chamberlain, Norman E. McClure (ed.), 2 vols. Philadelphia: American Philosophical Society, 1939.

Chapman, George, *Homer, Prince of Poets*, London: 1609.

Cleland, James, *A Monument of Mortalitie*, London: 1624.

Coke, Roger, *A Detection of the Court and State of England*, London: 1696.

Collections III: A Calendar of Dramatic Records in the Books of the Livery Companies of London, 1485–1640, Jean Robertson and D. J. Gordon (eds), Oxford: Malone Society, 1954.

Collections VI: Dramatic Records in the Declared Accounts of the Treasurer of the Chamber 1558–1642, David Cook (ed.), Oxford: Malone Society, 1961.

Cornwallis, Charles, *A Discourse of the Most Illustrious Prince Henry*, London: 1641.

_____, *The Life and Death of . . . Henry, Prince of Wales*, London: 1641.

Court Masques: Jacobean and Caroline Entertainments 1605–1640, David Lindley (ed.), Oxford: Oxford University Press, 1995.

Daniel, Samuel, *The Complete Works in Verse and Prose*, Alexander B. Grosart (ed.), 5 vols, New York: Russell and Russell, 1963.

Darcie, Abraham, *A Monumental Pyramide to all Posterities*, London: 1624.

_____, *Frances Duchesse Dowager of Richmond . . . her Funerall Teares*, London: 1624.

Davies, John, *Microcosmos: The Discovery of the Little World*, Oxford: 1603.

Dekker, Thomas, *The Dramatic Works of Thomas Dekker*, Fredson Bowers (ed.), 4 vols, Cambridge: Cambridge University Press, 1958–61.

Elizabeth, Princess, *The Correspondence of Elizabeth Stuart, Queen of Bohemia*, Nadine Akkerman (ed.), vol. 1, Oxford: Oxford University Press, 2015.

Ford, John, *Honor Triumphant*, London: 1606.

The Funeral of the High and Mightie Prince Henry, London: 1612.

H., W. *The True Picture and Relation of Prince Henry*, Leiden: 1634.

Hacket, John, *Scrinia Reserata*, London: 1692.

Halliwell, J. O., *A Copy of a Letter of News Written to Sir Dudley Carleton*, London: 1865.

Harrington, John, *Nugae Antiquae*, London: 1779.

Hayward, John, *The Lives of the III. Normans, Kings of England*, London: 1613.

Historical Manuscripts Commission, *Report on the Manuscripts of the Marquess of Downshire: Papers of William Trumbull the Elder*, vols 2–6, London: HMSO, 1936–89.

――――――――, *Calendar of the Manuscripts of the Marquess of Salisbury*, Pts 15–24, London: HMSO, 1930–76.

――――――――, *Supplementary Report on the Manuscripts of the Earl of Mar & Kellie*, Henry Paton (ed.), London: HMSO, 1930.

――――――――, *Report on the Manuscripts of His Grace the Duke of Portland*, vol. 9, London: HMSO, 1923.

――――――――, *Report on the Laing Manuscripts in the University of Edinburgh*, 2 vols, London: HMSO, 1914–25.

――――――――, *Report on the Manuscripts of the Earl of Mar and Kellie*, London: HMSO, 1904.

――――――――, *Seventh Report of the Royal Commission on Historical Manuscripts*, Appendix, London, 1878.

――――――――, *Third Report of the Royal Commission on Historical Manuscripts*, London, 1872.

Holles, John, *Letters of John Holles 1587–1637*, P. R. Seddon (ed.), 3 vols, Nottingham: Thoroton Society, 1975–86.

'Household Accounts of Ludovick Duke of Lennox, When Commissioner to the Parliament of Scotland 1607', in *Miscellany of the Maitland Club*, vol. 1, Edinburgh: 1833, pp. 161–91.

James, King, *By the King James by the grace of God, king of England, Scotland, France and Ireland*, Proclamation, London: 1605.

――――――, *Letters of King James VI & I*, G. P. V. Akrigg (ed.), Berkeley: University of California Press, 1984.

――――――, *The Letters of King James I to King Christian IV, 1603–1625*, Ronald M. Meldrum (ed.), Brighton: Harvester Press, 1977.

――――――, *Basilicon Doron*, James Craigie (ed.), 2 vols, Edinburgh: Blackwood, 1944–50.

Johnston, Robert, *The Historie of Scotland during the Minority of King James*, London: 1646.

Jonson, Ben, *The Cambridge Edition of the Works of Ben Jonson*, David Bevington, Martin Butler and Ian Donaldson (eds), Cambridge: Cambridge University Press, 2012.

_____, *Ben Jonson: The Complete Masques*, Stephen Orgel (ed.), New Haven: Yale University Press, 1969.

King of Denmarkes Welcome, London: 1606.

Letters and Papers Relating to Patrick Master of Gray, Thomas Thomson (ed.), Edinburgh: 1835.

Luna, Juan de, *Arte Breve*. London: 1623.

Mackguear, Patrick, 'Teares for the death of the most gracious Prince Lodowicke', broadsheet, London: 1624.

The Magnificent Marriage of the Two Great Princes, pamphlet, London, 1613.

The Magnificent, Princely, and most Royal Entertainment given to the High and Mightie Prince, and Princesse, pamphlet, London, 1613.

Marcelline, George, 'A Funerall Elegie vpon the death of . . . Lodowick, *Duke of Lennox*', broadsheet, London: 1624.

_____, *The Triumph of King James the First*, London: 1610.

Markham, Gervase, *Cavalarice, or, The English Horseman*, London: 1607.

Marston, John, *The Works of John Marston*, A. H. Bullen (ed.), 3 vols, London: 1887.

Martin, Richard, *A Speech Delivered, to the Kings Most Excellent Maiestie*, London: 1603.

May, John, *A Declaration of the Estate of Clothing*, London: 1613.

Middleton, Thomas, *The Collected Works of Thomas Middleton*, Gary Taylor and John Lavagnino (eds), Oxford: Oxford University Press, 2007.

Millar, Neill S., 'A Sixteenth Century Golf Match at Leith', *Through the Green*, December 2018, pp. 38–9.

Moysie, David, *Memoirs of the Affairs of Scotland*, Edinburgh: Bannatyne, 1830.

Munday, Anthony, *Pageants and Entertainments of Anthony Munday: A Critical Edition*, David M. Bergeron (ed.), New York: Garland, 1985.

Nichols, John, *John Nichols's The Progresses and Public Processions of Queen Elizabeth I: A New Edition*, Elizabeth Goldring, Faith Eales, Elizabeth Clarke and Jayne Elisabeth Archer (eds), 5 vols, Oxford: Oxford University Press, 2014.

_____, *The Progresses, Processions, and Magnificent Festivities of King James*, 4 vols, London: 1823.

Nixon, Anthony, *Great Brittaines Generall Joyes*, London: 1613.

Norwich 1540–1642, David Galloway (ed.), Toronto: University of Toronto Press, 1984.

The Order and Solemnitie of the Creation of . . . Prince Henrie, pamphlet, London, 1610.

Papers Relative to the Marriage of King James with the Princess Anna of Denmark, Edinburgh: 1828.

Peacham, Henry, *Minerva Britanna*, London: 1612.

Pett, Phineas, *The Autobiography of Phineas Pett*, W. G. Perrin (ed.), London: Naval Records Society, 1918.

Prayers appointed to be used in the Church . . . for the Queenes safe deliverance, London: 1605.

Price, Daniel, *Prince Henry His First Anniversary*, Oxford: 1613.

Quin, Walter, *Sertum Poeticum*, London: 1600.

The Register of the Privy Council of Scotland, David Masson (ed.), 14 vols, Edinburgh: HMGR House 1877–98.

Spottiswood, John, *History of the Church of Scotland*, 3 vols, Edinburgh: 1851.

Stow, John, *The Annales or Generall Chronicle of England*, continued by Edmund Howes, London: 1615.

Tailboys, Samuel, *A New Lachrymentall and Funerall Elegy*, London: 1624.

Taylor, John, 'True Louing sorrow, attired in a robe of vnfeigned griefe', broadsheet, London: 1624.

_____, *Heavens Blessng and Earths Joy*, London: 1613.

The Warrender Papers, Annie I. Cameron (ed.), 2 vols, Edinburgh: Scottish Historical Society, 1932.

Webster, John, *Monuments of Honor*, London: 1624.

_____, *The Works of John Webster*, David Gunby, David Carnegie and MacDonald P. Jackson (eds), 3 vols, Cambridge: Cambridge University Press, 1995–2007.

Wilson, Arthur, *The History of Great Britain . . . King James*, London: 1653.

Wotton, Henry, *The Life and Letters of Sir Henry Wotton*, Logan Pearsall Smith (ed.), 2 vols, Oxford: Clarendon Press, 1966.

SECONDARY SOURCES

Akrigg, G. P. V. (1962), *Jacobean Pageant: The Court of King James I*, Cambridge, MA: Harvard University Press.

Astington, John H. (1999), *English Court Theatre 1558–1642*, Cambridge: Cambridge University Press.

Barroll, Leeds (2001), *Anna of Denmark, Queen of England*, Philadelphia: University of Pennsylvania Press.

Bellany, Alastair (2002), *The Politics of Court Scandal in Early Modern England*, Cambridge: Cambridge University Press.

Bergeron, David M. (2021), 'Gerrard Herbert's Reports on Drama Performances (1617–19)', *Studies in Philology*, 118: 725–41.

_____ (2020), 'The Duke of Lennox and Civic Entertainments', in J. Caitlin Finlayson and Amrita Sen (eds), *Civic Performance: Pageantry and Entertainments in Early Modern London*, New York: Routledge, pp. 157–75.

_____ (2019), 'Pericles: A Performance, a Letter (1619)', in Sophie Chiari and John Mucciolo (eds), *Performances at Court in the Age of Shakespeare*, Cambridge: Cambridge University Press, pp. 107–19.

_____ (2017), *Shakespeare's London 1613*, Manchester: Manchester University Press.

_____ (2016), 'Court Masques about Stuart London', *Studies in Philology*, 113: 822–49.

_____ (2010), '"Are we turned Turks?": English Pageants and the Stuart Court', *Comparative Drama*, 44: 255–75.

_____ (2008–9), 'Creating Entertainments for Prince Henry's Creation (1610)', *Comparative Drama*, 42: 433–49.

_____ (2006), *Textual Patronage in English Drama, 1570–1640*, Aldershot: Ashgate.

_____ (2003), *English Civic Pageantry 1558–1642*, revised edition, Tempe, AZ: Arizona State University Center for Medieval and Renaissance Studies.

_____ (1999), *King James and Letters of Homoerotic Desire*, Iowa City: University of Iowa Press.

Bingham, Caroline (1979), *James VI of Scotland*, London: Weidenfeld & Nicolson.

Brown, Keith (2011), *Noble Power in Scotland from the Reformation to the Revolution*, Edinburgh: Edinburgh University Press.

Butler, Martin (2008), *The Stuart Masque and Political Culture*, Cambridge: Cambridge University Press.

Chambers, E. K. (1923), *The Elizabethan Stage*, 4 vols, Oxford: Clarendon Press.

Croft, Pauline (1992), 'The Parliamentary Installation of Henry, Prince of Wales', *Historical Research: Bulletin of the Institute of Historical Research*, 65: 177–93.

Cuddy, Neil (1987), 'The Revival of the Entourage: The Bedchamber of James I, 1603–1625', in David Starkey (ed.), *The English Court from the Wars of the Roses to the Civil War*, London: Longman, pp. 173–225.

Curran, Kevin (2009), *Marriage, Performance and Politics at the Jacobean Court*, Farnham: Ashgate.

Curran, Stuart (2006), 'James I and Fictional Authority at the Palatine Wedding Celebration', *Renaissance Studies*, 20: 51–67.

Donaldson, Gordon (1967), *Scottish Kings*, London: Batsford.

_____ (1965), *Scotland, James VI to James VII*, Edinburgh: Oliver & Boyd.

Donaldson, Ian (2011), *Ben Jonson: A Life*, Oxford: Oxford University Press.

Dutton, Richard (2016), *Shakespeare, Court Dramatist*, Oxford: Oxford University Press.

_____ (1991), *Mastering the Revels: The Regulation and Censorship of English Renaissance Drama*, Iowa City: University of Iowa Press.

Fraser, Antonia (1969), *Mary Queen of Scots*, New York: Delacorte.

Fraser, William (1874), *The Lennox*, 2 vols, Edinburgh.

Gardiner, Samuel R. (1965), *History of England, 1603–1642*, 10 vols, reprinted edition, New York: AMS Press.

Goodare, Julian (1999), *State and Society in Early Modern Scotland*, Oxford: Oxford University Press.

Goodman, Paul (2017), 'James VI, Noble Power and the Burgh of Glasgow, c. 1580-1605', in Miles Kerr-Peterson and Steven J. Reid (eds), *James VI and Noble Power in Scotland 1578–1603*, New York: Routledge, pp. 81–97.

Grant, Ruth (2010), 'George Gordon, Sixth Earl of Huntly and the Politics of the Counter-Reformation in Scotland, 1581–1595', Ph.D Thesis, University of Edinburgh.

Gurr, Andrew (2004), *The Shakespeare Company, 1594–1642*, Cambridge: Cambridge University Press.

Heaton, Gabriel and James Knowles (2003), '"Entertainment Perfect": Ben Jonson and Corporate Hospitality', *Review of English Studies*, 54: 587–600.

Hope, W. H. St John (1907), 'On the Funeral Effigies of the Kings and Queens of England, with special reference to those in the Abbey Church of Westminster', *Archaeologia* 60, pt 2.

Jansson, Maija (1988), *Proceedings in Parliament 1614 (House of Commons)*, Philadelphia: American Philosophical Society.

Knowles, James (2015), *Politics and Political Culture in the Court Masque*, New York: Palgrave Macmillan.

Lamb, Jonathan (2016), 'Ben Jonson's Dead Body: Henry, Prince of Wales, and the 1616 Folio', *Huntington Library Quarterly*, 79: 63–92.

Lee, Maurice (1980), *Government by Pen: Scotland under James VI & I*, Urbana: University of Illinois Press.

Limon, Jerzy (1990), *The Masque of Stuart Culture*, Newark: University of Delaware Press.

Lindley, David (1993), *The Trials of Frances Howard*, London: Routledge.

_____ (1986), 'Embarrassing Ben: The Masques for Frances Howard', *English Literary Renaissance*, 16: 343–59.

Lisle, Leanda de (2005), *After Elizabeth: The Rise of James of Scotland*, New York: Ballantine.

Lytle, Guy Fitch and Stephen Orgel (eds) (1981), *Patronage in the Renaissance*, Princeton: Princeton University Press, 1981.

McLaughlin, Adrienne (2017), 'Rise of a Courtier: The Second Duke of Lennox and Strategies of Noble Power under James VI', in Miles Kerr-Peterson and Steven J. Reid (eds), *James VI and Noble Power in Scotland 1578–1603*, London: Routledge, pp. 136–54.

MacLeod, Catharine (2012), *The Lost Prince: The Life and Death of Henry Stuart*, London: National Portrait Gallery.

Macpherson, Robin (2004), 'Stuart [Stewart], Ludovick, second duke of Lennox and duke of Richmond', *Oxford Dictionary of National Biography*, Oxford: Oxford University Press.

_____ (1998), 'Francis Stewart, 5th Earl of Bothwell, c. 1562–1612: Lordship and Politics in Jacobean Scotland', Ph.D thesis, University of Edinburgh.

Mantel, Hilary (2009), *Wolf Hall*, New York: Henry Holt.

Mathew, David (1967), *James I*, London: Eyre & Spottiswood.

Murray, John Tucker (1910), *English Dramatic Companies 1558–1642*, London: Constable.

Norbrook, David (1986), '*The Masque of Truth*: Court Entertainment and International Protestant Politics in the Early Stuart Period', *Seventeenth-Century*, 1: 81–110.

Orgel, Stephen and A. R. Braunmuller (eds) (2002), *The Complete Pelican Shakespeare*, New York: Viking.

Orgel, Stephen and Roy Strong (eds) (1973), *Inigo Jones: The Theatre of the Stuart Court*, 2 vols, Berkeley: University of California Press.

Orrell, John (1979a), 'The London Court Stage in the Savoy Correspondence, 1613–1675', *Theatre Research International*, 4: 79–94.

_____ (1979b), 'Antimo Galli's Description of *The Masque of Beauty*', *Huntington Library Quarterly*, 43.1: 13–23.

Peck, Linda Levy (1993), *Court Patronage and Corruption in Early Stuart England*, London: Routledge.

Reid-Baxter, Jamie (2000), 'Politics, Passion and Poetry in the Circle of James VI', in L.A. R. Houwen, A.A. MacDonald and S.L. Mapstone (eds), *A Palace of the Wild*, Leuven, Belgium: Peeters, pp. 199–248.

Rickard, Jane (2015), *Writing the Monarch in Jacobean England*, Oxford: Oxford University Press.

Somerset, Anne (1997), *Unnatural Murder: Poison at the Court of James I*, London: Weidenfeld and Nicolson.

Stewart, Alan (2003), *The Cradle King: The Life of James VI & I*, New York: St Martin's.

Strong, Roy (1986), *Henry, Prince of Wales and England's Lost Renaissance*, London: Thames & Hudson.

Ullyot, Michael (2004), 'The Fall of Troynovant: Exemplarity after the Death of Henry, Prince of Wales', in Alan Shepard and Stephen D. Powell (eds), *Fantasies of Troy: Classical Tales and the Social Imaginary in Medieval and Early Modern Europe*, Toronto: Centre for Reformation and Renaissance Studies, pp. 269–90.

Wallerstein, Ruth (1950), *Studies in Seventeenth-Century Poetic*, Madison: University of Wisconsin Press.

White, Hayden (1978), *Tropics of Discourse: Essays in Cultural Criticism*, Baltimore: Johns Hopkins University Press.

White, Paul Whitfield and Suzanne R. Westfall (eds) (2002), *Shakespeare and Theatrical Patronage in Early Modern England*, New York: Columbia University Press.

Wilks, Timothy (2007), *Prince Henry Revived: Image and Exemplarity in Early Modern England*, Southampton: Southampton Solent University.

Williams, Ethel Carleton (1970), *Anne of Denmark*, London: Longman.

Williamson, J. W. (1978), *The Myth of the Conqueror: Prince Henry Stuart, a Study in 17th-Century Personation*, New York: AMS Press.

Willson, David Harris (1956), *King James VI and I*, New York: Oxford University Press.

Wormald, Jenny (1988), *Mary Queen of Scots: A Study in Failure*, London: George Philip.

_____ (1985), *Lords and Men in Scotland: Bonds of Manrent, 1442–1603*, Edinburgh: John Donald.

_____ (1983), 'James VI and I: Two Kings or One', *History*, 68: 187–209.

Young, Alan (1987), *Tudor and Jacobean Tournaments*, London: George Philip.

Index